पुरातत्त्व

पुरातत्त्व

PURĀTATTVA

Bulletin of the Indian Archaeological Society

No. 29 1998-99

Editors

K. N. Dikshit & K.S. Ramachandran

D.K. Printworld (P) Ltd.
New Delhi

Cataloging in Publication Data — DK
[Courtesy : D.K. Agencies (P) Ltd. <docinfo@dkagencies.com>]

Purātattva : bulletin of the Indian Archaeological
Society, no. 29, 1998-99 / editor, K.N. Dikshit &
K.S. Ramachandran.
p. cm.
Includes bibliographical references.
ISBN 8124603049

1. Archaeology — India — Periodicals. 2. India — Antiquities — Periodicals. 3. India — Civilization — Periodicals. I. Dikshit, K.N. II. Ramachandran, K.S. (Kattalai Sivasubramanium), 1939- III. Indian Archaeological Society.

First Published in 1999
First Reprinted in 2005
ISBN 81-246-0304-9
Price for volume 29 (1998-99): Rs. 800 US $ 40

Reprint authorised by
Indian Archaeological Society
New Delhi - 110 016

Purātattva is published annually.

Manuscripts (whether in the form of articles or notes or book reviews) offered for publication should be sent to the Editor, Purātattva, Indian Archaeological Society, B-17, Qutab Institutional Area, New Delhi - 110 016.

Published and printed by:
D.K. Printworld (P) Ltd.
'Srikunj,' F-52, Bali Nagar
New Delhi – 110015
Phone : (011) 2545 3975, 2546 6019 Fax : (011) 2546 5926
E-mail : dkprintworld@vsnl.net
www. dkprintworld.com

PURĀTATTVA

CONTENTS

Obituaris

Dr. S.A. Sali
(1927-1999)

In the passing away of Dr. Shankar Appaji Sali on 30th June, 1999 at Domiwali, Bombay, archaeological fraternity has lost a brilliant and self-made archaeologist whose contribution in the domain of prehistoric and protohistoric archaeology will long be remembered. He was born on May 5th, 1927.

Shri Sali was born in a very humble family of weavers. With great difficulty Appaji educated his son who matriculated from Pepit High School. He managed to get a petty job of Field Assistant in the local Agricultural Bank and started his career of visiting villages in the neighbourhood for popularising improved seeds and providing loans. During one such routine visit, Shankar Sali chanced to go to a village called Jorwe and he was surprised to see a sprawling mound, locally called as Jarcsandhachi Nagri, spread over with pottery, including large painted jars, burials and host of other antiquities. This aroused his curiousity and forthwith he published a letter in one of the Marathi newspapers. As luck would have it, we chanced to read that letter and immediately contacted Shri Sali and visited Jorwe in his company. The find of painted pottery perplexed me as it did the late Dr. H.D. Sankalia as no site with painted pottery of the type encountered at Jorwe was reported so far from Deccan. Subsequently, Deccan College excavated the site of Jorwe and the well-known Jorwe culture of the Deccan Chalcolithic period came to be established.

Seeing his genuine interest in sending me voluntarily reports, we offered him the position of Caretaker, Kanheri Caves in 1950 and there was no looking back for this young man. He took special interest in excavations and explorations at Bahal, Tekwada and Prakash. In 1956 he was selected for the post of Exploration Assistant.

Later, he learned under the guidance of Dr. Sankalia. His research project involved a small excavation at Pante, Taluk Chalisgam, District Jalgaon, where he brought to light a succession of cultures starting with Middle Palaeolithic, Upper Palaeolithic to Mesolithic with stone tools and Ostrich egg-shell in Upper Palaeolithic levels.

Dr. Sali was held in great esteem by his colleagues, the Survey and Deccan College. We pay homage to this brilliant gentle and genuine scholar.

M.N. Deshpande

Dr. Tribhuan Nath Roy
(20 July 1930 - 14 May 1998)

Tribhuan Nath Roy passed away at his home in Varanasi on May 14, 1998 at the age of 68 years. Dr. Roy was born at village Kashipur in district Kanpur Dehat (U.P.) on 20 July 1930 in a family of educationists. He received his early education at the Queens' College, Varanasi. After obtaining Master's Degree in 1956 from the Deptt. of Ancient Indian History, Culture and Archaeology of the Banaras Hindu University, he joined the same Department as Research Fellow in 1957. He received practical training in Archaeology at the Indian School of Field Archaeology at Ujjain during 1957-58 under Dr. N.R. Banerjee of the Archaeological Survey of India. Dr. Roy joined the Department of AIHC & Archaeology, B.H.U. as Assistant Director-cum-Lecturer in 1960 and was promoted as Reader in November, 1983. He was engaged in teaching of Archaeology and conducting archaeological excavations and guiding research till his retirement on superannuation in July 1990. He was re-appointed by the B.H.U. for a period of three years and thus he was in active service of the B.H.U. upto 1993.

Ever since his appointment Dr. Roy was associated with archaeological field work. He participated in excavations at Rajghat (1960-67), Sarai Mohana (1967-68), Ayodhya (1969-70), Kampilya (1975-76) and Bhitari conducted by the B.H.U. He conducted independent excavations at Takiyapar, district Chandauli, during 1971-72 and at Manjhi, district Saran, Bihar, during 1983-85. This field work of more than two decades gave him first-hand knowledge of ceramic industries and antiquities of the Middle Ganga plain of early historical period. Dr. Roy was particularly interested in the stratigraphy and chronology of PGW and NBPW sites which resulted into his two books namely ***The Ganges Civilization***, (New Delhi, Ramanand Vidya Bhavan, 1983) and ***A Study of Northern Black Polished Ware Culture*** (New Delhi, Ramanand Vidya Bhavan, 1986). Dr. Roy will be remembered for the publication of excavation reports of Rajghat (Parts I and II) dealing with the Strata & Structure and the Pottery and the excavation report of Prahladpur - all with Prof. A.K. Narain. He reported his findings of excavation at Manjhi in Puratattva, No. 16 (1985-86) and of Takiyapar in ***IAR***, 1971-72. Besides actively participating in seminars and conferences, he published more than a dozen research papers. Dr. Roy is survived by his wife, a son and a daughter.

Dr. Roy briefly visited Ankara, Turkey during 1970-71 as a Government Scholar and also participated in the Conference of South Asian Archaeologists held at Rome/Venice in July 1987. Dr. Roy was a sincere and dedicated field worker and an admirable colleague. His untimely death has created a void which will be difficult to fill for years to come. His death will be deeply mourned by his friends, colleagues and students of South Asian Archaeology.

Purushottam Singh

Professor Ram Lal Parikh
(18 April 1927 - 01 November 1999)

Professor Ram Lal Parikh left for his heavenly abode in the morning of 1st November, 99. He is survived by his wife, Smt. Padma Parikh and four daughters.

Professor Parikh was born on 18th April 1927. He passed M.A. in Ancient Indian History and Culture from teh University of Bombay in 1951 A.D. He also earned post graduate experience in Field Archaeology under such doyens as Dr. H.D. Saukalia and Dr. B. Subbarao. He got his 'doctorate' in peace education and Diploma in Management.

Basically starting his career as a teacher, he rose to be the Principal of Mahadeva Desai College of Social Sciences, Vice Chancellor of Gujarat Vidyapeeth, and, a member of Rajya Sabha. He had been a member and chairman of many educational and cultural institutions in India, and abroad.

During his long-acedamic career of five decades, he won the following awards :

1. Peace Meneuger Award from U.N.
2. Padma Krupaskaya Levin Award for Literacy from U.N.E.S.C.O.
3. J.M. Award for literacy from Indian Adult Education.
4. Great World Peace Award for International Association of University Presidents, Seoul, Korea.
5. Viwa Gujrati Award in 1991.
6. National Citizens Award of 1991.
7. Morarji Desai Award for peace, education, and international understanding in 1992.
8. U.P. Government's Kabir Award for development of Hindi.
9. Victor Johnson Award of ICEA, England.
10. Lifetime Literarcy Award by the Ministry of HRD, Govt., of India.
11. Pranavanand Award by the Government of India
12. Manubhai Pancholi 'Darshak' foundation award in 1998.

His dedication to the cause of research and education in India, the sincere adherance to Gaudhian principles like 'Ahinsa', and humility, his integrity and gentle nature will be long remembered by his friends, colleagues, and future generation of students.

Rasesh Jaminder

Shri Sital Banerjee
(1912 - 1999)

Shri Sital Banerjee was born on 21.1.1912 at Shilpur, Howarah, West Bengal. He died on 4.2.1999 at his residence in Shalimar Bagh, New Delhi.

In the death of Shri Sital Banerjee, archaeological world of India has lost a very dedicated field-worker who served Archaeological Survey of India for around 40 years. He was associated with the excavations conducted at Taxila, Ropar, Lothal, Purana Qila (New Delhi), Kailbangan and several others.

Sital Babu was always made incharge of pottery and antiquities recovered from excavations and explorations conducted by Archaeological Survey of India and other agencies. He handled these objects very carefully, so much so that no scholar could work on any subject concerning field-archaeology without consulting Sital Babu. Infact for all the trainees who joined the first school for field Archaeology under Sir Mortimer Wheeler at Taxila, he was the friend, philospher and guide in matters concerning the upkeep of pottery. He was trained by Wheeler himself, about the selection and division of pottery according to trenches, layers, fabrics and typology.

Sital Babu also kept all the minor antiquities in systematic fashion according to trenches, locus and area which has been the model for the A.S.I. for the last more than 50 years.

Sital Babu was very pleasing personality, always ready to help young and old scholars. Even after his retirement, we used to go and ask Sital Babu all about the potteries and antiquities of different sites housed at various places in India. His memory was very sharp and his attitude was very helpful.

We all pray for the peace of the departed soul.

S.P. Gupta

Professor Lallanji Gopal
(1934-99)

Prof. Lallanji Gopal was one of the eminent historians of India, respected nationally and internationally for his scientific and unbiased approach. A great teacher, he inspired generations of students, researchers and scholars in India and Abroad. He produced about hundred Ph.Ds and his research scholars came from different Asian and Continental Countries as well as USA.

Born on June 15,1934 in a family of lawyers, Lallanji Gopal in his very school days chose to study Sanskrit. He lost his mother, Smt. Surya Devi, when he was a couple of months old. Brought up by his grandmother Smt. Mahadevi Madan Gopal, a very religious minded lady he grew as a pure Vaisnava not eating even onion in his brahmacarya asram. His father Dr. Hanuman Prasad shaped his life and career.In Allahabad University he distinguished himself by winning the most coveted awards and scholarships, such as Jubilee scholarship and Dr. Tara Chand gold medal for securing highest marks in history as also the Subbarao best graduate medal in the BA examination in 1951. He bagged the UP State Scholarship and Chancellor's Medal (for being the best Postgraduate student in all four faculties - Arts, Science, Commerce and Law) of the Allahabad University and Shankar Saran best post-graduate medal in 1953.

He completed his D.Phil in 1957 under the supervision of Prof. G.C. Pande, on "Some Aspects of Economic Development in Ancient India.c.400 BC to 700 AD." from the Allahabad University. He was the first recipient of the Government of India Humanities Research Scholarship (1954-56). In 1960 he got the British Council Scholarship for advanced research in the United Kingdom, where he completed his Ph.D in 1962 in the record time of 20 months under Prof. A.L. Basham on "Economic Life of Northern India (c.AD 700-1200)" from the School of Oriental and African Studies, University of London.

Prof. Gopal started his academic career at the Allahabad University as Lecturer in Ancient History Culture and Archaeology in 1956 and switched over to Banaras Hindu UNiversity as Reader in History in 1963. In BHU he was appointed on top academic posts in four departments - Reader in History and Ancient History; Sayaji Rao Gaekwad Professor of Indian Culture and Civilization in 1970, (a post occupied first by S. Radhakrishnan), and Head, Department of Indian Philosophy and Religion, Director, Advanced Centre in Philosphy, and, Professor, Head and Co-ordinator of Special Assistance Programme in Ancient Indian History, Culture and archaeology. He was also the convener, Purana Research Committee, BHU, 1966-67 and 1970-1994.

Besides these he also acted as Director, Wisconsin University year in India Programme, 1966-67, Director, Short Term Course for San Francisco University teachers 1976, and, North Carolina University Group 1977.

Economic Life of Northern India c. 700-1200 AD, the Gurusamita Sukranti : A Nineteenth Century Text, Aspects of History of Agriculture in Ancient India, Studies in the History and Culture of Nepal (joint author

Dr. T.P. Verma), Pulastya-Smrti-Sangraha (joint author Prof. K.K. Gopal), Early Mediveal Coin types of Northern India, and, Vejrasuci-a manifesto on social equality are some of his works. He wrote three books under a UNESCO scheme and two of his books were published by the National Book Trust of India and are available in 6 languages. Out of the four books which were in press at the time of his sad demise one Prachina Bharatiya Rajnitika Vichardhara has came out, the other three Retrieving Sankhya History, Lokaprakash and Vrkshayurveda are in each proof stage and will be coming shortly. About half a dozen important books remained unfinished.

Dr. Gopal was a pioneer among the economic historians who never relinguish the totality of the historical situation and goes deeper than any of the groups that adhere to one particular ideology. He was infact one of the foremost historians who demonstrated the limitations and short-comings of the narrow and political conceptions of history. By his researchers on the history of science and technology, he exposed the superficial interpretation which was in vouge for some decades. Besides he has shown that history, economic history especially, is not governed by materialistic factors alone. It has to be studied as influenced by thought: social, economic, political, religious and even philosophical.

Under the auspicies of the Kashi Raj Trust, Ramnagar, Varanasi, he organised an International Seminar. Its proceedings have been published as *Ayodhya: History, Culture and Archaeology*, which offers in a scientific historical manner the facts regarding the much debated Ayodhya problem.

Dr. Gopal was not restricted to any one aspect or discipline of history. He was expert for epigraphy, numismatics, archaeology, archival studies and museology also, having been connected in an official capacity with the main organisations and bodies of these disciplines. The holistic approach as contrasted with the fragmented and peace-meal treatment was his hall mark.

He was appointed U.G.C. National Lecturer in history twice in 1977 and 1986. He also delivered lectures as Visiting Fellow, and Special Endowment lectures at Vishwa Bharati, Bhandarkar Oriental Research Institute and the Institute of Culture, Ram Krishna Mission, Calcutta. For the Academic Staff College Programmes he gave lectures at the Universities of Allahabad, Jaipur, Jodhpur, Aligarh and Banaras. He gave extension lecturers at several Universities in the country, Sri Lanka, and Tribhuwan University, Nepal. Under the Cultural Exchange Programmer he gave lectures at Universities in Yugoslavia and Czechoslovakia in 1976. In 1977 he participated in the International Seminar on "Movement of people in the second millennium B.C." held at Dushanbe.

During the last two decades new honours came unsought to Prof. Gopal in World-wide recognition of his massive contributions to Indological Studies. The Supreme Sangha Council of Sri Lanka conferred on him honrary (D. Litt.) Vidya Chakravarty in 1981 for his contributions to Buddhist Studies. In 1985 he was awarded the Chakravikarm Gold Medal, the highest award for his outstanding contributions to numismatics by the Numismatic Society of India. The Hindi Sahitya Sammelan Prayag conferred the degree of Vidyavacaspati in 1996.

He was the member of the Executive Council of the Banaras Hindu University twice 1975-78 and 1991-94. President of India appointed him Rector and Acting Vice-Chancellor of the Banaras Hindu University in 1993. In 1998 he was nominated as member of the Executive Council of Jamia Millia Islamia University, New Delhi.

With the sad demise of Prof. Gopal India has lost a great scholar of Indology, whose place cannot easily be taken by any other person.

S.P. Gupta

PURĀTATTVA

Number 29 1998-99

Editorial

The ushering in of the new millennium coinciding with the completion of our building in every respect augurs bright academic prospects for our society.

In spite of many hurdles, mainly financial, the building has come up in its grandeur and is ready for occupation during the first month of the 21st century.

Here we would like to record our sincere gratitude for the untiring efforts, labour and single-minded perseverence(among all odds) to Dr. Swarajya Prakash Gupta (Chairman) but for whom the building would not have seen the light of the day.

Passing on to our activities during the year, we wish to record that we have taken up the job of chemical preservation of antiquities etc in the Sattaras in the Majuli islands, the biggest island in the Brahmaputra. This being carried out on receiving a grant from the National Museum, New Delhi.

We have set up a museum called 'Indraprastha Museum of Art and Archaeology' to highlight our culture particularly the heritage and vestiges around Delhi - the ancient Indraprastha.

We intend to setting up a fully equipped laboratory for chemical preservation of archaeological specimens in all media-stone, terracotta, ivory, paper, cloth etc. The preparations are progressing on a fast track.

The current issue of Puratattva carries articles and notes etc. spanning over a vast period right from the prehistoric to modern times. Of particular importance will be the report on the further excavations at Rakhigarhi, which is an on-going project and the other a long informative write up, comparing Dholavira and Banawali.

Depending upon the accrual of revenue we intend in future to conduct seminars , workshops and give lectures on Indian archaeology, art and sculpture. Besides we will also prepare and publish tomes on specialised subjects.

Finally we would record our sincere thanks to the Archaeological Survey of India Govt. of India for a generous grant for printing Puratattva no. 29 and also to the Indian Council of Historical Research for sanctioning money for the publication of Puratattva no. 28. However, we wish to put on record that these two organisations are not responsible for the views expressed in the Puratattva; individual authors are responsible.

Special thanks to Smt. Anita Mehta and her staff for their cooperation in bringing out the issue on time.

We wish our members and readers a happy new year, century and prosperous millennium.

KND
KSR

A New Acheulian Site at Kolihal : Hunsgi Valley, Karnataka

K. Paddayya and Richa Jhaldiyal*

In this paper the authors wish to bring to the attention of prehistorians the disovery of a primary Acheulian site near the village of Kolihal in the Hunsgi valley. Kolihal is a new type site which preserves evidence of tool manufacture on a large scale.

The Hunsgi and Baichbal valleys are located in the Shorapur taluk of Gulbarga district, Karnataka. These valleys are erosional in nature and together with the tablelands enclosing them cover a total area of over 1000 sq. km. They are separated from each other by a narrow strip of shale-limestone plateau but otherwise form a single geomorphic unit. A quarter century of intensive fieldwork in this area comprising foot-survey and excavations has brought to light, apart from other Stone Age sites, well over 120 Acheulian sites[1] (Fig. 1).

There are several features of these Acheulian sites which are worth emphasising. First, unlike most of the known Lower Palaeolithic sites in the subcontinent these sites are located in a non-riverine setting. The two valleys constitute the headwater zone of a tributary (called the Hunsgi nullah) of the river Krishna which flows 30 km away, to the south of this region. Secondly, they are buried under 1 to 2 m thick silt deposit and are in many cases exposed to the surface in recent times due to the removal of this sedimentary cover by surface run-off and land modification processes like levelling and ploughing. Thirdly, these valleys have provided a stable landsurface which promoted continuous occupation of the region by the Stone Age groups and also contributed to the preservation of the sites in their original depositional contexts. Another unique feature of the Acheulian sites of these valleys is the use of siliceous limestone as the principal raw material for the manufacture of tools.

Pooling together the field data pertaining to the distribution pattern of sites (dispersed or clustered) in relation to the location of raw material sources, seasonal or perennial sources of water, as provided by seep-springs, and availability of wild plant and animal foods (as extrapolated from ethnographic data), it has been possible to reconstruct the Acheulian culture of the area from the settlement system perspective. The main observation emanating from this study is that the Acheulian groups of the two valleys adopted an annual resource management strategy consisting of wet season dispersal all over the valley floor and dry season aggregation near perennial water sources[2].

Since 1987 additional work has been undertaken in this area, with the specific objective of understanding the variability in the locational and sedimentary contexts of the Acheulian sites. It is for the first time in the Indian

*Department of Archaeology, Deccan College, Pune-411006

context that the Stone Age sites are being studied from the recently developed perspective of site formation processes. The results of these recent studies are very encouraging[3]; and have set in motion a new trend in Indian prehistory. Due to the adoption of this approach it has been possible to detect a wide variety in the natural processes which are responsible for the variability in the depositional context of the sites. The sites have been classified into four main contexts i.e. fluvial and colluvial where artefacts occur in a secondary context, and sheetwash and deflationary where artefacts occur in their primary context either on the surface of bedrock, calcrete or on the surface of soft sediments like silt deposits and travertines. Likewise it has been possible to understand the site variability from the point of view of cultural processes on the basis of which sites have been classified as occupation sites, single episode activity sites, food processing sites and caches.

In continuation of this work, further field investigations were undertaken in the Hunsgi valley with the two-fold objective of having a more refined understanding of the geoarchaeological contexts of the sites and identifying undisturbed sites to reconstruct hominid adaptations.

One of these included an Acheulian locality near the village of Isampur (Lat. 16° 30′ N and Long. 76° 29′ E). The site is situated in a narrow sub-valley in the north-western part of the Hunsgi valley (Fig. 2). It is enclosed by shale-limestone uplands on all sides and is drained by a seasonal stream called the Kamta Halla. The site is located on the valley floor at a distance of 150 m from the left bank of the Kamta Halla.

Our detailed field research for three seasons (1997-1999) at this site comprising both intensive survey and excavation proved to be very instructive[4]. From our geoarchaeological studies it is clear that the site lay on the edge of a palaeodrainage tract which was filled with brown/black silt deposits in the post-Acheulian times. The site forms part of farmland covered with 1 to 1.5 m thick silt deposit and occupies on areas 3/4 of a hectare. The Stone Age cultural material was exposed to the surface due to quarrying of silt deposits by the Irrigation Department and erosion by a field nullah.

Our studies brought to light well-preserved evidence of tool manufacture at the raw material source. Here the limestone blocks derived from the weathered bedrock of the valley floor served as cores. Surface observations and test pits revealed several dozen artefacts comprising cores, finished tools, flake blanks and a large amount of debitage, which suggested that the site witnessed large scale and prolonged manufacturing activity. Moreover the fresh physical conditions of the artefacts indicated that the site is in a primary context.

Five regular trenches were excavated at the site. The principal results of this work are as under. First, it was possible to identify the criteria of site selection employed by the Acheulian groups – recognition of a raw material source occurring in the form of a large number of highly siliceous limestone blocks of suitable sizes and shapes; location of the site close to the drainage tract which served as a source of water as well as aquatic foods; and, easy accessibility to both the uplands and the valley floor for purposes of hunting and gathering. Secondly, excavations at this site has enabled us to identify intrasite variability in the preservational context of the Acheulian horizon; it ranges from the fluvially rearranged contexts through ones which are partially modified by past and contemporary disturbance processes to situations where the assemblage is still preserved in its original context with a minimum amount of disturbance by post-depositional processes. Thirdly, this site probably served as a localised centre for tool production and from here flake blanks and finished tools were being regularly transferred to other sites and locations in the region.

A detailed study of the cultural material has allowed us to reconstruct various stages of the lithic production process viz. transformation of limestone blocks into regular cores by knocking of irregular angularities and corners, removal of flake blanks of various sizes from cores, preparation of tools like knives and chopping tools on large flake blanks by chipping one of the thicker sides to secure a butt end, and manufacture of bifacial tools on flakes of suitable sizes and shapes by subjecting their surfaces and margins to elaborate secondary chipping. The by-products of all these stages of the reduction sequence are found at the site.

As a part of the detailed field studies at the site of Isampur, explorations were conducted in various segments of the Isampur valley to identify additional Acheulian localities. These exploration led to the discovery of two new sites and half a dozen non-sites of isolated occurrences of Acheulian artefacts. There is the likelihood of some more located in the Isampur valley while the non-sites lie either in the valley or on the surrounding uplands. These new sites, considered together with the major workshop site of Isampur described above, lead to a more elaborate understanding of the organisation of both technological and settlement system of the Acheulian groups.

Kolihal is one of these new sites(Lat. 60° 30′ N and Log. 76° 28′ E) and was discovered in November 1997. It compares well with Isampur in terms of the nature, spatial extent and density of cultural material. A brief note is given below about the locational setting and cultural features of this site.

The site within the revenue limits of the village of Kolihal is located on the footslope of the plateau flanking the Isampur valley on its southern side. It lies 1.5 km due west of the major site of Isampur and about 700 m to the west of the Narayanpur Left Bank Canal forming part of the Upper Krishna Irrigation project. Here the valley measures about a kilometre wide (north to south). The site forms part of a farmland strip measuring about 250 m east-west and 150 m north-south and is covered with half a metre thick black silt. The farmland has an elevation of 475 (above Mean Sea Level) on its southern side and slopes down by 1 to 2 m on the northern side where it borders upon the Kamta Halla. It is defined on all four sides by one to half-a-metre high field bunds made up of limestone blocks and soil. The site has a characteristic topographic setting: it lies at the junction of the valley floor with the lower slopes of the plateau (Fig. 3). Further up the limestone gradually rise and attain an elevation of 500 to 520 m on the plateau top which is capped by the Deccan Trap. The plateau slopes are drained by unchannelised surface runoff and rills and are sometimes covered with a loose deposit of black soil (20-30 cm. thick).

On account of ploughing activities and slopes-wash processes a considerable amount of cultural material has been exposed to the surface in the southern part of the farmland. Our careful foot-survey revealed that the original extent of the site measures about 100 m east-west and 30-35 m north - south. A large amount of cultural material comprising 30-40 large cores, half-a-dozen bifacial tools, over 100 flake-blanks and debitage consisting of large and small flakes was found scattered in this part of the farmland. In particular large clusters of artefacts were noticed in those patches where the overlying silt deposits were eroded away due to surface run-off and action of rill. It was also noticed in that the landowner while clearing the farmland had shifted most of the large cores form their original location and dumped them on the field edges to form part of the field bunds. These disturbances notwithstanding, it is almost certain that systematic excavation will expose a regular Acheulian horizon at the site. This horizon overlies the weathered limestone pediment surface, the broken/disjointed blocks of which served as cores for tool manufacture. As at the site of Isampur, it is most likely that the cultural horizon lies within a carbonate rich matrix.

There are a few features of this new site at Kolihal which are worth highlighting. First, this is a primary context site which is located on the footslopes of the limestone plateau. Barring the small degree of smoothening which has developed on the surfaces of some of the artefacts due to removal of sediment cover and their exposure to sub-aerial weathering processes, the assemblage is preserved in its original depositional context. A considerable portion of the site still preserves cultural material underneath black silt; this part of the site is ideally suited for purposes of excavation. The second aspect is that like Isampur, this locality also appears to be a workshop meant for the production of flak-blanks and their transformation into bifacial tools and other implements. The third and perhaps the most important aspect of the site is that in terms of technology the site is widely separated in time from its counterpart at Isampur. There are several technological features which clearly suggest that the Kolihal assemblage is an advanced one. For example, almost all the cores noticed on the surface belong to the discoidal/circular forms (Fig. 4.1) ranging in diameter from 15 to 25 cm. They are mostly flaked unifacially by subjecting them to convergent flaking. Cores showing 2 to 4 negative flake scars are common. In spite of their large sizes these cores present an overall symmetrical appearance. There are a few cores which show careful surface dressing to facilitate removal of well-shaped (oval/round) flakes (Fig. 4.2). This is the prepared core technique, foreshadowing the later Levallois technique. Another feature justifying as well as the shaped bifacial tools are relatively smaller in size and also have thinner cross-sections (Fig. 5).

Considering the large size of the site and its good preservational context as well as the evolved typo-technological features of the lithic assemblage, the authors propose to undertake a small excavation at this place in the near future.

Acknowledgements

We would like to thank S.A. Pradhan, D.V. Karanjkat, B.S. Waghmode and D.D. Phule for preparing the drawings and Shri Sunil Jadhav and Shri Ravi Dhamapurakr for attending to the photography work.

REFERENCES

1. Paddayya, K. 1977. An Acheulian Occupation Site at Hunsgi, Peninsular India: A Summary of the Results of Two Seasons of Excavation (1975-6). *World Archaeology* 8 pp. 344-55; also 1979. Excavation of a New Acheulian Occupation Site at Hunsgi, Peninsular India. *Quartar* 29-30 pp. 139-155; [1982. *The Acheullian Culture of the Hunsgi Valley, Peninsular India: A Settlement System Perspective*. Pune: Deccan College; 1987a. The Stone Age Cultural Systems of the Baichabal Valley, Gulbarga District, Karnataka: A Preliminary Report. *Bulletin of the Deccan College Post-Graduate and Research Institute* 46,pp, [77-100 pp. 1987b. Excavation of an Acheulian Occupation Site at Yediyapur, Peninsular India. *Anthropos* 82,pp, 610-614 pp. 1987c. The Place of the Study of Site Formation Processes in Prehistoric Research in India, in D.T. Nash and M.D. Petraglia (Eds.), *Natural Formation Process and the Archaeological Record,* pp. 74-85. Oxford: BAR International Series 352; 1989. The Acheulian Culture Localities along the Fatehpur Nullah, Biachbal Valley, Karnataka (Peninsular India) in J.M. Kenoyer (Ed.) *Old Problems and New Perspectives in the Archaeology of South Asia* pp., 21-28 Madison: University of Wiscons in Press.
2. Paddayya. 1982. Ibid.
3. Paddayya. 1987c. op cit.; also Jhaldiyal, R. 1998, Formation Process of the Prehistoric Sites in the Hunsgi-Baichbal Basin, Gulbarga District, Karnataka. Unpulished Ph.D. Thesis, University of Pune; 1991. The Acheulian Culture of the Hunsgi-Baichbal Valleys, Peninsular India: a Processual Study, *Quartar* 41/42 111-138; Paddayya, K. and M.D. pp, Petraglia. 1993. Formation Processes of Acheulian Localities in the Hunsgi and Baichbal Valleys, peninsular India, in P. Goldberg, D.T. Nash and M.D. Petragila (Eds.), *Formation Process in Archaeological Context.* pp. 61-82. Madison: Prehistory Press; Paddayya, K. and M.D. Petragila. 1995. Natural and Cultural Formation Processes of the Acheulian Sites of the Hunsgi and Baichbal Valleys, Karnataka, in S. Wadia, R. Korisettar and V.S. Kale (Eds.) *Quaternary Environments and Geoarchaeology of India* pp. 333-351. Bangalore: Geological Society of India.
4. Paddayya, et al. 1997 and 1998, Ibid; Paddayya, K. and M.D. Patraglia 1997. Isampur: and Acheulian Workshop Site in the Hunsgi Valley, Gulbarga District, Karnataka, *Man and Environment* 22(2): 95-100; Paddayya, K. and M.D. Petraglia 1998. Acheulian Workshop at Isampur, Hunsgi Valley, Karnataka: a Preliminary Report. *Bulletin of the Deccan College Post-Graduate and Research Institute* 56-57 (1996-97) pp. 3-26; Petraglia, M.D., P. Laporta and K. Paddayya 1999. Isampur. The First Acheulian Quarry in India: Stone Tool Manufacture, Biface Morphology and Behaviours, *Journal of Anthropological Research* 55, pp. 39-70; Paddayya, K., R. Jhaldiyal and M.D. Petraglia. 1999. Geoarchaeology of the Acheulian Workshop at Isampur, Hunsgi Valley, Karnataka. *Man and Environment.* In Press.

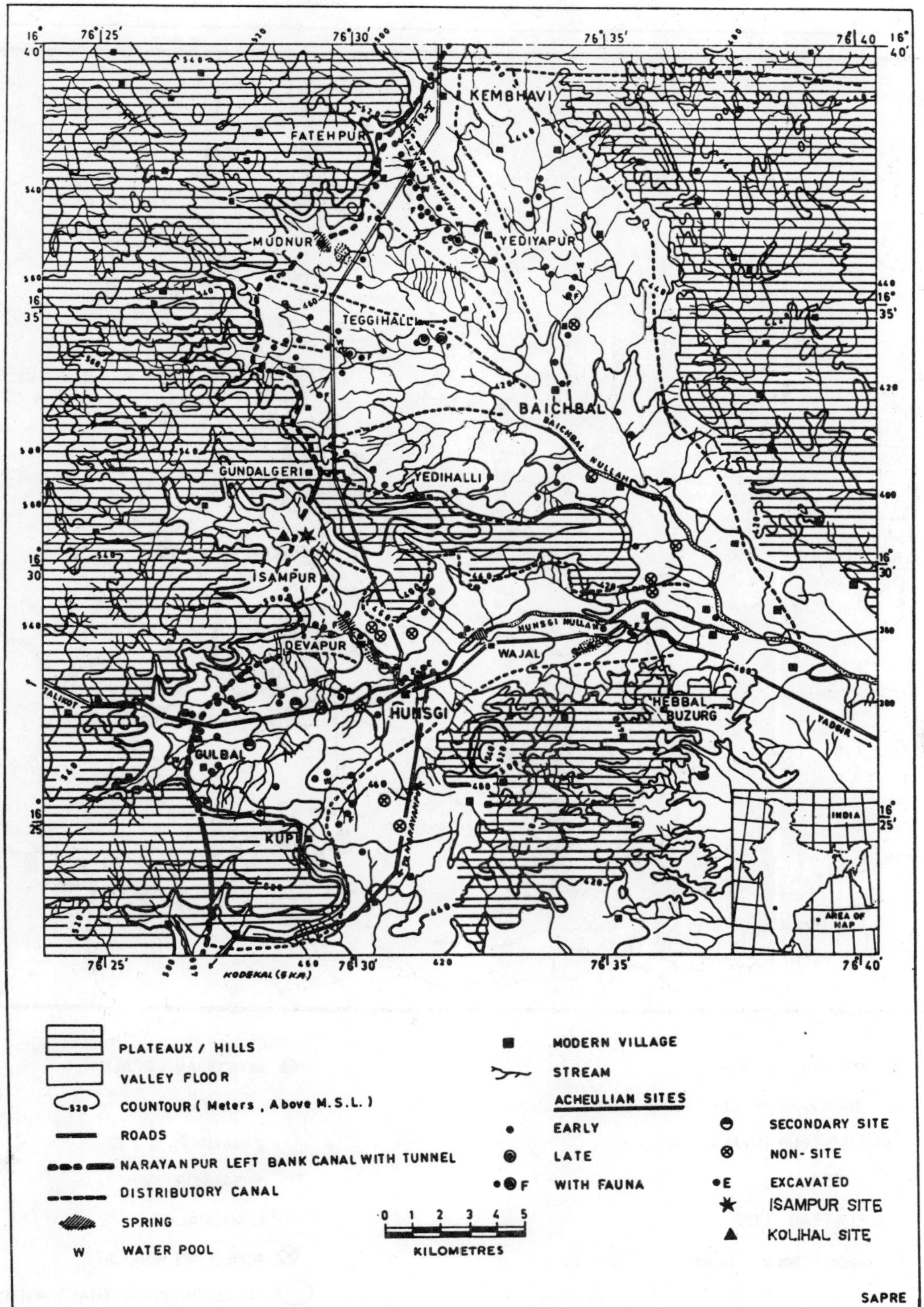

Fig. 1 Map showing the distribution of Acheulian localities in the Hunsgi and Baichbal valleys

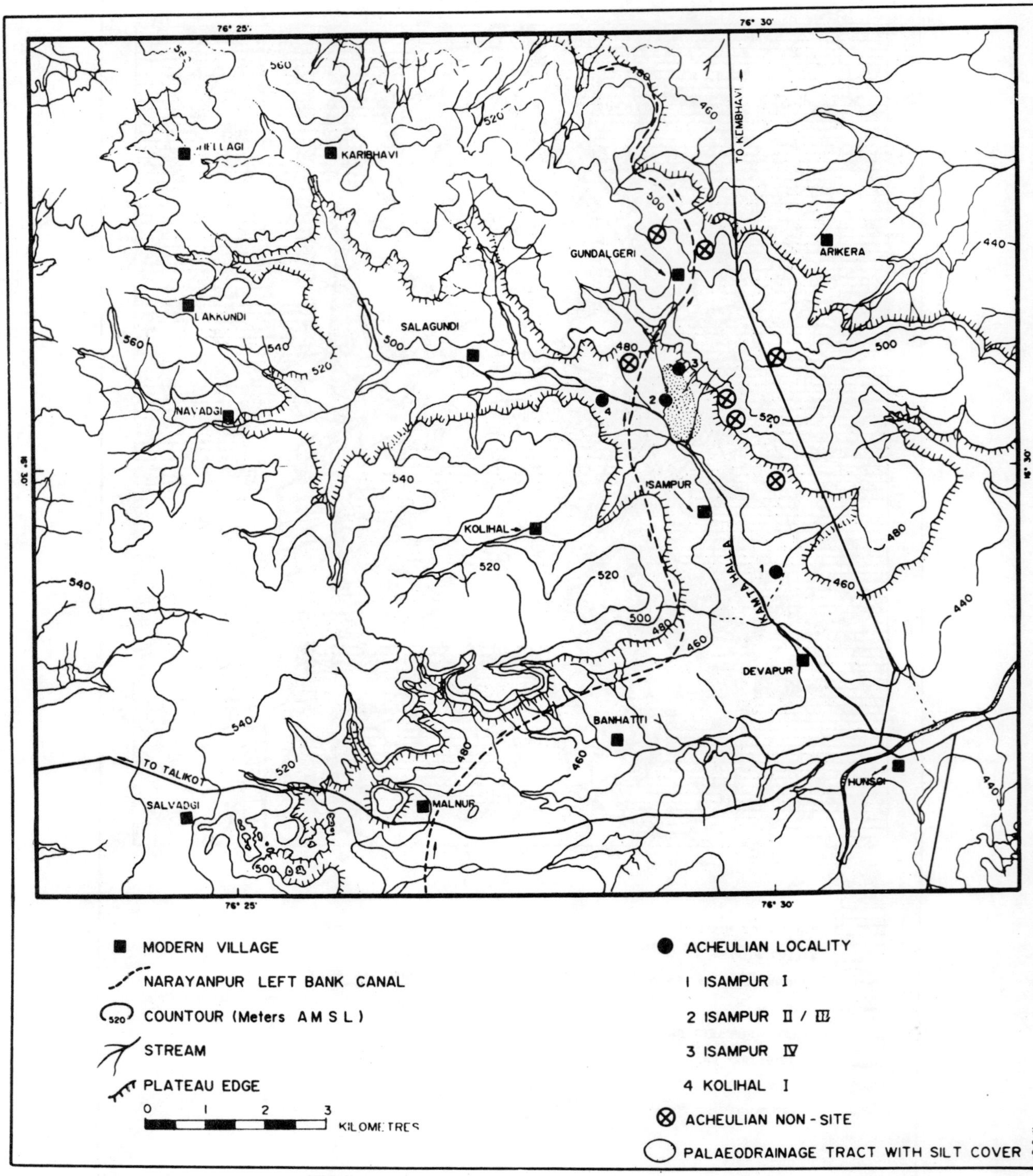

Fig. 2 Map of Isampur sub-valley showing the distribution of Acheulian localities

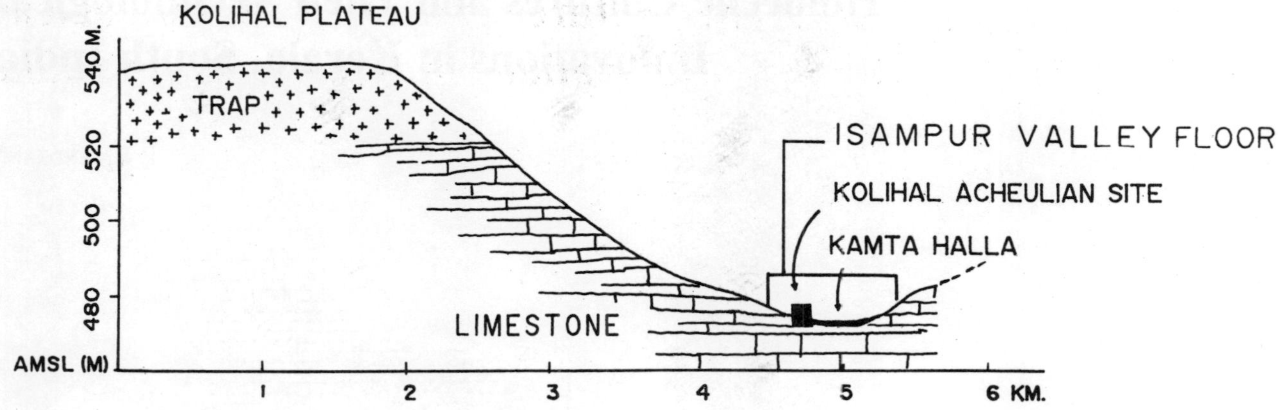

Fig. 3 Profile showing the location of Acheulian site at Kolihal in relation to the valley floor and surrounding uplands

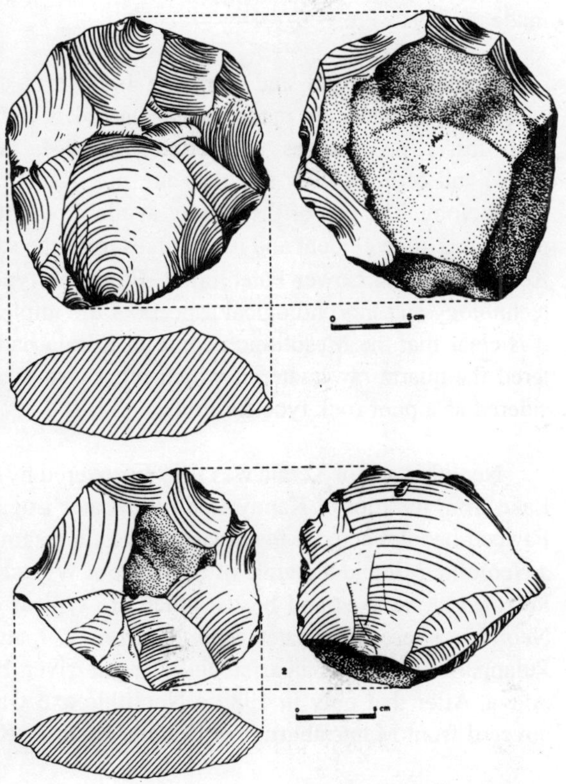

Fig. 4 Artefacts from Acheulian site at Kolihal: 1, prepared core and 2, flake removed from a prepared core

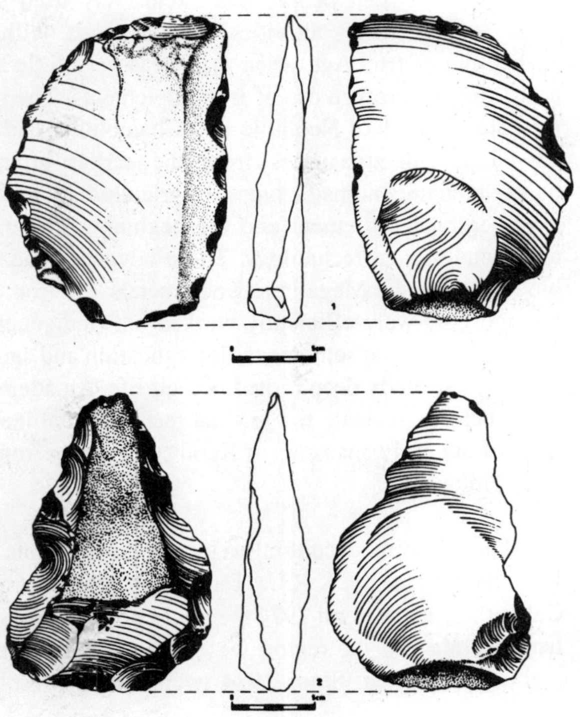

Fig. 5 Artefacts from Acheulian site at Kolihal: 1, flake and 2, handaxe on flake

Holocene Cultures and Their Technological Innovations in Kerala, South India

P. RAJENDRAN*

Introduction

The Holocene cultures in Kerala mainly include the Mesolithic, Neolithic, Chalcolithic and the Megalithic. The discussion starts with the pure Stone Age–Mesolithic – when people had exclusively used stone tools for all their activities, and it ends with the Megalithic or Iron Age when there was very little stone tools; instead profuse use of iron implements. The intermediate stages like Neolithic and Chalcolithic had witnessed several transitions from the earlier group of hunter-gatherers nomadic types to agriculture, domestication, seasonal settlement and the beginning of ceramic and metallurgical technology. These advances had their bloom during the Megalithic when metals like iron, copper and gold were efficiently worked out (indigenously) for their needs and settlement, domestication and agriculture were strongly deep rooted in their life. An attempt is made here to evaluate the gradual technological innovations of our early ancestors of Kerala, beginning from the early Holocene.

The Mesolithic cultural evidence from Kerala was first discovered by K.R.U. Todd from Chevayur near Calicut[1]. Since then till 1974 there was no such discovery from Kerala and the region was rather neglected in the prehistoric studies. Since 1974 twenty-three Mesolithic sites have been discovered by me from various physiographical zones including from rock-shelters. Almost all the Mesolithic sites have yielded implements made exclusively on quartz except at two places where a few tools made of chert were.[2]

Unlike in central and northern India this coastal Mesolithic artifacts are made mostly on flakes (69.44%) with lesser percentages on nodules (16.94), pebbles (8.64) and blades (4.98) and they are not microlithic in morphology. The use of the locally available quartz raw material is quite evident and it continues to be the same in Kerala since the Lower Paleolithic[3]. From the typology, technology and morphological aspects of the implements it is clear that the Mesolithic people in Kerala had mastered the quartz raw material which otherwise was considered as a poor rock type for tools

Neolithic axe in Kerala was first discovered by Philip Lake from the foot of Kannyakod hill[4]. Later Logan and Fawcett had collected a few quartz flakes, a fragment of a Neolithic celt and a couple of beads from Wynad area[5]. Polished stone axes and beads which are typical of the Neolithic phase were later reported from Kalpatta and Pulappalli in Wynad district and Periyar river bed in Aluva. After that only in 1989 a Neolithic axe was discovered from Mantrothuruth in Kallada basin in Kollam

*U.G.C. Research Scientist-C, Dept. of History, University of Kerala, Trivandrum- 695 581.

district, and it was the first Neolithic discovery from south Kerala[6]. This site lies hardly 10 km inland from the Arabian sea. Though in limited number[8], all the three physiographical zones, viz., Lowlands, Midlands, and Highlands of Kerala have yielded Neolithic evidences. Neolithic axes were made either on gneiss or granite rock which are locally available.

Megalithic discovery in India had initially taken place from Bangla Mottaparamba in Chirakkal taluk of Cannanore district in north Kerala. Hundreds of Megalithic burials have been reported from different parts of Kerala after the first discovery of it by Babington[6]. Some of the earlier discoveries from the region include ancient pottery from Malabar[8], Urn burial excavations at Feroke and Porkalam.

Different types of Megalithic monuments have been recorded from the region and they include Rock-cut caves, Rock-cut pits or chambers, Urns, Umbrella-stones, hat-stones, Dolmens; Cists, Menhirs, Hero-stones etc. The above types, in fact, indicate that the Megalithic people in Kerala had made various sepulchrals or monumental structural forms, and good percentage of them were built with laterite. Megalithic monuments made with laterite are the earliest evidence for the utilization of laterite by man for structural purposes. Studies conducted on the Rock-cut caves of Kerala by Logan[10] Sharma, John etc. have revealed the peculiar architectural features of the Megalithic monuments of Kerala.

My Recent Discoveries of Various types of Megalithic monuments from south Kerala include cists, urns, laterite rock-cut chambers, laterite rock-cut domes and Menhirs. Dolmens are also reported from Idukki district. They have yielded various types of hand-made and wheel-made potteries, iron implements, ornaments of gold and copper, human bones of adults and children, cereals and pulses, and rarely stone tools. Here Megalithic evidences are found even 2 km inland from the sea to the Highlands near the Western Ghats while the Mesolithic and the Palaeolithic evidences are, till now found only from the Midlands and Highlands.

Material Culture

Mesolithic

Kerala Mesolithic artifacts are mostly fashioned on the locally available quartz raw material. Different forms of quartz are seen in Kerala as boulders, cobbles, pebbles, gravels and as veins. They include both milky and transparent varieties and among them there are fine grained, and coarse grained types. Eventhough weathering has affected certain quartz pieces people were intelligent enough to discard the weathered ones and select the best. Irrespective of varying qualities of quartz such as compactness, grain size, transparency, weathering etc., the Mesolithic industry is found very rich with different types of implements and it, in fact, proves their mastery over the selection of good quatz raw material for fabrication.

Kerala Mesolithic implements are mostly made on flakes and the tool types mainly include bifacial points, blades, lunates, borers, burins, backed-knives, scrapers, discoids and small choppers made on medium pebbles. Absence of geometric types such as triangles and trapezes are conscpicuous while the presence of bilateral symmetric bifacial points is quite notable. Allthough very less in percentage lunate is represented in almost every site. Unifacial choppers made on small pebbles are peculiar to Kerala unlike other regions of India. Although the industry is primalily on flake the use of blade technology is evident from the presence of flutted cores and blades. Varieties of scrapers on flakes do indicate the richness of the industry.

Some of the Mesolithic rock-shelters in Kerala bear artistic expressions in the form of paintings and carvings which reflect their aesthetic sense. Carvings or petroglyphs are found both in relief and incision . Depiction of floral motives is mostly seen in petroglyphs while animal motives are seen in petrographs while animal motives are seen in petrographs in different colours.

Neolithic

Stone axes are the main type of artifact obtained from Kerala Neolithic cultural phase. At a few places flake and blade tools are also found with stone beads along with stone axes. These stone axes are well made through flaking, pecking, grinding, and polishing. Finished axes are of symmetrical nature and their working edge is well polished. Some of the tools bear use mark as striations at the convex working edge in right angle.

Chalcolithic

A distinct Chalcolithic phase in Kerala has not yet

been discerned. However, a few bronze/copper artifacts have been found in certain Megalithic sites in the region[11]. Since they are seen along with the Megalithic artifacts their separate identity has not yet been ascertained. Whether they fall exactly between the Neolithic and the Megalithic is a matter yet to be proved. One thing is certain that our early ancestors in Kerala too had used such utensils which were made either here or brought from outside. It is pertinent to note that the bronze/copper products were in vogue in several other sites in the country even before the Megalithic times[12]. Some of the human bone remains from Urn burial in Kerala show greater antiquity, probably of the Chalcolithic phase[13].

Megalithic

It is one of the richest prehistoric cultural phases noted in Kerala. Its artifactual richness has been seen in various types of hand-made and wheel-made pottery, different types of heavy and light duty iron implements and ornaments of semi-precious stone beads, copper and gold. Development in metallurgy of copper, iron and gold was important during this period. Besides these artifacts the organic remains of humans and food materials were also recovered from the Megalithic sites[14]. Above all the construction of various types of burial monuments reveal the architectural development during this period. Changes have also been noticed in their settlement, subsistence, domestication, agriculture, beliefs etc.

Technological innovations

Mesolithic culture in Kerala reaches its zenith in the early Holocene and it continued till 3000 BC[15]. Stone tools are the prime indicators of their technical skill. In the case of Kerala they could fabricate most beautiful and effective implements on quartz. Even from the Palaeolithic times Kerala pre-historic people had used quartz as the main raw material for tool-making. This, in fact, reflects dependence on the locally available raw material, and also the innovation and development of suitable stone fabrication technique. Eventhough the utilization of quartz, especially during the Mesolithic has been noticed in various parts of south India it forms only in lesser percentage unlike in Kerala. Other regions, of course, have many other raw materials including the cryptocrystalline types.

Among the tool-types the bifacial points and small choppers are remarkable and they are not commonly seen in other parts of India except Tamil Nadu. The backed-blades, scrapers and lunates are also good examples of their technical skill on quartz. The availability of smaller blades and fluted cores among other artifacts definitely shows the presence of blade technology. However, the blade production was very less. More percentage of flake artifacts perhaps show the necessity for such implements in the then existed ecology to exploit the subsistence. This may be one of the reasons for the morphological and typological changes in the Stone Age industries of different regions.

Mesolithic art in Kerala includes both the petrographs and petroglyphs. Petroglyphs are found at Edakkal in Wynad district, Tenmala in Kollam district, and Ankode in Trivandrum district while petrographs are recorded only from Marayur in Idukki district. Rock incisions in these sites range in age from the Mesolithic to early Historic, and it remains the same in the case of paintings. Eventhough no convincing stone tools are reported from within the Edakkal and Marayur rock-shelters they are found in stratified context at Tenmala and Ankode rock-shelters[16]. Above all the Mesolithic cultural deposit at Tenmala has been dated by ^{14}C to 5210 BP[17] and thereby an indirect date to the prehistoric artistic expression on the same shelter has also been obtained. Charcoal remains within the habitational deposit at Tenmala rock-shelter again confirm the use of fire by the Mesolithic people.

Mesolithic peoples' interaction or mobility between Kerala and Tamil Nadu has been proved with the stray finds of chert implements from Malampuzha open-air site in Palghat district and Ankode rock-shelter site in Perumkadavila in Trivandrum district. Chert is not a locally available rock type in the geological formations of Kerala while it is found in Tamil Nadu. As such the very few chert implements found in these two sites might have their origin in the eastern side of the Western Ghats either as raw material or as finished tools. A few number of chert implements in Kerala point to the fact that the mobility of people between these two coastal regions during the Mesolithic was only of a limited nature unlike in certain other regions. It further explains that probably the people might not have felt the need to search for a better raw material, and their technology was quite apt to fabricate the desired types of tools on quartz. Thus the over all characteristics of the Mesolithic industries in Kerala present certain peculiar features which might have been suited to the regional ecology.

Eventhough the Neolithic artifacts from Kerala are very much limited they represent as the clear indicators of their technical skill. It is testified in the stone Axes, flakes, blades, and beads. Probably some of the artistic expressions in the rock-shelters are also the product of the Neolithic culture. Thus the Neolithic finds recorded till now from Kerala show that there was an almost parallel cultural development as in other regions of south India.

Among the prehistoric cultures Megalithic is the richest cultural phase recorded from almost all places of Kerala. The artifactual richness is rather amazing with the various types of potteries. iron implements, a stone tool and ornaments of gold, copper and beads. The monumental structures are, infact, the true representation of their engineering skill. The secondary burial practices and the funerary materials testify to their faith in 'life after death'. Since no human bone is charred it is certain that they did not practice cremation. The material cultural remains of the Megalithic people speak a lot their status, burial practices, subsistence, settlement, domestication, agriculture, trade, art, architecture, metallurgy etc., indicating a rapid stride towards progress.

Pottery types are of various nature and consist of both hand-made and wheel-made varieties. Pottery jars are generally thick walled with several applique marks and they are partly burned. Small potteries are wheel-made and well-baked and they constitute even the very thin walled types equal to the thickness of egg shell. Black-and-red polishing on potteries are superb, and black polishing is generally seen on the inside surface of the utensils. In certain cases both the surfaces are black polished. The red glaze is generally seen on the outer surface of the pottery. However, applique decorations are seen even on smaller potteries. But no cord or incision marks are seen in any pottery associated with the Megalithic finds in Kerala eventhough such types are found along with the Chinese celadon wares discovered from Tangasseri in Quilon District[18].

Varied types of vases, cups, lids, bowls, pot-rests, etc are the remarkable products of rich ceramic technology. Red ware, black ware, black-and-red ware and grey ware are commonly found. A peculiar type of pottery containing quartz grains on the outer surface is also rarely seen. Some of the sites have yielded good number of pottery indicating more availability of them. This perhaps show the local production and as such the people might be aware of advanced ceramic technology. Lateritic soil and clay which are commonly seen in Kerala were the raw materials for pottery making.

Iron implements of the Megalithic culture include both heavy and light duty tools like swords, daggers, spear-heads, axes, sickles, plough-share, knifes etc. Some of them are offensive and defensive weapons while others are for agriculture and household purpose. They have well made handle and certain tools retain remnants of wooden portions of them. Certain sites have good number of iron implements which again show more availability of them probably due to the indigenous production. Tools have geometric shape and they have the characteristic of beaten iron.

Ornaments of gold, copper and beads of stone and carnelian and shells are sparsely seen with the funerary materials. Among them the gold ornaments like slotted ear-rings, and flower motives are excellent results of perfect metallurgy. They are made with pure thin gold foil and in the case of ear-rings each one has a small slotted copper ring inside which is covered over with the gold foil. Such simple slotted rings mights have used to clip the ears. Gold foil over the ear-rings is cent percent pure gold, having 0.0075 mm thickness and they appear as the products of an advanced technology[19].

Monumental structures like cists, Dolmens, Toppikkals, Kodakkals, Rock-cut caves, Rock-cut Chambers, Domes, Menhirs, Urns, etc. are good examples of their architectural and engineering skill. Cutting of laterite blocks and their balanced placing for hat-stones, umbrella-stones and menhirs as also the shaping of laterite domes and chambers did show a lot of engineering skill. Heavy iron implements and more man power might have used for such work.

The prehistoric method by which large rock slabs were cut for the preparation of cists and dolmens still remains a puzzle. Specialised weapons and high technology are needed to cut such bigger slabs of uniform thickness and shape. Probably some of the heavy iron implements which are seen in the Megalithic context might have served the purpose. Above all more manpower was needed to carry them to the site and for their placing in proper order both in the case of cists and dolmens. Standardised alignment pattern in their construction, whether in clockwise or anti-clockwise, is common everywhere. These kinds of monuments reflect our ancient architectural excellence besides the population strength and teamwork. The complexity of structures and their funerary materials show the status of the dead.

Conclusion

The foregoing account presents some of the salient features of the rich prehistoric cultural heritage of Kerala during the Holocene period. They are quite discernible in the case of Mesolithic, Neolithic and Megalithic. The technological developments during these cultures appear remarkable and they show more or less a separate identity. Dependence on the local environment, in fact, appears to be more prominent here. The pre-historic site-scatter in Kerala does not show any concentration of sites in particular regions instead they are found all over in limited numbers. This again obviates any belief on large scale migration from other regions through certain Gaps in the Western Ghats[20]. Above all there is nothing substantial to show greater mobility of people between the adjacent regions. The material remains of various prehistoric cultures from Kerala point to the fact that the region had witnessed several remains of various prehistoric cultures from Kerala point to the fact that the region had witnessed several technological innovations and developments to cope with the local environment.

REFERENCES

1. Allchin, B. and Allchin, R. 1968. *The Birth of Indian Civilization.* London.
2. _________ 1989. *The Pre-historic Cultures and Environment.* New Delhi.
3. _________ 1981. The Palaeolithic Industries of North Kerala *Bulletin of the Deccan College Research Institute* - 40, pp. 145-64. Poona.
4. Philip, L. 1891. *The Geology of South Malabar, between the Beypore and Ponnani rivers.* Geological Survey of India. Memoirs-24 (3) pp. 221-37. Calcutta.
5. Fawcett, F. 1901. Notes on the rock carvings in the Edakal Cave, Wynad. *Indian Antiquary-XXX* pp. 409-21.
6. Rajendran, P. 1990. Neolithic artifacts in Kerala. *Science Today* 2001 (6), pp. 31. Bombay.
7. Babington, J. 1823. Pre-historic Antiquities. *Tran Lit. Soc. of Bombay* 3, pp. 324-30.
8. Logan, W. 1879. Finds of Ancient pottery in Malabar. *Indian Antiquary,* pp. 309-11. Bombay.
9. Aiyappan, A. 1933. Rock-cut cave tombs of Feroke, Malabar. *Quarterly Journal of Mythic Society* 22, pp. 299-314 Bangalore.
10. John, K.J. 1974. Rock-cut cave tombs of Citrari. *Jour. of Kerala Studies,* 1 (4) pp. 383-7. Trivandrum; Logan, 1879 op cit. Thappar, B.K. 1952. Porkalam 1948: Excavation of a Megalithic Urn-burial. *Ancient India,* 8 pp. 3-16, Sharma, Y.D. 1956. Rock. cut caves in Cochin. *Ancient India,* 12 pp. 93-115; Raghavan, M.D. 1936. The Rock-cut caves of Malabar. *Dr. S. Krishnaswami Aiyangar Commemoration Volume:* 384-89; Rea, A. 1911. Excavation; Prehistoric caves, Perungulam and Excavation; Ancient remains, Kaniyampundi. *Annual Report of Arch Dept.,* Southern Circle pp. 10–13, Madras, also Aiyappan op. cit; 1982.
11. Rajendran, P and A. Kshirsagar. 1993. Poredam Urn burial – A Chalcolithic Culture. *Current Science* – 64 (3) pp. 148-9. Bangalore.
12. Sankalia, H.D. 1874. *Prehistory and Protohistory of India and Pakistan.* Deccan College, Poona.
13. Rajendran and Kshirsagar 1993, op. cit.
14. Rajendran, P and G.L. Badam. 1995. A note on the Megalithic Cultural remains from the Cist burials at Arippa in Kollam District of Kerala, South India. *Current Science,* 68 (7) pp. 684-6. Bangalore.
15. Rajendran 1983 op cit,
16. _________ 1995. Recent Discoveries of the Pre-historic and Proto-historic sites including the Rock Art Sites in Kerala and Their implications. *Review of Social Sciences* 1(3) pp. 52-7. Trivandrum.
17. _________ 1984, 1987 and 1989 op cit.
18. _________ 1996. Ancient Chinese Trade Links. *Jour. of Marine Archaeology* - (5-6) pp. 67, 72-3. Goa.
19. _________ and C.S.P. Iyer. 1997. A Preliminary report on the characterization of Copper and Gold ornaments of

Arippa Megalithic Culture, Kollam District, Kerala, South India. *Man and Environment,* 22 (2) pp. 61-5, Deccan College, Poona.

20. _________ et al. 1993, op cit.

Dholavira and Banawali: Two different paradigms of the Harappan Urbis forma

R.S.Bisht*

Dholavira and Banawali have revealed, of late, two altogether diverse models of the Harappan Urban planning. Indeed, there are certain notional features such as a provision of a 'citadel' and a 'lower town', both secured by formidable defences with corner towers, salients and gateways, and both having a cognisant system of streets, lanes, residential sectors and minimally necessary arrangement for sanitation as well as surface water drainage, which are common to both the models but for the difference in configuration. The Banawali model is different insofar as the outer form, inner layout and location of citadel *vis-a-vis* lower town are concerned. All these features, like in many other cities and towns of the Harappans are, however, present at Dholavira too but in perfect traditional setting and conformation in addition to many more new features which are yet to be found elsewhere in the Harappan context. There is a planner's-dream-come-true situation at Dholavira which has manifested an exquisite and fully advanced example of classical formalism, while at Banawali, there is a departure from conventional regimentation and yet regard for the tenets of utilities in a different modulation indeed. Penchant for orthodoxy in case of the former and wish for resilience and experimentation in the lattar are obvious.

In fact, in either case, there had been antecedents which contributed towards shaping the consecutive forms till the full-blown stage of planning came by. It is, therefore, desirable to describe each against its natural and historical perspective.

BANAWALI

The protohistoric mound at village Banawali (29^0 37 5 N and 75^0 23 6 E), district Fatehabad (earlier Hissar), Haryana, which lies on the right bank of the 'lost' Sarasvati, has provided a nearly complete plan of a pre-Harappan as well as mature Harappan settlements (Fig 1.). For a better appreciation of the changing or evolving patterns of layout, it is necessary to understand the sequence of cultures which run through the pre- Harappan (periods IA & IB), the proto-Harappan or transitional (period IC), the mature Harappan (period II) and the post-Harappan (period III) periods. Furthermore, in order to follow the growth of the successive settlements superimposing each other at the site better, it is also imperative to briefly describe the configuration of the town of the mature phase for the reasons : Firstly, it was probed considerably over different areas; Secondly, the layout of the antecedent settlements can be understood better in relation to it; and thirdly, the unusual planning of the Harappan town was considerably influenced by the overall form of the pre-Harappan habitation.

*Director, Archaeological Survey of India, New Delhi

Like many Harappan sites, the Banawali town too consisted of two distinct components viz., the citadel and the lower town; but, unlike any but for Lothal, it did have them as two seperately located entities (Fig. 1). Rather, it had its citadel as provided well within its town— the former thus being an important subdivision within the latter itself. Both were, as usual, boldly delineated by their respective fortification systems each of which has presented a glaringly unusual formation— an apsidal citadel in a trapezodial town. The citadel occupied a higher and comparitively much larger south-central area of the town in which the former was embraced by the latter from three sides, i.e., the eastern, the northern, and the western. However, on the south, along the river front, the defence along with some some other structures were found to have been destroyed. If the unavailable topographical features together with extant archaeological evidence are relied upon, the citadel and the outer town might have shared a common wall on that side. An attempt is being made in the following account to explain the natural as well as man-made factors responsible for the unusual planning of the Harappan town and its salient features in proper perspectives of the past (Pls. 1-5)

The Pre-Harappan (Kalibangan 1) Period

The juvenile dune upon which the first settlement of Banawali was laid out determined the unusual form of the successive settlements-to-be. Initally, during period IA, it was an open village having no circumvallation. Nothing much was known about the streets and houses owing to the limited nature of the work. Whatever little information that has come by indicated that the house walls followed nearly the cardinal directions and that the principal building material was the sun-dried mud-bricks set in mud mortar, although the manufacturing of fired bricks was not unknown. Interestingly, all the bricks, albeit showing various sizes, were made in the moulds of a definite ratio of 3:2:1 in respect of length, width and thickness. While looking at the general thickness of the walls being made usually of single courses of headers, it may be believed that the houses were low and squat with a light roofing.

Period IB starts with the construction of a comparatively thin boundary wall that was thrown around the settlement. Initally, it was only 1.40 m wide with no tapering on either side. Due to its faulty construction, it soon started developing signs of tilting and a vertical cleavege down the middle and thus necessitating its augmentation by raising a low fender wall along the inner foot. This measure could not alleviate the problem. The outer face of the wall was damaged by water action. At this stage, the boundary wall was built into a massive fortification wall by adding brick-work from outside. This evidence came handy in a section cut across the fortification wall at its apex in the north where its extant width was noticed to be 2.50 to 3.20 m. It may not be the actual breadth which was intentionally reduced by way of chiselling out or slicing away the outer portion to a varying depth by the builders of the succeeding period IC when that deep dressing was carried out for adding from outside another brick-work with a view to obtaining a considerably wide and strong defensive wall. So far the total width of the wall of period IB is concerned, at one place, it was found to be about 3.60 m.

Making a large westward curve from its northern apex, the defensive wall of period IB has been found running for about 230 m of length beyond which it has been washed away completely. Out of that length, an arm admeasuring 150 m runs from the north-east to the south-west and from there, possibly making another apex lying in the west, it takes a south-westerly course for over 40 m. Along the eastward curve, it could be seen running from the north-west to the south-east for about 40 m beyond which it had been superimposed probably by the wall of the mature Harappan period. It was only nearer the south-eastern end that it was found reappearing for about 15 m of stretch all through which it made a tortuous curve from the north-east towards the south-west. Beyond that, it was destroyed by large pits dug up there by the post-Harappans.

Curiously enough, whenever the defensive wall has been exposed, it was found to have delimited the habitation of period IB. As already indicated, all along the eastern side, the wall still remained untraced. The probings that were made there on either side of the later-day citadel wall, revealed the structures of the period IC lying under the mature Harappan ones and overlying the pre-Harappan deposit particularly in the western part of the east-central zone which otherwise too registers an elevated topography. It strongly suggested that the habitational area of periods IB and IC was extending on to the East. That extended area was perhaps left out from the Harappan citadel. If that be so, the fortification wall of these periods was making a larger and a more tortuous curve towards the east where it was most plausibly following the contours of the dune and thus making the outline of the enclosing fortification more likely an oblong oval having its longer axis from east to west.

If to look elsewhere for comparision, Rehman Dheri, Kot Diji, Kalibanga, Balu and Harappa are some of the sites where some sort of fortification around a settlement of the times preceding the mature phase of the Harappa culture are known to be existing to a varying degree of exposure. At Rehman Dheri, it is appears to be fairly rectangular. A somewhat similar situation might have prevailed at Kot Diji. However, Kalibanga has revealed almost a complete formation of the fortification which is designed like a pentagon with straight arms. At Balu, an adequate uncovering still remains a desideratum. So far Harappa is considered, only a little segement of what appears to be a perimeter wall at the north-western corner of the mound E is laid bare. Curiously enough, enough of the southern and eastern arms of the succeeding mature Harappan habitation are exposed and particularly the former shows a cursive run which might have been dedicated to be so due to a similar nature of the pre-existing wall which perhaps lies concealed within as well as under the exposed one : Banawali has presented a most unusual pattern so far.

So far as the other details of the layout within the pre-Harappan settlement at Banawali are concerned, the picture that emerges is as sketchy as it was during period IA. At the initial stage of the defence phase (period IB), there existed some structures abutting the defensive wall. However, later on, a narrow street running along the inner side of the defensive wall was maintained always. At one point on the north, a narrow ramp-like structure made of *pucca* bricks with a brick lining has been found piercing through the wall. Since there are no side walls to that structure, it cannot be taken for a drain. Possibily, it was a narrow postern entrance suficient only for admitting a file of single individuals. In any case, it could have drained out the surface run-off as well. On the other side of the wall, there was found brick-on-edge paving abutting the fortification wall. A little farther, near the northern apex of the perimeter wall, there was found cut into the ground a drain-like feature with slanting sides and a flat bottom running at a distance from and parallel to the wall. It was perhaps meant for letting out the rain-water. This feature was got filled up with brick masonary subsequently during the period IC while the defensive wall of the preceeding phase was being widened.

There was found beside the northern apex of the wall a house gutted in fire. The burnt debris that was found inside a room showed that the roof of the house was made of wooden poles, twigs and grass and plastered over with the straw mixed earth. The houses were generally remained quite low in height as the thin walls indicated. For construction, besides those of the ratio of 3:2:1 there were a few bricks of square surface made the ratio of 3:3:1.

Thus, the evidence of planning and architecture whatever meagre was significatant.

The Proto-Harappan Period

The succeding phase, i.e., period IC, showed up itself as a transitional phase, or rather a stage of introduction of the proto Harappan elements in an otherwise continuing ceramic *milieu* of the preceeding culture. It is characterised by drastic changes in planning, architeture and antiquities. It is singularly significant, not only in that it witnessed the debut of certain typical items such as the bricks marked by a novel ration of 4:2:1, triangular cakes and 8-shaped nodules of terracotta, chert blades and a few proto-Indus pottery forms and designs which would become later on regular and standard cultural companions of the following mature Harappan period, but also in that the entire settlement was enlarged into a bipartite township. The interior of the settlement was planned and constructed *de novo*. All the pre-existing residential houses were razed to the ground and fresh ones were raised with the newly introduced bricks and with thicker walls of better workmanship. The general orientation of houses was also underwent a trifling change. Furthermore, a new street system was introduced although not enough could be gathered about that. However, the antecedent fortification wall was spared from demolition. It was rather appropriated as it was widened almost twice as much. It was in fact during this significant phase that the precedent fortress, thus reinforced and rebuilt, was converted into citadel, and on three sides viz., the east, north, and west the lower town was laid out within a larger framework of fortification, designed like a trapezoid, within which the citadel, planned in the form of a horseshoe with its apex towards the north, occupied a large south-central area. On the south, along the river front, as stated already, the outer town and the citadel might have shared a common wall which had since been erased partly by the flows and partly by the post-Harappans who caused a large-scale destruction of earlier structures and accumulation in that area particularly. It is also evident that the radial arrangement of streets in the lower town came into existence during the phase. The curvilinear nature of the pre-existing fortification wall which was adopted and widened by the proto-Harappans was largely responsible for this novel street system.

As said before, the houses of this phase were generally oriented slightly differently from those of the preceding times and the masonry work was also far more improved. Besides several partially exposed structures, there has been fully exposed a modestly large house having seven enclosed spaces. The house occupied a vantage location in the north-eastern corner of the local town. In fact, it was surrounded by the two major streets, one each on the east and the north . and two lanes on the remaining sides. Significantly, the major streets were found running respectively along the eastern and northern arms of the outer fortification and the lanes emanated from either of them. The house was provided with a room at each of the four corners in addition to two large ones, running parallel and lying side by side on the west, and a much larger courtyard, designed in the form of the Roman 'T' that lay in the east. Furthermore, there was a small cubicle that is built in the wall probably as a silo for storing foodgrains. Outside, on one of the lanes, there was attached from the outside to the house another cuboid for keeping firewood or fodder. The house must have belonged to a wealthy person or a high offical. Unfortunately, nothing could be gathered about the furnishings and provisions of the house which had been eroded to the level of the substructure which could be found in foundation only expecting a part of the countryard in which some traces of a fire-place were seen.

Inside the citadel, close to the fortification wall at the northern apex, there were laid bare a few curious apsidal structures, each normally with a smaller apsidal construction as a fire-place provided in the apse. Such structures were surely related to fire-activity. However, on the basis of the associated material, those appeared to be industrial rather then religious in nature.

This entire phase was rather found devoid of the mature Harappan objects but for the bricks, etc; as has already been discussed briefly.

The Harappan Period

Period II ushered in the Harappan culture at Banawali in its full-blooded form. But now, the change was rather sweeping both qualitatively and quantitatively. And yet, there was a strong element of continuity in that the Harappan generously accepted in bequest from their predecessors the outlines of the town albeit with marginal modifications here and there. These changes necessitated redefining of street system as well as concomitant residential sectors. Once again, all the houses of the preceding phase were demolished and new ones were built. Once that was done, the Harappans scrupulously maintained that planning all throughout the five months of their regular habitational deposit that contained therein six or more building phases, spanning a time period of about five centuries or so.

Two altogether different forms— the apsidal one for the citadel and trapezoidal for the general town— determined the unusual inner layout of the Harappan settlement. In the whole scheme, the citadel being the original, pre-eminent form and surely the seat of authority, it became the nucleus around which a new system of streets and attendant sectors was developed. The divergent formation of the outer town also brought about some moderation in the planning.

Salient features of the planning of the Harappan town at Banawali

1. Now that the outer fortification has revealed three out of its four corners lying in the south-east, north-east and north-west respectively, its trapezoidal conformation has became amply obvious. There were no two arms which were found to be either parallel to each other or equal in length. While the eastern and the northern walls were found to have measured 240 m and 250 m for their respective lengths, the western one could be ascertained for a run of about 300 m beyond which it was seen to

have been washed away. So far the missing wall on the south is concerned, its existence in the past on the strength of the evidence that was partially brought to light at the south-eastern corner cannot be denied. For poor results on that count, inadequate probings admittedly and large-scale vandalism wrought by man and nature are largely responsible. Now, relying on the prevailing contours, as well as general nature of the layout of the fortification, together with closely located structures and streets, we have been not less but more than 385 meters. Regarding total area of the town including its fortifications and the in lying acropolis, it is estimated to be somewhere around 8.8 to 9 hectares.

2. Another innovation of special significance was the provision of a V-shaped moat which may have surrounded the circumvallation of the town. The moat has been duly vouched for in the dig cut across at three far-flung locations along the entire length of the eastern arm, while it has already taken a westerned turn at the north-eastern corner to run compliantly along the northern one. Furthermore, its presence along the western wall as strongly suggested by the derbis resembling the moat's fill in a small gash which could not be expended owing to the then prevaling constraints. So far the southern side is concerned, no attempt was made to look for it due to the large-scale destruction of the contemporary archaeological deposit that was caused in the past. It is, however, not certain whether the moat should be running along there too where the Sarasvati might be flowing perhaps. It is not an improbability either. It perhaps depended largely on the nature of the water volume and physical situation of the river of yore.

So far other details are concerned, there always maintained a road between the moat and the defensive wall. It not only served the purpose of providing easy movement of security guards, maintenance staff and others but also functioned as a berm to safeguard the fortification against water action. More importantly, the moat may have formed a formidable first line of defence in the wake of an attack.

On the present showing, the moat has shown 5.70m to 6.50m for the width at the top and 3.60 m for the depth. The earlier contention based on the interpretation of the existing stratigraphy that it was a later introduction at the site of the moat were found neatly dressed in all the three digs. it is an inexplicable situation indeed because unlined sides of a *cutcha* moat are extremely vulnerable to erosion by water. it is, therefore, certain that the Harappan must have resorted to periodical clean shaving of the sides and in the process causing progressive windening of the moat and narrowing of the lateral road and thus obliterating the evidence of original cutting of the moat.

Flaring sides of a water channel effectively control velocity and thrust of water and its erosive power too. Besides, slanting sides with an acute angle the bottom in the moat made the crossing or scaling not only difficult but served as trap for the trespasser too.

Another interesting feature was a shallow yet more or less equally wide channel running parallel to the moat at a little distance away to the east. It was perhaps meant for draining out the surplus water or surface run-off, or to feed water to the moat. It is not yet probed elsewhere to see whether or not it was just a local feature.

3. Standing out majestically on an elevated ground, a vantage location in the much larger area in the south central zone of the town, the citadel, truly as an acropolis, domineeringly commanded over the entire townscape and the surrounding landscape including the Sarasvati flowing past to south. Much has been said about its horseshoe-like or apsidal formation. To be more precise in delineation, the citadel looked in a prostrate archway having its pointed curvature on the north and its somewhat straight arm (and a corresponding feature existing in the north-west may as well be a possibility). The eastern arm of the citadel, which might be having a much pronounced curvature during the preceding phases seems to have been shifted westward for straightening it out by way of adding from outside, i.e., the town-side, a series of right-angled projections and recesses which were gradually shifted towards the west while along the inner side the existing curvature was allowed to exist as may be seen at the south eastern area of the citadel wall.

Another noticeable feature was that the builders made efforts to make the graduatedly straightened eastern arm of the citadel to be parallel to its counterpart of the outer fortification, however, curiously enough, only for so long as the former ran fairly straight, but as soon as it took a sweeping curve towards the north-west, the eastern town wall too started to re-orient itself to be slightly moving off to the east and yet maintaining its straight run upto the north eastern corner. The space between the straight walls of the citadel and the town has measured 68m to 70m.

Another interesting feature was obvious that only about 25% of the area lying in the east-central zone of the citadel now contains the Indus structures. Of course, it is this area of the division which still retains mounded surface intact, while the rest of the area has been considerably destroyed for making terraced fields for cultivation. Earlier, it was surmised that hapless removal of the ancient accumulation had caused the disappearance of the Indus remnants beyond redemption. But, subsequent excavation and surface study indicated that the entire area of the citadel was never made crowded with houses. Had that been so, the western slopes of the undisturbed mound should have yielded the Indus structures. But there are none. One comes across directly with the houses of period IC on the margins or with those of the pre-Harappans all over the leveled area further down. Secondly, such a wholesale dislodgment of the 5 m of the Indus and 1 m of the proto-Indus debris would have caused an extensive and high ground replete with antiquarian remains outside the confines of the ancient settlement. Thirdly, the Sarasvati may not have washed away that debris entirely nor the normal process of erosion would had caused such a disappearance of it. This longish explanation is necessary because we believe that at least half the area, or even more of the Harappan citadel might have been maintained as an open space to whatever use, maybe to multi-purpose use. Such an provision at Dholavira may be seen pratically in its every division of the Harappan city.

The maximum span along the east-west in the citadel as obtained so far has measured 300 m while it should go upward of 310 m further down along the suspected base line. The north-south distance has been confirmed for 175 m to which another 10-15 m may be added. The total area of the citadel may thus account for 2.7 to 2.8 hectares.

4. If the estimated area of the citadel is compared with that the entire town, it approximated to one-third of the whole.

5. Coming to the construction of the defences, true to the Indus norms, all the Walls were entirely made of moulded bricks set in mud morter and finally plastered over with mud mortar mixed with husk and dung (Pl.1). Further, the walls rose from a broader base with a taper on either side. Yet another important feature of the planning was the peripheral road running all through uninterruptedly on either side of the fortifications whether it appertained to the town or the citadel. Like any other road, street, or lane, the outer ring road too was carefully maintained even by raising it periodically. Additionally, this arrangement must have served the useful purpose of guarding as well as maintaining the defences besides facilitating easy movement of inhabitants and goods. Besides, it should have been a protective berm for the defences against the erosion by the water of the encompassing moat. Such a provision may have been a standard practice at some or many of the Indus towns and it must, therefore, be looked into elsewhere too.

6. Streets at Banawali too played a vital role in the urban planning of the Harappans. Banawali was no exception to that. It has rather accentuated the role of streets all the more in such a configration of the town which is so different from the monotonous formalism the Harappan have been known for. Banawali has rather offered a pleasant mix of prescriptions, that too quite paradoxically. It may be seen that the citadel has, notwithstanding its curvatural delineation, resolved itself in a formal arrangement of streets and lanes which ran straight almost along the cardinal directions and cut each other at the right angles and thereby determined a fairly rectangular form for individual housing sectors of which six units can be easily identified and a few more conjectured on the site plan of the Banawali town. On the other hand, the lower town, being trapezoidal in conformation and thus somewhat yet other hand, the lower town, being trapezoidal in conformation and thus somewhat yet closer to the conventional parallelogram for outline, has exhibited a nucleated radial layout of streets and lanes which, in turn, demarcated a series of triangulate of acutely trapezoidal residential sectors.

In this unconventional layout, there were seen certain focal points for streets, like spokes of wheel, to converge on or radiate from. They, therefore, made an acute or obtuse angle at the point of bifurcation. Futher, the focal points were determined by important architectural features such as gates.

In the lower town, one such focal point was near the

impressive 'east gate' where five major streets— three coming fronm the interior of the town and two running along the fortification wall— met with the passageway of the gate on a broad piazza (Pl.2). To that may also be added the outer ring road which too might be bringing the travellers from two opposite directions to the passageway. It hardly needs an emphasis that the gate should have been connected to a highway or highway which too should be bringing travellers, traders and others from the countryside and other urban centres as well as facilitating an outflow likewise. The importance of the piazza was further enhanced by the find of a well, the solitary one found thus far at Banawali, was provided there.

Another piazza in the lower town was found under the shadow of the enormous partition wall of the citadel. It lay in the south-eastern zone of the town. At that place, there was exposed a much eroded stairway going up across the wall for providing intercommunication between the two division of the town. On the side of the citadel there was laid bare an extensive mud-brick platforn which once might be furnished with a flight of steps which has since been eroded completely.

As a rule in general, no streets showed use of vehicular traffic at all. It must not have been permitted. The kind of entrances that are uncovered so far lend credence to this belief. The only expception was seen in the outer street near the northern apex of the citadel wall. There were found several pairs of rut marks cut deep into successive street floors. Signifiantly, the distance between the two corresponding ruts conformed to what a resent-day bullock cart causes, It can be opined that plying of vehicles was restricted to some special streets only.

7. The elaborate gate-complex constructed in the thickness of the eastern town wall is an important architectural marvel. It was provided with a frontal moat, flanking bastions, a broad passageway, a postern stairway and a storm-water drain. The passageway was furnished with a longitudinal drain (Pl.3) and a latitudinal tie-wall both of which were made of pucca bricks set in mud mortar. The drain showed five phases of rebuilding. During each phase, it should have been rendered concealed under a ramp, or more plausibly, under a flight of steps of which the tie-wall may have been the first one from the inside. The moat that passed by in the front yielded among other things a mandible of a young elephant. It could not, however, be determined as to how one got across the moat to reach the gate. Possibly, there was a wooden bridge.

8. Despite the restricted nature of the excavation in both the divisions of the town, it may be recorded that there was seen no appreciable difference in the quality and types of houses (Pl.4). There are carefully made, impressive and large vis-a-vis less ostentious houses in both the parts. The only difference was seen that there are quite a few bathing platforms made of fired bricks in the toilets of the citadel houses whereas, in the lower town, none of them have been found so far. Instead, there were ordinary platforms spread with terracotta nodules and potsherds. For sanitatiion, pottery jars, connected to house drains of baked bricks, were placed on the streets or lanes. However, for letting out the surface water, the Harappan made regular and broad drains with or without aprons in front of the head- all made of baked bricks. Such drains were found piercing through the defences of under the passageway of a gate. In the streets and lanes, the rain-water was allowed to flow freely and cause gushes and pot-holes at will.

Overall picture that emerges is that Banawali was a small prosperous town, a seat of authority and a centre of trade and commerce. Its layout has indeed shown an unknown example of urban planning of the Harappans. So far the period III which belonged to a post-Indus stage as it yielded nothing of the classical attributes such as planning, architecture and antiquities is out of the scope of this essay. It may however be added that it was a small village consisting of pise houses of little pretension.

DHOLAVIRA

An enormous accumulation caused by successive settlements of over one a half millennium has revealed seven significant cultural stages documenting the rise and fall of the first Indian urbanization that is what the Harappan civilization (Pl. 6-15). Besides, it has brought to light a major as well as a model Harappan city which is remarkable for its exquisite planning, mounumental structures, aesthetic architecture and amazing water-management system .It also enjoys the unique distinction of yielding an inscription made up of ten large-sized signs of the Indus script. A variety of funerary structures is yet another features of exceeding importance as it is likely to throw new light on the socio-religious practices and beliefs, and, therby indicating the presence of a more diverse social matrix in the Indus population.

The ancient site at Dholavira (230 53' 10" N; 700 13' E), Taluka Bhachau, district Kachchh in state Gujarat, lies in the north-western area of the island of Khadir which, it turn, is strongly isolated by the cheerless and barren salt waste of the Great Rann of Kachchh. Lying ot the north of the village, the ancient settlement is embraced by two storm-water tunnels, namely, the Manhar in the south and Mansar in the north. Originating in the low chain of the hills running along the northern edge of the both descend through a short course into the Rann in the west. The ruins, including the cemetery, lie half-way down the slope and are spread over an area of about 100 hectares half of which was apropriated by the articulately fortified settlement of the Harappans alone.

Layout of the city

The salient components of the full-grown cityscape consisted of a biapartile 'citadel', a 'middly town' and a 'lower town', two 'stadia'— one wide and extensive, the other much smaller and compact— an 'annexe', a series of reservoirs— all of them set within enormous fortification running on all four sides (Fig. 2). The city was perhaps configured like a large parallelogram boldly outlined by massive walls with its longer axis being from the east to west. On both sides of the city-wall, there was provision of a broad road running all around. On the bases of their relative location, planning, defences and architecture, the three principal divisions are designed tentatively as 'citadel', 'middle town', and 'lower town', which temptingly sound analogous respectively to three interesting terms in the Rigveda viz., 'parama' 'madhyama' and 'avama' (which are used in all three genders as adjectives or nouns denoting three different categories of zones, regions, stations, even settlements or building, whether divine, ethereal, terrestrial or human).

The citadel at Dholavira, unlike its counterparts at Mohenjodaro, Harappa and Kalibangan, was laid out in the south of the city area. Like Kalibangan and Surkotada it had two conjoined subdivisions, tentatively christened as 'castle' and 'bailey' , laocated on the east and west respectively, Both are fortified ones. The former is the most zealously guarded by impregnable defences and aesthetically furnished with impressive gates, towers and salients while the latter is lower in height and enclosed by compatatively less thick walls. To the north of the citadel was provided a broad and long ground which may have been put to multiple purpose such as for community gathering on festive or special occassions, a stadium and a marketing place for exchanging merchandise during trading seasons (s). Further north, there was laid out the enwalled middly town, and to the east of it was founded the lower town. The last - mentioned one did not have an appurtenant fortfication though, it was set within the general circumvallation running around the entire city. These three major built-up divisions made together an L- shaped design : the citadel and the middly town forming the shorter line from the south - north and the middle town and the lower town forming the larger stroke along the west-east axis.

Besides, to the south of the castle, across the adjoining reservoir, there was raised another built-up area runing along the city wall. It should, as it appears, have been an annexe meant for housing the retainers and menials attending on the privileged occupants of the castle of a warehouse.

Growth and Decline of the urbanism vis-a-vis the settlements

The layout that is briefly described above pertained to the fully-developed form of the Harappan city, the Harappa culture as well as urbanization. There are identified seven major cultural stages signifying gradual rise, culmination and fall of the Urban System of the Harapan civilization vis-s-vis the settlement. This sequence in its entirety is best documented in the occupational debris lying stratified in the castle which alone withnessed all the vicissitudes spread over a time period of one and a half millenniums (Fig. 3). The total artificial accumulation works out to about 15 m out of which only 11.30 m accounted for regular occupation, while the remaining one goes with the one-time raising of 2 m in addition to the higher ridges of the defensive walls.

The first settlements that was raised at the site in Stage I was a strong fortress now lying buried in the citadel mound. A part of the southern arm of its fortification, running along the east-west axis, was laid bare near the south-western cornet where its basal width measured 11.10 m from where the wall with tapering sides rose to the extant height 4 m. It yet showed sign of further rising. This fortification perhaps covered a somewhat larger area, particularly in the east, where remains of a massive wall of identical nature and orientation has been found running further eastward beyond the south-eastern corner tower of a later date.

The foundation of the planning that was laid in Stage I formed the nulceus on which the subsequent settlements of the later stages expanded gradually. Even the building materials, whether standardized bricks (9 x 8 x 36 cm, ratio 1 : 2 : 4) or stone, both undressed and dressed, ramained in use.

The authors of this stage were fully well-versed in copper working, stone-dressing, bead-making, shell working and advanced ceramic technology as well as in planning and architecture. Our earlier statement of designing it as a "Non-Harappan' or Pre-Harappan' stage (as reported in this bulletin, No. 20-1989-90) now stands revised. While non-Harappan character of the ceramics is admitted in general, there were seen many an element which strongly suggested a formative stage in which the classical Harappan items had their origins : monumental and massive fortification with a broad accompanying street, use of moulded bricks yielding the well-known ratio of 4 : 2 : 1 in respect of length, width and thickness, presence of perforated jars, dish-on-stand, basins, the 'reserve slipped' ware, triangular terrocotta cakes and chert blades, occuring from the beginning. All those items would proliferate and get standardized successively and become essential cultural companions of the Harappa culture all throughout in time and space. Thus, Dholavira had stooped to evolve the Harappa culture in no uncertain terms.

In stage II, a 2.80 m thick brick masonry wall was added to the pre-existing defensive wall from the inner side and the face of it was plastered over with fine paste of white and pink clays at least as many as thirteen times. There is another significant development that took place. A residential area was coming up to the north of the walled settlement. Besides, pottery forms and antiquities diversified as well as increased in both quality and quantity.

Stage III was a most creative and important one in many respects : the southern arm of the antecedant fort-wall was further widened from the inner side with an additional brick-masonry of about 4.5 m and the existing walled settlements was made into a castle and another walled subdivision, arbitrarily called as bailey,was added to it from the west. In the north, the extended residential area of stage II was cleared of structures for carving out a multipurpose ground. Further north, the extensive walled town (which would become middle town subsequently) was founded. Reservoirs were created on the south, west and north of the built-up divisions. And, finally, an outer fortification in order to surrounded all those components was constructed, during this stage, for the first time, three steatite seals with figures but without inscriptions appeared in addition to a potsherd bearing Indus signs and a cubical weight. Besides, a good number of classical Harappan pottery forms with painted motifs made their debut.

When the town of Stage III had lived two-thirds of its life, it was immensely damaged by a natural catastrophe, most possibly by an earthquake of intense magnitude, Its tell-tale marks are distinctly present in the defensive wall of the castle. Repairs were undertaken and lower town was added and the city-walls were extended further eastwards in order to enclose as well the newly found division of the settlement. As a result, the erswhile town attained full cityscape that dominated the cultural scenario for centuries through Stages IV and V. In stage III B itself, certain more qualitative changes took place, as if under new dictates for planning, so as to obtain fresh prescribed ratios and proportions within each as well as amongst different divisions of th enlarged city. It shall be dealt with later on. Likewise, it brought about some modifications and alterations practically in each of the earlier division and subdivision of the settlement.

It is significant to note here that uptill then, through all the three stages., i.e., I, II and III, the inhabitants exhibited an abiding preference for colourful clays. e.g., white and pink structures such defensive walls, roads, streets or the ceremonial ground, or to the walls and floors of private houses. In this situatuion, we may infer that even roof tops of house were also being treated similarly.

But, this tradition came to an abrupt end with the end of Stage III, as if under a royal decree or by a resolute public consensus. In this case, we are tempted to think loudly that there came about a drastic, rather an almost revolutionary, or reactionary change verging on political, social or religious fervour or commotion. We would soon witness more changes coming close on the heels. However, before that, the cityscape had attained its fullest growth.

Stage IV belong to the classical Harappan culture which is so widely familiar with from a large number of excavated sites. Almost all the salient features of the city-planning were scrupulously maintained alongwith the monumental structures such as gateways, fortification, drainage-system. Those elegant pillar members as well as freestanding columns were the creations of this stage or that of the preceding one. The famous ten-signed inscription was surely in use in this stage. All the classical Harappan elements such as pottery, seals, weights, beads, items of gold, silver, copper, ivory, shell, faience, steatite, clay and stones are found in abundance.

Stage V is characterized by the gereral decline particularly in the maintenance of the city. It is more vividly reflected in the citadel. The other items such as pottery, seals, weights, etc., continued in use.

This stage was followed by a temporary desertion of the site, perhaps not lasting more than a few decades before the Stage VI ushered in.

Stage VI presents a state of transformed Harappa culture which is so widely distributed in Gujarat. New ceramic traditions coming from the sides of Sind, Rajasthan and other parts of Gujarat made appearance. The one-time city shrank into a smaller town which became confined to the citadel and the southern margin of the middle town where they delimited it by raising a wall of an entirely different workmanship. The classical planning was largely given a go-by. Only the fortifiction of the castle, the bailey, and partly that of the middle town and partly of the city, which were still standing with their gates, were appropriated for use. Domestic buildings were laid out in a different planning. And, those were, by and large, rickety and jerry-built. Bricks were no longer in use. While many of the pottery forms together with distinct decorative motifs were still in vogue, the fabric had certainly underwent a perceptible change. In addition, new ceramics in the form of white painted black-and-red and white painted grey wares along with a coarse ware bearing incised or applique or both kinds of designs made their appearence. Many other traditional items continued in use though the seals underwent a change. Rather being square in form, those were long rectangular with a flat or triangular back. Those still bore nicely cut inscriptions only and no figures. Their shapes always became smaller and simpler. Stone cubical weights were still in vogue in addition to those out of potsherts. Overall picture that is projected is that impoverishment and rapidly crumbling urbanism. Having lived there for about a century, the late Harappans of Stage VI abandoned the settlement.

The desertion that followed was certainly a longer one. How long? it is not certain at present. The new comers of Stage VII had forgotten the classical Harappan fabrics, shapes and designs. Strangely enough, the new - comers built their houses in an entirely new form that was circular (Pl. 15). No planning as such is discernible. All the urban attributes became conspicuous by their absence.

Thus the urbanization that made its humble beginnings in stage I and went on progressing through Stages II, III and IV, started decaying in Stage V and underwent a transformation in Stage VI with a feeble revival only to become totally de-urbanized in Stage VII. The site was never occupied thereafter.

Planning : A Resume

At the outset, it may be stated that the measurements of general features and important structures were taken by a single team with the aid of the same set of instruments and tools including the measuring tapes so that the margin of error remained uniform. Tools were simple and ordinary. To the maximum possible extent, measurements between distant or near features were obtained at contemporaneous working levels. Results were cross- checked geometrically with the grid-plan. Still a good deal of cross-checking is necessary both on the ground and with the numerous detailed drawings of the collection. Therefore, the measurements will remain subject to correction. So far the error is concerned, the measurements obtained may be slightly on higher side, if not lower. Margin of error in respect of longer distances particularly may be higher at most by 0.2 to 0.5 percent.

For recording, in the first year of excavation, Wheeler's system of grid-plan was adopted. It did not work satisfactorily at an extensive site like this. Therefore, a new system, named as GSQ, was devised. One square kilometer of area bearing antiquarian remains was brought within the GSQ system and divided into 100 grids- each measuring 100x100 m; each grid was further divided into 100 squares of 10x10 m each; and each square, as usual, was subdivided into quadrants of 5x5 m each. Both grids and squares thus had rows of tens either-way. Serial numbers denoted by arabic numerals ran from north to south starting from the north-east. In case of quadrants, numbering was clock-wise from the north-east. To elucidate, 11.20.4 represents the 4th quadrant of 20th square of 11th grid.

For excavation, five rows of squares criss-crossing the entire settlement in a tic-tac-toe fashion in order to cover principle features and divisions, etc. were chosen for excavation.

Needless to say, it helped to conjure up an overall picture. The GSQ plan was laid out 40<50 off the orientation of the visible features of architecture and planning.

Fortification

Lying in between the storm-channels and half-way down between the hills and the Rann, the site with a few rocky proturberances and ridges and naturally deposited sediments was ideally suited for a settlement having fortifications, built-up areas and artificial dams and reservoirs. The fortification walls, both inner and outer, were in fact solid structures made of proportionately moulded mud-brickes set in mud mortar. Successive courses of brick-work were laid in a recessed manner. As a result, both the faces registered a marked taper, While the outer faces of the inner ones were plastered with clay. Only in the event of repairs or where the walls or bastions were susceptible to erosion the builders resorted to stone facing.

The outer wall which was constructed in Stage III and remained in use throughout Stage IV and V and partly during Stage VI runs for a length of 781 m along the east-west axis on the north and 630.50 m along the north-south on the west. The southern arm is traceable for a distance of about 600 m and the eastern one for 210 m with a vague indication for another 100m. In the east, the ground being higher and more vulnerable to surface water and wind action, the eastern wall and half the northern wall had suffered considerably to the extent of being oblitewrated for stretches. In the south-eastern quarter, particularly across the Manhar nallah, the wall, if existed at all, is not traceable now. Another, interesting feature is the provision of projectiong salients almost at regular intervals. Depending on the presence of vaguely to fairly observable remains there were provided, excluding the corner towers, 11 salients along the northern and 9 ones along the western arm of the city-wall, roughly at a distance of 50 to 52 m. Similarly, salients can be seen along the extant segments of the other arms too.

Likewise, there were 5 salients along the northern and 4 along the western arms of the middle town. Barring a smaller one in the south, no other gateways pierceing through the outer walls has so far been exposed although there are certain prospective points. Of course, one gate provided in the east arm of the middle town is laid bare while a few others are suspected in the other arms as well. In the castle, there was provided an impressive gate somewhere in the middle of each arm, although in the eastern wall a wide opening furnished with a flight of broad steps going down thickness of the defensive wall in addition to a regular gate. But, surprisingly, the steps in this gate under reference stopped on the outer edge of the wall and never descended onto the lower ground level on the east—thus rendering its function indeterminate.

Ratios and Proportions

The city of Dholavira in its fullest form was a precisely proportionate whole and proportionality resolved configuration following a resolute set of principle of planning and architecture with mathematical precision and perhaps with astronomically established orientation.

Of the city, at present, three corners with partially eroded towers but fully intact inner corners are fairly traceable and thus confirmed by excavation, Those are ltying in the north-east, the north-west and the south-west. They together have provided the northern and the western arms of the outer fortification. When measured on the ground from the inner corners to the corresponding inner corners, the E-W length along the northern defensive wall and N-S one along the western one worked out to 771.10 m and 616.87 m, respectively—thus giving the precise ratio of 5 : 4. Similarly, the other divisions of the city also revealed amazing ratios and proportions which rather provided in all other major and minor entities of planning and architecture. However, in the following table only some principle features are taken into account

Sl. No.	Division	Width	Length	Ratio
1	City Internal	616.85	71.1	4 : 5
2	Castle Internal at available top	92	114	4 : 5
3	Castle External as per present exposure	118	151	4 : 5
4	Citadel (castle+bailey) External approx. (incl. bastions)	140	280	1 : 2
5	Bailey Internal	120	120	1 : 1
6	Middle Town +Stadium Internal	290.45	340.5	6 :7
7	Middle Town excl. Stadium Internal	242	340.5	5 : 7
8	Stadium Internal	47.5	283	1 : 6
9	Lower Town Built-up area	300	330	10 : 11

While respective proportions in each case are sigfnificant, more interesting is the inter relationship among all the divisions and subdivisions. Of all, the most important is the relatioinship between the city and the castle, the latter being the most important as a center of the supreme authority of the settlement. As already seen, both the city and the castle provided the same ratio, i. e., 5 : 4 in respect of their respective length and width. But a closer examination reveals that the outer length of the castle is 1/5 of that of the city area while the inner one is 1/7 and the same is the case in regard to the respective measurements of contemporaneous level. So far the castle is concerned, the inner measurements are obtained at the extant upper top and the outer ones at the hitherto exposed levels. In no case, the level of original construction is reached so far. Against this background, an explanation is necessary. The outer area of the castle provides the measurements of 151x118m, which ideally should be about 154x123 m. Similarly, the inner measurements could be 10x88 m. Keeping in account the sharp taper on both faces of the fortification walls as well as the seven to eight meters of thickness of the occupational deposit inside the castle, the measurement in both cases should be what are visualised above. If that be so, as it should be, the ratio of 5:4 is highly significant. In other words, the ratio is 1.25 to 1. Conversely, that is one to one-and-a-quarter. The latter is an auspicious figure symbolizing increase and prosperity because there is by twenty five percent increase to one to make one-and-a-quarter which stands in this case for width and length respectively. It is, therefore, presumed that width was measured first and followed by length towards the east which is the quarter of the rising sun.

We have seen the precisely proportional relationship between the castle and the city. It should be worthwhile to find out whether there existed a similar inter-relationship in terms of locational disposition as well. It did indeed. The diagonal drawn between the two opposite angles made by the north-eastern and the south-western corners of the city touched the north-western corner of the castle. Of the remaining two, the south-eastern corner is still missing, or nor found out. Therefore, a line bisecting the angle of the remaining city corner in the north-west into two equal halves was extended towards the south-east. Surrisingly, this line not only bisected the angle of the corresponding north-western corner of the midddle town and further on cut across a crossing of major streets in the same division but also struck the north-eastern corner of the castle. This could have been achieved by mathematical calculation and drawings.

The second noteworthy fact is that the above proportions between the city and the castle were obtained by making alterations in the planning at the time when the lower town was added towards the close of stage III. In the whole scheme, the enwalled area of the castle became 49th (7x7) part of that of the city and total built-up area of the former 25th (5x5) part.

The two third of the middle town was laid out with three bold projections and two recesses provided on either side of the arterial street running from east to west. It can be better visualized if one recalls the indented ground-plan of a developed Indian temple having projections and recesses on all four sides. In the middle town, there are seen two full and one half such units of which the slightly smaller one is in the western part, larger one in the middle and the half on th east where the last-mentioned one is bounded by the inner peripheral street that runs along the eastern defensive wall of the town. Another significant feature is the arterial street that run across axially from west to east dividing all the above-mentioned units and sub-unit into two equal halves, and a north-south street, perhaps somewhat staggeredly, further subdivided each unit : Thus, rendering each unit having four built-up areas subdivided by streets. This kind of layout of the town helped carve out six open spaces in between the surrounding fortification walls and the built-up areas. However, on the southern margin of the town the resolution seems to have been entirely different in that there was a straight, continous and rectangular built-up area running from one end to the other between the bounding fortification walls running along on the eastern and the western sides. This built-up area was also subdivided by a street into two equal halves along the east-west axis. These observations are based on the meagre excavation in proportion to the wide expanse of the middle town. Indications are also available to state that each bold projection of a unit might be having likewise a series of minor projections and recesses in each case.

What was the ultimate use fo those open spaces provided in the middle town remains yet to be revealed by excavation. Whatever meagre work was done on the margins had demonstrated that the inhabitants were dumping the household refuse onto that part of the open space which was immediately adjoining their houses. Whether the entire area of a modestly large open space was being used likewise is premature to opine. Not unlikely that the central part of such a space might have been for special public utilities such as for having a well, for example.

More or less in a similar way, rather in a little more complicated fashion, the lower town too was resolved into several units. That network of units still remains to be studied. Each unit seems to be having likewise projections and recesses and in turn demarcating an open space, of course. The arterial street of the middle town passed through a gate in eastern fortification wall and then went on running across the lower town albeit with a few turns, each at the end of a residential sector. The street, however remained uninterrupted. Other major and minor streets and a lane shot off from the axial street for making a defined network of housing sectors.

Water Harvesting System

The kind of efficient system that the Harappan of Dholavira developed for utmost conservation, harvesting and storage of water speaks eloquently for their advanced hydraulic engineering given the state of technology in the third millennium B. C. This concern for water also tells for the contemporatry environment which may not have been glaringly different from what prevails now. The water must heve been a precious commodity as of now. Seated on the margin of the monsoon belt, Kachchh experiences poor, often erratic summer precipitation. Failure of monsoon, sometimes for consecutive years, is quite a phenomenon. There are no perennial rivers, lakes or springs. The ground water is, by and large, brackish and saline and unfit for human and animal consumption and even for cultivation largely. The winter rainfall is almost absent. Therefore, droughts are frequent and so are famines. On the whole, the environment is harsh and hostile to human existence. In such a rid Kachchh, the Khadir Island where Dholavira lies, is the second poorest in rainfall which only averages to 262 mm per annum.

It is quite surprising that the Harappans made such a Kachchh as a density area which has yielded as of now as many as sixty sites most of which flourished during the mature phase. Should one believe that was a happier time so far the rainfall is concerned. The latest researches in the area of palaceoclimate indicate that the wetter phase all over the globe was over by 6000 B. C. and the present-day conditions had, more of less, stabilised by 3000 B. C. and continued as such of another 1000 years. Thereafter, arid conditions become more severe for some centuries before another spell of wet phase re-occurred. In this circumstance to think of better mansoon condition prevailing around 3000 B. C. when the early Harappans had started to pour in and settle down in Kachchh seems to be a distant possibility. At best, one may think of better living conditions as the natural environment was yet unspoilt by human interference. Hence better soil cover, better forest cover, better pasture lands and richer acquifers, and may be slightly better climate and rainfall. However, the rainfall should not have been prolific. This can be visualized by glancing at the tremendous efforts put in by the Harappans towards water management within as well as without their magnificent city.

A good deal of forethought must have gone into selecting the site even for the first settlement which was by far a fortalice only. The early Harappan chose a higher ground by the side of the Manhar, one can see that an (or rather the) inundation channel, if not the main channel itself, was flowing in the east and then running along the south of the site of the first settlement. The first settlers who had developed expertise in Baluchistan and Sindhi Kohistan before coming to Kachchh may have successfully dammed the Manhar and deepened its bed by cutting the basal rock in order to carve out a large reservoir spreading over in the east as well as the south of their fortress. Perhaps, the aberrantly cut deep tank, a lower part of what can seen inside the subsequent rock-cut reservoir to the south of the castle, is the remnant of the first experiment. Surely, the selection of such a site beside a smaller torrent having potential of being tamed was a well-considered decision. Otherwise, there were existing many a deeper and broader channels having voluminous flood regime but those were certainly too difficult for harvesting water as the builders did not possess the knowledge of raising durable dams for want of dependable cementing material. This choice of site naturally suited well to all the successive Harappans who gradually developed it into a town and then a city. Given a slopping nature of a wider ingeniously encompassed all the principal divisions of the expanded settlement. In order to harvest more water, they reached out to the Mansar which too was dammed for filling the reservoirs. In fact, the Manhar has evidenced for three and the Mansar for two places where the dams were raised across their channels. At the prospective site of the lowermost dam thrown across the Manhar there were exposed lower remnants of several closely adjoining parallel walls in the river - bed by simply removing the sand accumulated over them. Nearby and further down stream, a scatter of huge stone blocks of different geological formations other than those found in the vicinity may be seen lying helter-skelter in the bed. Those blocks, some of them cut to size, are too heavy for being tranported over distance by the flood waters of the channel. Similar situation prevails at the other dam sites too. Close to the lowermost dam site across the Manhar, an enormous bounding wall with a neatly plastered face and having an inlet channel higher up for letting surplus of the dammed-up water into the southern series of the reservoirs was laid bare. The deposit accumulated on the other side of the inlet channel vividly showed the angle and depth of fall as well as the force of water.

Excavation, particularly in the east has amply shown artificial removal of an enormous pile of alluvium to make room for as the pottery of different 'stages' have been still sticking to the underlying bed-rock and embedded in the subsequent water-borne deposit. The said deposit contained potsherds of all Stages from I to VI and even VII. As late as in Stage VI, the people attempted to raise a check-dam at that far east. Looking at the depth of 3.5 m in the eastern zone against the depth of 8m or even more of the westernmost reservoir of the eastern series, one can visualize existence of a descending cascade of reservoir many of which are awating the archaeologist's spade.

Before coming to the details of two excellent reservoirs it would be proper to state in general about the system.

The Harappans, during their hey-day, created within the city walls in all sixteen or more reservoirs of varying sizes and arranged them, along the northern and western and largely along the southern sides of the main settlement and to the east of the citadel. An ingradient of 13 m lying between the higher north-east and the lower south-west was ideally suited in ~~selected~~ tanks instead of letting it spread out over larger area as a thin sheet which should be highly susceptible to quick evaporation and seepage. Many of the reservoirs might not be meant for storing water all the year round as they were carved out by removing the top soil down to the bed-rock which does not behave evenly nor lies adequately deep all over. Possibly, to get all the reservoirs filled with water might have served multiple purposes : first, to utilize the water for large scale repairs to private houses and public structures as soon as the rainy season was over; secondly, for the irrigating summer crops; and last, if not the least, to enrich the ground water reserve.

In the whole scheme, the city walls, particularly on the west and its adjoining quarters, played a crucial role. Apart from providing formidable protection to the city, they functioned as strong *bunds* made of millions of moulded mud-bricks carefully laid in mud mortar. The inner peripheral road lined with stone masonary saved the walls from the water scoring as well.

A tentative estimate indicates that the reserviors account for about 10 hectares, working out approximately to 10% of the total area covered under the city. Our earlier view that the north-eastern quarter across the Manhar housed a large reservoir was not substained by the sporadic digs that were made there.

Recent excavation has brought to light two excellent examples of reservoirs. One of them lying astride to the east of the castle, and by the side of the small stadium has been exposed partially while its northern embankment along with the adjoining flight of 31 steps descending to the rock - bottom was confirmed for its full width of 24 m and extant depth of 7.50 m the eastern one was laid bare just for 5m only (Pl. 6). Both the embankment and the steps were built in stone-masonary of superior workmanship. It appears that nine steps of the original flight have been washed away along with the upper part of both the embankments. If the surface study is believed, the reservior should be at least 70m broad on north-south axis. Further work promises of many more interesting features of this water structure. As already indicated, this is the westernmost of the eastern series of reservoirs.

The other one is the earliest ever rock-out example that too on a grand scale. It lay along and in between the castle and the annexe (Pl. 7). So far its length along the east-west is concerned, it has already been confirmed for a run of 95 m upto the western end where it was connected to a long and modestly wide spill-channel which, in turn, conducted the surplus water into another reservoir which must be lying buried under the modern cultivated field lying between the bailey in the north and the city wall in the south. At the western end, the rock-cut reservoir has revealed a width of 11.42 m for the upper part and 10.80m for the lower and vertically deeper part while the depth varied from 1.95 m on the north to 4 m on the side. This variability was due to the sloping nature of the bed rock which seems to have been left intentionally untampered with as it was the area which had to bear the heaviest thrust of the water flowing into or standing in the reservoir. However, the cutting made in the central zone of the open space has provided more information about the rock-cut reservior which, on one side, was overlooked by the concealed gate peirced through the castle wall higher up on the north, and, on the other was accessible through a narrow unpretentoius gate in the city wall along which, was raided the annexe. A flight of wide steps descended from the concealed gate of the castle to the brim of the reservoir. All those architectural features had their origin in Stage III. The said castle gate seems to have been closed sometime later in Stage IV or Stage V. Cut in a stepped fashion, the main portion of the reservoir measured 9 m across while the upper part with a ledge on the either side was about 12 m. Curiously, there was cut out in the general bottom of the reservior that aberrantly oriented trough which rather runs obliquely across in a manner that its north-western part becomes flush with the northern side and the opposite one seems to be touching the other side of the reservoir. However, it had its beginning in this exposed part only, and therefore, was a local feature only.

Regarding this feature it has already been held that it could be a creation of Stage 1 and even II. However, it could be contemporary to the main reservoir for a special purpose of storing water in a deeper and smaller trough at least while the larger one has gone dry. So far, its oblique orientation made it possible for it to touch both the sides, it was obvious that it was intended to facilitate the people to draw up its water from both the sides.

Strom - Water Drainage

The citadel has yielded an effective system for collecting the rain water and conducting it through a network of drains to a reservior carved out in open space provided in the bailey. Small and big drains coming from different areas of the castle were linked to an material one. Infact, two principal drains have been exposed considerably. One of them originated from a stone-paved platform provided atop the eastern fortification wall near the east gate (Pl. 8). The rain-water falling on the top of a part of the wall may have been collected there from where, through a beautifully cut-stone cascade, the water flowed into a covered underground drain running under the boundary of the castle. Running towards the west, the drain met somewhere near the centre with another principal drain which was found, in turn, to be issuing from two interconnected chambers made of stone. The clay deposit in the chambers was found throughly churned up as if under the force of water falling from a height. There was apparantly no source of water. To explain, it may be added that, to the north of the chambers, there was running pathway opposite to each other. It is surmised that these columns, one set abutting the fort wall and the other side wall of the chambers, supported conduits made of pottery, wood or stone to conduct the rain water from the superstructure of the gate and the wall and let it fall with a force into a chamber(s) from where the water flowed into the large covered drain. To that, another drain, having its head in the form of steps at a short distance away in the east met nearly half way down. The combined water of these two drains joined that the flowing in the arterail drain coming from the eastern wall (Pl. 9). The arterial one running all through under the broadway towards the west hit the side wall of the stepped pathway near the west gate and then turned at a right angle to take southerly course. Some distance short of the south-western of the castle, it again took a right angled turn to pierce through the western castle wall. Before that, just at the turn, it received another underground drain coming from the east. The united water of the drains was then falling through a cascade into a drain in the bailey and finally into a *kaccha* reservoir in the bailey itself.

All the drains were made carefully with so much floors, side walls, roofing with capstones of this elaborate network. Their purpose of letting out the rain water is undeniable as all of them contained clean fresh water deposit, not sewage or household waste. If a small segement of a principal drain did yield some doubtful material, it offered cut images and related material as well, In fact, one or two of its apertures remained exposed during Stage VI definetely and in Stage VII possibly. Any abuse was not all impossible. It must also be borne in mind that none of the drains of the network were found connected to domestic houses.

So far disposal of the household waste is concerned, the middle town, the lower town and the annexe have presented the evidence of sanitary jars or tanks placed or provided on the street sides as usual at many a contemporary Harappan centre. Mohenjo Daro was indeed an exception.

So far the domestic architecture of the citadel is concerned, its uncovering is far too inadequate to know about its drainage or disposal system.

More Water Structures

Two water tanks and one well which together make an interrelated complex have set an example of a kind. All those are located in the south-western quarter of the castle (Pl. 10). On the north, it was bounded by the broadway, on the south and west by the fortification and on the east, perhaps by the residential houses which yet remain to be probed. All those water structures as they were found and so far probed were in use during Stages IV, V and VI.

The well which is the focal feature in the complex has come out in the Harappan context the largest and best equipped example as it had became somewhat misshapen by the lateral thrust, its inner diameter measured 4.25 m along one direction and 4 m on the other, thus suggesting to make to 4.125 m by averaging. On the south-western face which is best preserved by far has evidenced the highly skilled masonry work. As of now, it has been evaluated to a depth of 13.60 m. In view of the present level of the ground water in the locality, the well-head can be struck at another 10 m. At the south western top, it was found equipped with a trough made a basal slab supporting two vertically placed ones. The trough is placed with an outward stant. Its perfect prototypes can be seen all over the tanks constructed a little distance away. On the sides of the well, there were found the debris of stone masonry columns fallen in *situ.* The basal slab of the trough bore shallow rope-marks. All evidence strongly pointed that the water may have been drawn with aid of a leather bag having two months, one big and another small, both fitted with thicker and thinner ropes respectively. On the present analogy, those ropes get the mouths tied up when the water filled bag is pulled up and the smaller one gets loosened as soon as it starts rolling over a wooden roller fitted across the mouth of the trough. And, for lifting or letting down the leather bag with the aid of strong rope, a wooden pulley fitted high on a horizontal wodden pole supported by masonry or wooden columns on the sides of a well is necessary. One end of the rope is tied to the bag and the other is used for pulling it by men or animals drafted for the purpose. The provision of this kind of water drawing device becomes explicitly vivid at the Dholavira well. At Dholavira, the water thus drawn was stored in a large tank which was found well-provided with skillfully made floor with smoothered stones, the sides upto certain height lined with large limestone slabs and the superstructure with dressed stones. On one side from the north, a flight of steps was provided half-way down, not up to the floor. In the centre of the rectangular tank, there was a well-made pit which was perhaps used to let the dirty water accumulate therein during periodical mopping of the tank. For an easy disposal of the bulk of water in the tank, a small aperture was also noticed. It was perhaps connected to a waste water drain under the nearby broadway. In order to make the tank leak-proof, a sticky, grey-coloured clay which is highly impervious to water is used in the masonry work.

The smallest tank beside the larger one is also connected to a high inlet drain. The construction was, more or less, similar with the exception that the stairway, provided with gentler steps of low rise and good tread, descended into the tank. For stepping in a cylindrical stone block was placed on the floor near the stairway. It not only facilitated an easy descent but could also be used as a seat by the user because we postulate that the tank could be for bathing purpose. Anyway, it is also interesting to note that the said cylindrical stone concealed an aperture which may be connected to a drain for flushing out the used water.

Further digging in this area may reveal a few more interesting features. Already, traces of some fire-places perhaps used for heating water have been observed. Besides, some small cubicle-like constructions which were once fitted with stone slabs were seen in the area lying between the well and the tank. Those could be bathrooms.

In the foregoing account, we have tried to recount the cultural progression, the highlights of planning and the freshly discovered system of water harvesting. Each one has added a new facet to the personality of the Harappa culture. It may be well rounded off by recapitulating about the gates and stadia which too are marvels of planning and architecture.

Gates

In all fourteen gates, some elaborate and some simple, have been laid bare in different divisions and area of the Harappan city of Dholavira. The break-up is : Castle 5; Bailey 2; Stadium 4; Middle Town 1 and Annexe 2; and none so far is the lower town.

The Castle was found provided with five gates pierced through the fortification. Each one has revealed a distinct design. While the eastern arm has yielded two gates, there was one in each of the remaining three walls.

The south gate has a concealed passageway with an ordinary doorway at its southern end where it was connected to a flight of wide steps descending to the northern embankment of the rock-cut reservior. As already stated, it was in use during Stage III but was sealed off something in the following stage or Stage V.

The West gate which afforded intercommunication with the bailey was in the form of a 9m long and 2.2 m wide passageway with a small guard room carved in the southern wall while the northern side was found washed away completely to the floor level of the passage. The sloping passageway has a few steps at the outer end which was provided with the steps made of large limestone slabs one of which may be seen as a planoconvex with rounded sides placed as the lowermost steps as of now. Earlier, during exploration in 1984, we had seen there the lowermost step being in the form of a developed moonstone or *chandrasila.*

The East Gate one of the two principal ones, had a large chamber consisting of an elevated side-chamber on the south and a collatoral sunken passageway on the North (Fig. 4). The passageway was connected to a flight of 14 steps at the inner end while it was fitted with a door-sill made of large limestone slabs at the outer one. At both the ends, it must be having huge doors. At either end on top of the side wall of the elevated side chambers, there was found a set of nicely cut and smoothened limestone block of rectangular shape. The topmost block bore two long sockets one each on two sides and parallel to each other. As evidence had it, each set of the blocks was the base for a pilaster, made of mud-concrete bricks, and built to the ceiling of the gate chamber. Each pilaster was probably veneered with a wooden casing which was closed fit by a grooved and tongued joint into the couple of sockets. In the centre of the side wall was found another limestone blocks supporting a beautifully carved and polished pillar base having a pronounced concave profile and straight-sided bottom and top surfaces were flat. The top surface bore in the centre a 5 mm circular hole. By the side of it, two large-sized pillar members with rounded sides and flattened top and bottom were found lying disloged. Each flat surface of both the members also showed a similar hole for receiving a domel. In front of the gate, there was exposed a high terrace raised between two massive flanking bastions. The provision for access made in the form of jerry-built set of steps at the southern side of terrace was a creation of Stage VI while the original approach seems to be lying still concealed under the late Harappan structures. It must be added that, during Stage V, a number of domestic / industrial buildings were raised on the terrace of the gate.

The East Gate 2 was brought to light recently. It is provided with a series of broad steps going down from the top but terminating higher up on the outer edge of the defensive wall without yielding any evidence of descending to the ground level on the east. It remains an enigma so far.

The North Gate (Fig. 5 and Pl. 11) was found to be the most majestic, most elaborately designed architectural construction which commanded over the stadium, the middle town, the lower town and further beyond the picturesque landscape. In the thickness of the wall, it consisted of two elevated chambers flanking a sunken passageway which, in turn, was furnished at the inner end with a limestone door-sill flanked by a set of limestone blocks each bearing pilasters sockets on two sides - thereby suggesting the existing of two enormous columns (made of stone masonry) encased by wooden panels. Those columns may have supported the heavy door - frame fitted with two door leaves. A similar provision seems to have been made as well at the outer end of the passageway as evidenced by the door sill with a limestone block bearing sockets at one end, while the other one was replaced with ordinary blocks at a later time. As the east gate had marvelous bases of a central pillar and two pilasters on the elevated chambers of the north gate as well, although not found intact due to the vandalism wrought by the late Harappans of Stage VI. Similarly there was a 12 m wide and perhaps 33 m broad and 5.6 m high front terrace majestically overlooking the stadium. On the east and along the high fortification wall, the terrace was connected with a 9 m wide 'ceremonial' pathway descending onto the stadium or 'ceremonial ground' through a gate wide as much (Pl. 12). It was, however, reduced in width in Stage V or VI. At the inner end of the passageway of the north gate, there was an L shaped staircase having 10 steps, a landing and then another flight of 13 steps turning at a right angle towards the west.

Barring the southern one, all the other three gates remained in use from Stage III to Stage Vi although the last occupants neither maintained them well nor spared them from misuse.

The north bailey gate was constructed under the shadow of the towering north - western corner of the castle. A flight of steps gave access to 7.30 long and 2.30 m to 2.55 m wide passageway which too was flanked by chambers. It facilitated intercommunication between the bailey and the stadium.

The south bailey gate was likewise built under the shadow of the south western corner of the castle. Further details of the gate are yet to be collected by further excavation.

The east gate of the stadium was also an impressive construction with a guard room on the southern side and a santry post set in the northern wall (Pl. 13). The passageway measured 12.20 m long and 3.80 m broad.

The west gate as a simple opening was to provide movement between the two stadia.

The east gate of the middle town was flanked by two bastions. Originally, it was comprising two flanking chambers which were got filled up with stones subsequently. At its outer end, there were fitted stone slabs across the width. Those slabs bore two set of grooves perhaps for receiving tongs of some sorts of wooden planks for closing the gate.

The south gate through the city wall provided access to annexe and the rock cut reservior towards the outside it, however, opened on to a large enwalled area attached to the city wall from the southern side. The subjoined area perhaps housed the state animal farm. Another gate in the annexe area was laid bare in the western bounding wall which lies N - S, joining the city wall with the citadel wall.

Another gate, not yet fully exposed, stood to provide movement between the smaller stadium and the reservoir area lying to the east of the castle.

Yet another gate undercovered this year offered approach to the stadium as well as to the settlement of Stage VI.

Staduim

The earliest and the largest stadium found so far perhaps accredited to the Harappans. Lying between the citadel and the middle town, it measured about 283 m E W and 45 m to 47.50 m N S. Almost on all sides, excepting the stretch of a 80 m appropriated by the north gate and the appurtenant ceremonial pathway, it was provided with stands for seating of spectators. The broadcast one, 12 m wide, having three or rather four continously running tiers or terraces, in ascending order, was made abutting the defensive walls of the castle and the bailey. Steps for seating have been seen also atop the enormous defensive wall that stood to the east of the stadium. A similar arrangement of steps is slowing emerging at the west end too. The stand that lay along the middle town or on side of smaller stadium did not show the stepped construction due to perhaps the erosion of the centuries.

The smaller stadium lay under the shadow of the pre-eminent castle. It was created in the area that was extending from the north-western corner and the east gate 2 of the castle. It was provided with two gates : one for inner communicating with the larger stadium and the other with the eastern outfield and the reservoir area lying extending to the east of the castle.

As held before, those stadia which were multi-purpose grounds perhaps are altogether new features of the Harappan planning as well as architecture.

Select Bibliography

BANAWALI

Bisht, R.S : 'A New Harappan Site in Harayana', Man and Environment, vol. II, 1978

'Banawali and some Other Recently Excavated Harappan Site in India' (Jointly with Sahshi Asthana) South Asian Archaeology : 1977, (ed.) Shri. M. Taddei, Neples (Italy), 1979.

'Excavations at Banawali : 1974-77' Harappan Civilization, (ed.) Gregory L. Possehl, New Delhi- 1982 and in the second revised edition, 1993.

'Structural Remains and Town Planning of Banawali', Frontiers of the Indus Civilization, (eds.) B.B. Lal and S.P. Gupta, New Delhi, 1987.

'Further Excavation at Banawali 1983-84', Archaeology and History, (eds.) Shri B.M. pande and Shri B.D. Chattopadhyaya, Delhi, 1987.

Indian Archaeology A Review :
1983-84, 24-29; **1986-87,** 32-34; **1987-88,** 21-27;

DHOLAVIRA

'The Harappan Colonization of the Kutch : An Ergonomic Study with Reference to Dholavira and Surkotada', History and Art, (ed.) Shri. Krishna Deva and Lallanji Gopal, Delhi- 1989.

'A New Model of the HArappan Town Planning as Revealed at Dholavira in Kutch : A Surface Study of Its Plan and Architecture', History and Archaeology, (ed.) Bhaskar Chatterji, Delhi, 1989.

'Dholavira : New Horizons of the Indus Civilization', Puratattva, No. 20, New Delhi, 1989-90.

'Dholavira : Harappa Sabhyata Ke Naye Ayam', Aj Kal, October, 1993, New Delhi, 1983.

'Dholavira Excavations : 1990-94', Facets of Indian civilization - Recent Perspectives (Essay in Honour of Prof. B.B. Lal), vol. I (Chief ed.) Shri J.P. Joshi.

'Urban Planning at Dholavira : A Harappan city in Ancient Cities', Ancient Skies, IGNCA Pub. (In press).

Indian Archaeology A Review :
1967-68, 14-16; **1984-85,** 14-17; **1987-88,** 16; **1989-90,** 15-20; **1990-91,** 10-12; **1991-92,** 26-35; **1992-93,** 27-28

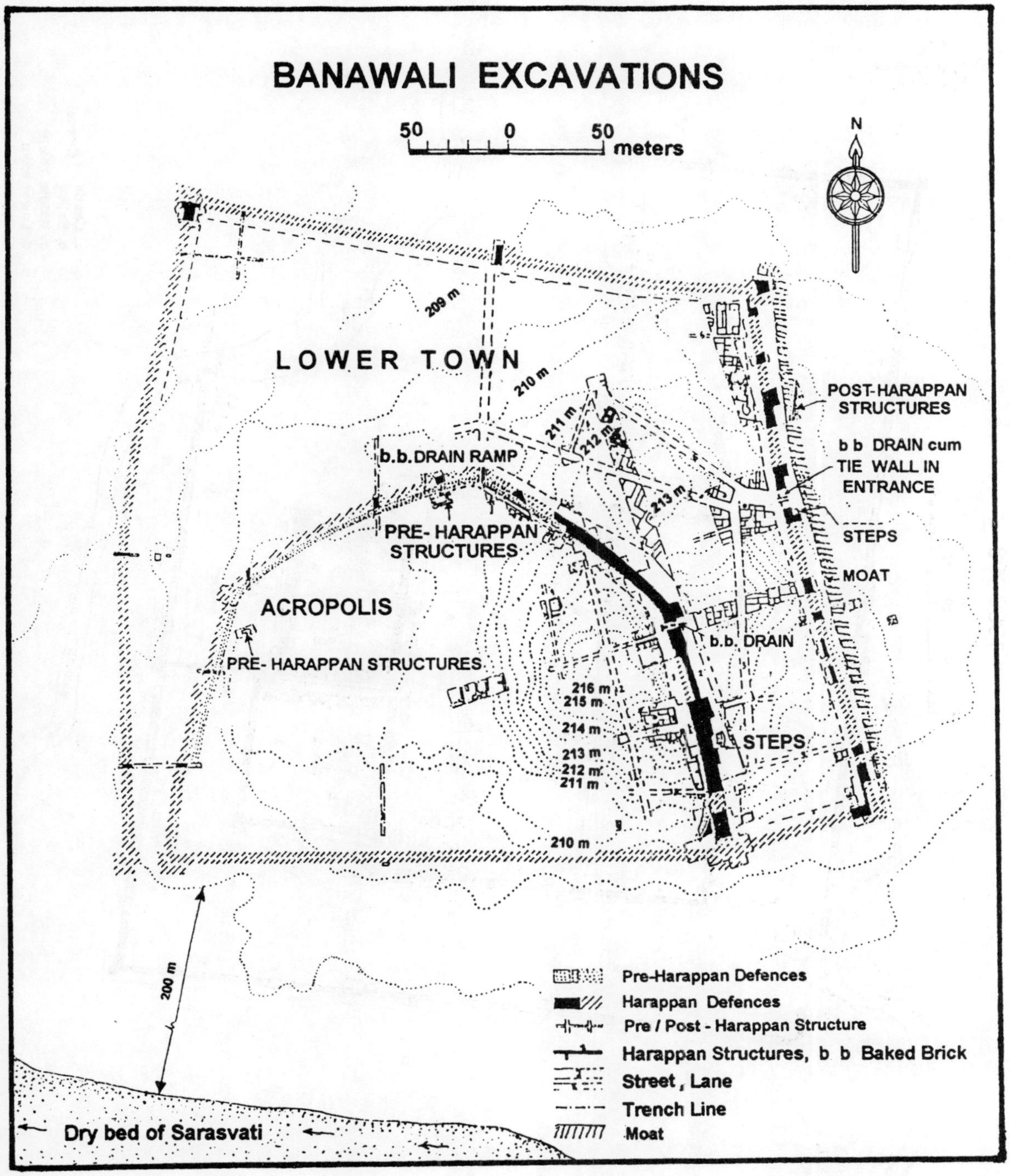

Fig.1 Banawali Excavations

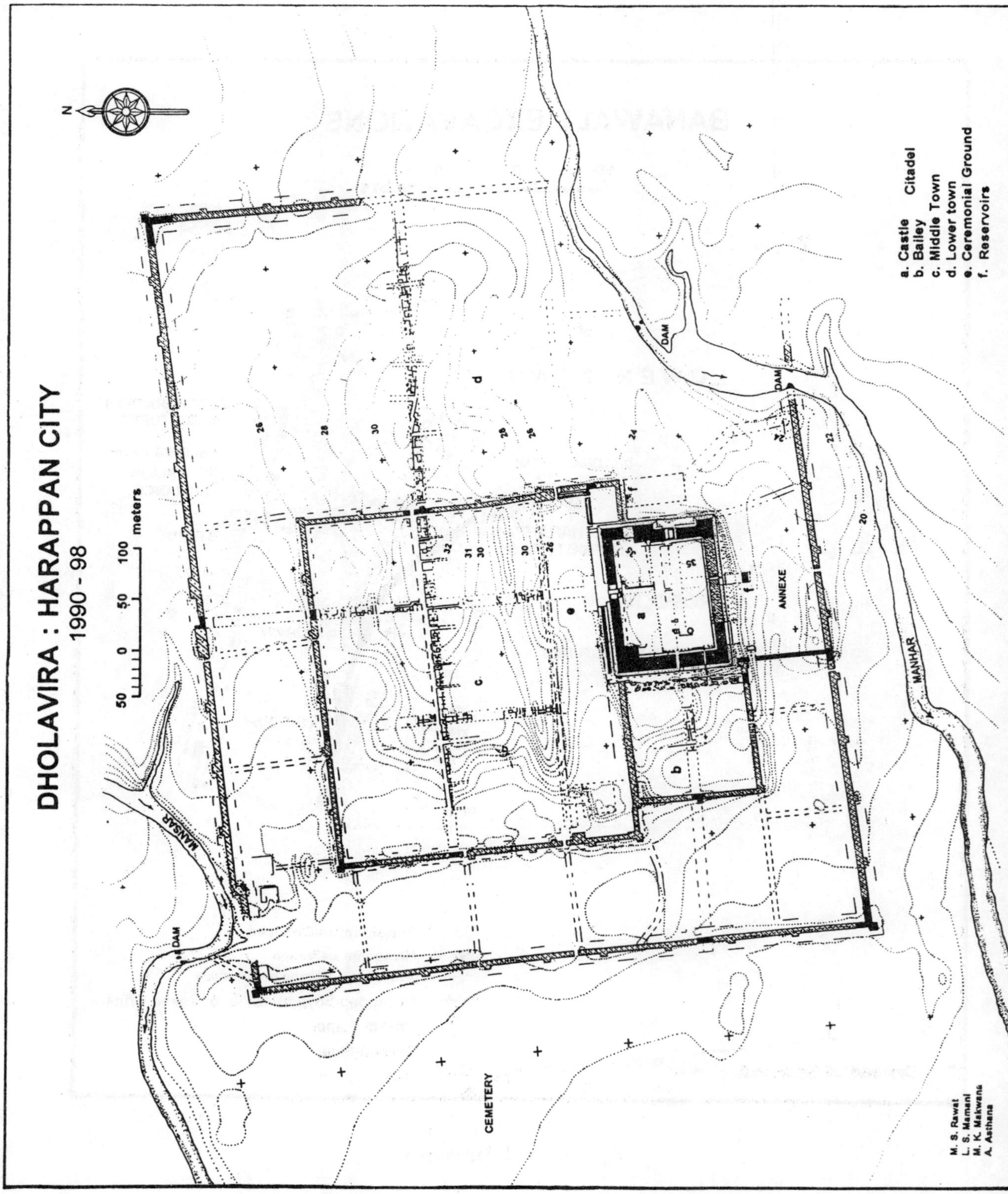

Fig.2 Dholavira : Harappan City

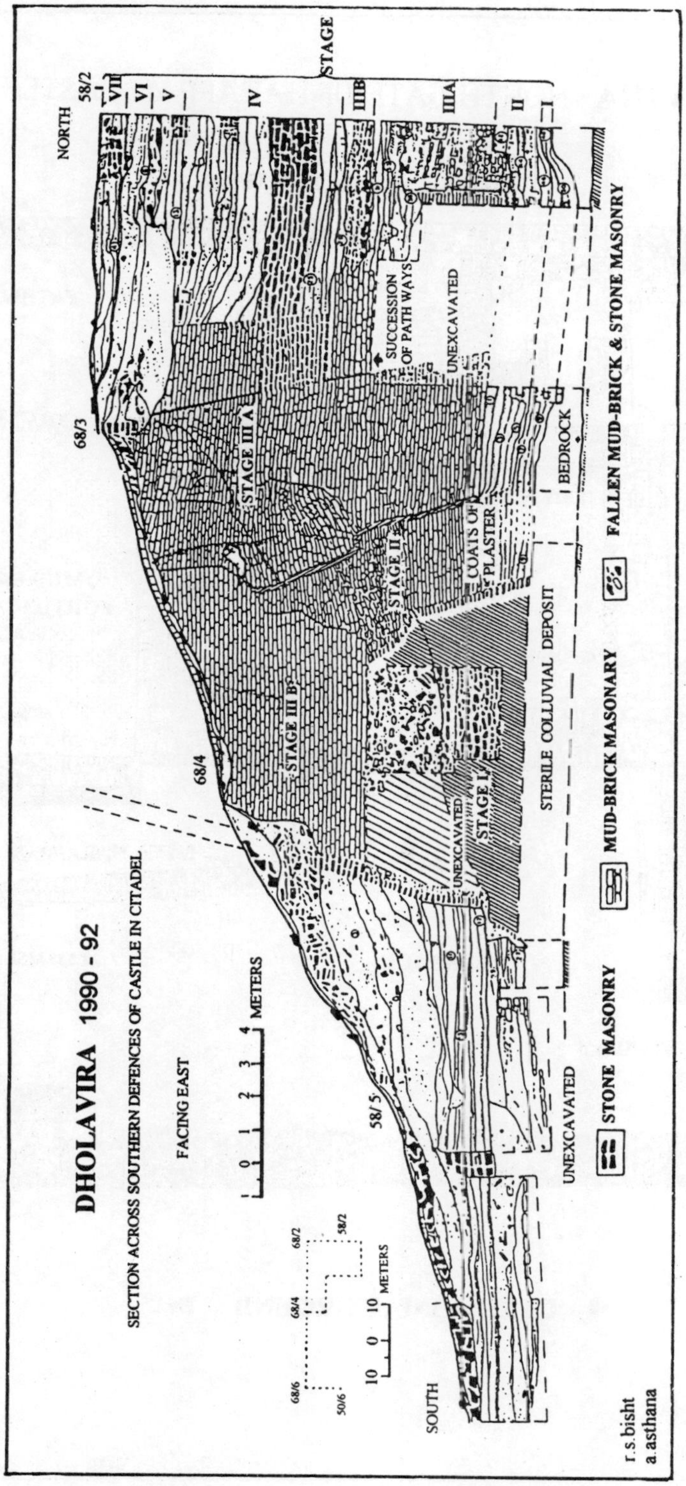

Fig.3 Dholavira 1990-92

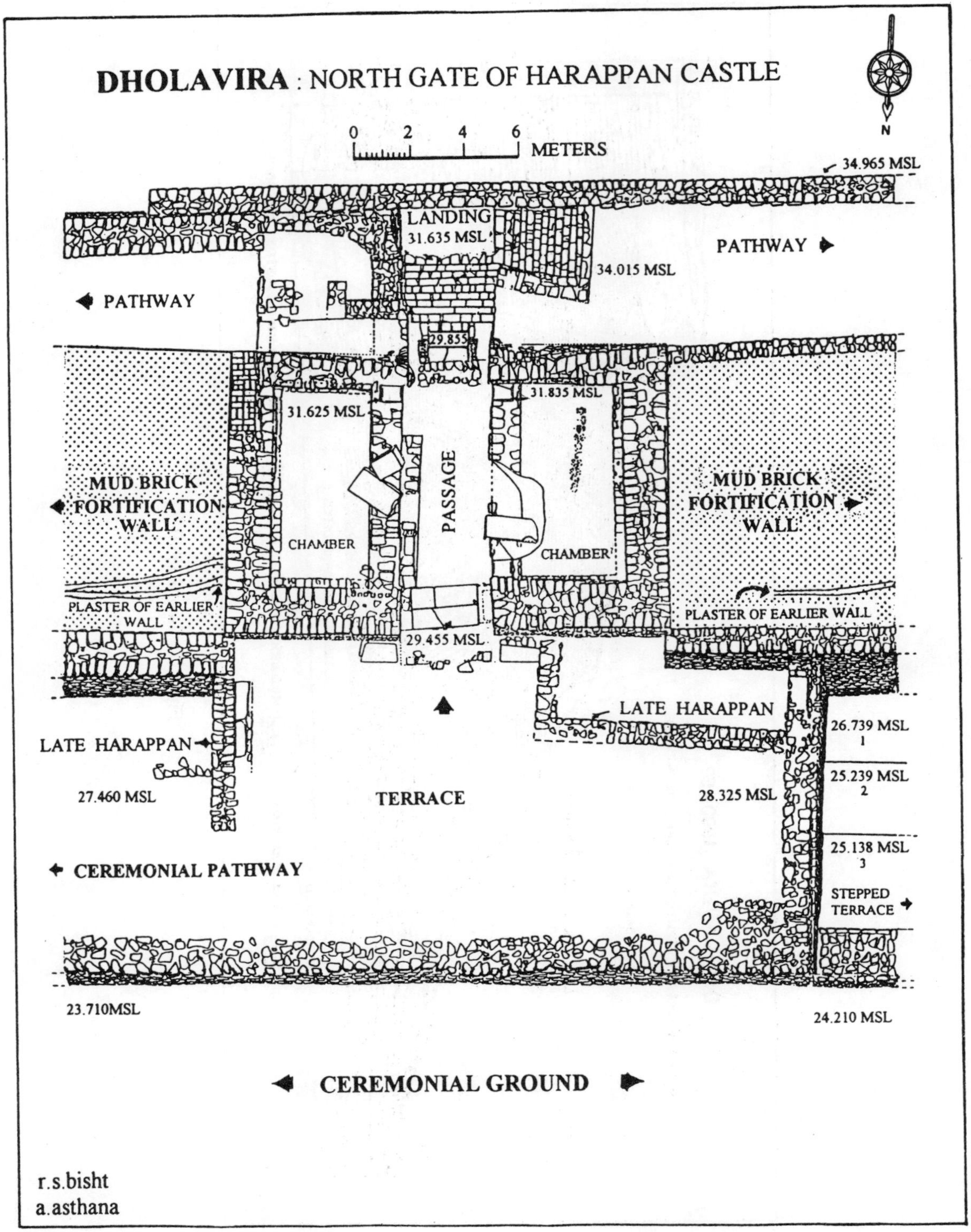

Fig.4 Dholavira : North Gate Of Harappan Castle

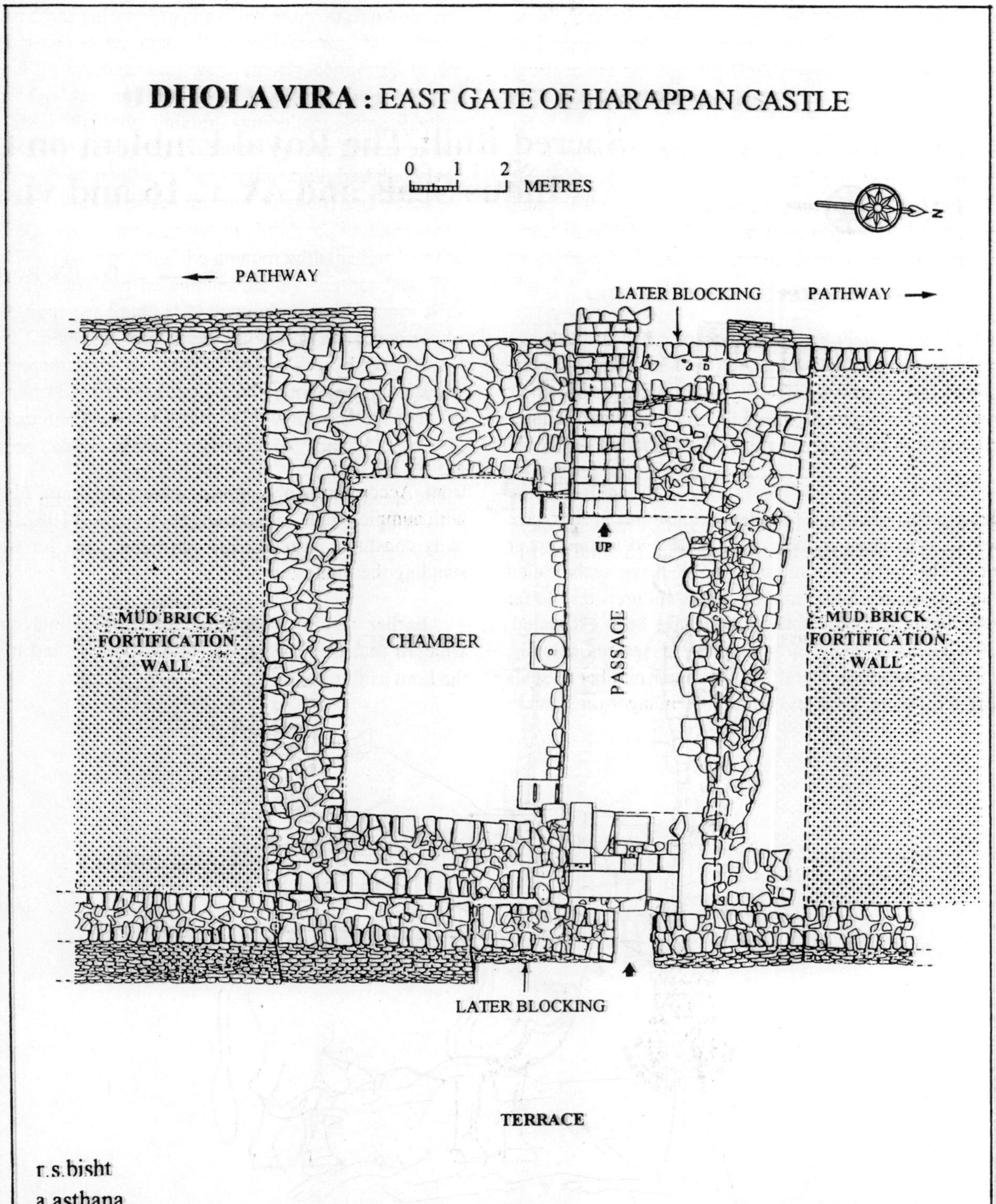

Fig.5 Dholavira : East Gate Of Harappan Castle

Sacred Bull: The Royal Emblem on the Indus Seals and AV V. 16 and VI. 86

DR. P.V. PATHAK*

Excavations at the major city-centres like Mohenjodaro, Harappa, Kalibangan, Dholavira etc. have yielded very large number of steatite and some copper seals. The terracotta impressions of these seals called sealings, are available from the Indus culture sites. So far more than 2500 seals and sealings have been excavated. Although these seals carry pictures of various animals, grotesque figures and graffitti, the major number of seals carry a figure of humpless bull with a manger-on-stand in front. According to the present author the count of seals with humpless bull with a manger on stand is 1082. These seals constitute a major and important clue for understanding the Indus culture.

Earlier Roy had expressed that the animal on the Unicorn seal being wild ass (*Eqqas asinus)* and treated the horn as fictitious.[1]

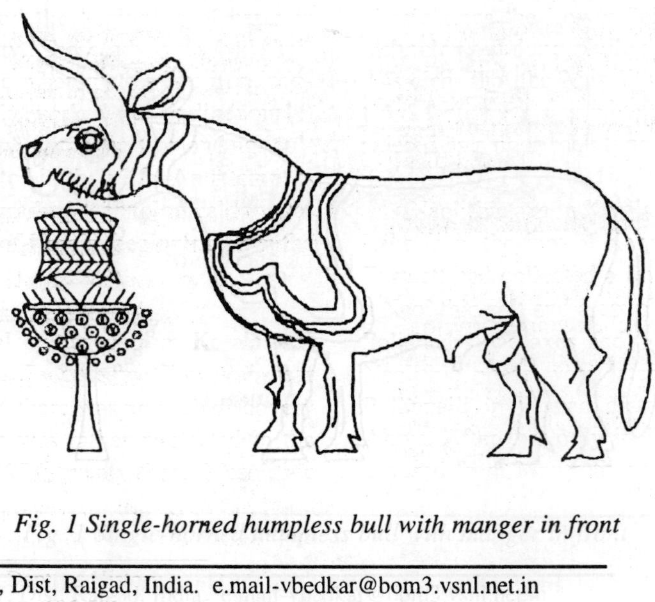

Fig. 1 Single-horned humpless bull with manger in front

*'Sitai', Prabhu Ali, Pin. 402107, Dist, Raigad, India. e.mail-vbedkar@bom3.vsnl.net.in

Atre has referred to the *Dictionary of Symbols and Imagery* and states that, "It is well-known that animals like bull, goat, deer etc. were closely connected to the Mother Goddess and fertility cults all over the world and it is likely that the unicorn symbolizes some Mother Goddess — he can only be caught by a virgin preferably naked, who lures him by her virgin smell; he falls asleep in her lap (often after sexual manipulation) and weeps for joy. The hunters then step out and kill him."[2] According to Atre "The assumption of the unicorn with the Earth or the Virgin goddess can be emphasised by another fact. The female figurines found at Mohenjodaro and Harappa with typical fan shaped headdress and which are suggested to be representatives of the Mother Goddess, differ sharply from matronly figures found at other archaeological sites. These are indicative of virgin deity who presided over the religious cults at Mohenjodaro and Harappa."[3]

The present author has refuted all assumptions about the Mother Goddess and virginity cult by Atre earlier.[4] It is suffice to state here that there is not a single seal to establish relation of the so called Mother Goddess with the Unicorn seals or virginity cult. The terracotta female figurines are not Mother Goddesses. They were toys for the female kids in those cities.

The animal on the seals is decisively a humpless bull *(Bos primogenus)* figure.[5] It can be determined by the shape of the body, head, sex organ, hooves and tail. The aspect in which it differs form the normal bull is the single horn which is the unique feature of this animal. (Fig. 1.)

Grigson has also expressed her views that the bull figure is possibly *Bos primogenus.* She has given pictures of the Middle Eastern bulls *(Bos primogenus)* from a relief at Nimrud where the bull with single horn is drawn (Fig. 2). The shape of its horn is very similar to the single-horned bull on the Indus seals.[6]

More than 90% of these bull figures are accompanied with a figure of manger-on-stand inscribed in front. The

Fig. 2. Sketch of two Middle-Eastern Bulls (Bos Primigenus). From a relief of a hunting scene at King Ashurnasirapal II's palace at Nimrud.

different variations of manger on stand are drawn on seals.

There are bull figures with two distinct horns. These bull figures are also shown without a prominent hump. They are shown with a flat tray-like (¬__⌐) manger on the ground before them.

Some of the two-horned bull figures are shown with a manger-on-stand in front.

There are 89 seals with bull figures with two horns; out of these, 10 bull seals are with manger on stand in front.

There are typical Brahmi bull figures *(Bos indicus)* with prominent humps. All these are with two horns. These seals are 53 in all. Not a single seal of the Brahmi bull carries the figure of manger-on-stand.

Fig. 3 Fabulous animal with horn and tasselled mane. Decoration of the body by blanks. Wing-like drawing on the back. Tail with lateral tuft at the upper bend, kneeling on one leg. Height 30 cm. Made by pecking altar rock above Thalpar bridge. Middle of the first millenimum BC.

There are seven seals with bull figures shown with multiple heads. Six out of these seals are shown with full body. One circular seal shows six bull heads up to the neck attached to one another in hexagonal pattern.

These multiple-headed bull seals are dealt in depth later in this article.

It is to be noted here that the total bull figure seal count is 1231 and it points to the great importance attached to the representation of bull in the Indus culture society.

So far the bull figures with single horn have been labelled by all the earlier authors to be ***unicorn seals.*** The present author differs with this nomenclature for the following reasons:

1. The concept of unicorn is invariably associated with horse. All the single-horned figures in Indus seals are typically the humpless bull figures. The anatomical features of the horse and the bull are distinct and they differ from each other.

2. The unicorn is usually shown with a straight horn. The bulls on the seals are shown with bent horns.

3. Unicorns are always shown with tasselled manes without any ornamentation, while the Indus seals are shown without manes and are often ornamented with ring-like or 'W' shaped decoration around the neck.

It is accepted that the concept of unicorn originated in India.[7] The recorded picture of a typical straight-horned tasselled mane unicorn in the Indian subcontinent dates back to the middle of the first millennium BC. One such specimen of rock carving along the Karakoram highways is given in Fig. 3.[8] This picture is made by pecking Altar-rock above Thalpar bridge. In the European mythology the unicorn was treated as sacred symbol and source of manly vigour.

Taking this into consideration, the present author is of the opinion that it is misnomer to call the Indus seals showing bulls with a single horn unicorn seals. He prefers to call them the ***Sacred Bull*** seals for the the reasons outlined below.

Central Authority and Governance

It is accepted that Indus culture which occupied the continental area had a central authority and a governing system. It can be attested from the civic set up, town planning techniques, sanitary system, layout of the city centres like Mohenjodaro, Harappa, Lothal, Kalibangan, Dholavira etc.

Another important aspect of the Indus culture is long distance trade in various commodities. Many commodities were exported by the Indus-merchants to the Middle

East.[9] That there was a substantial internal trade is confirmed by the fact that a uniform system of weights and measures prevailed at many Indus culture locations. The system of weights and measures was in operation over hundreds of years of its existence implying the strict control by the authorities. The authorities controlled the export trade. It is attested by the fact that:

1. At Tepe Yahya IV C, about twenty-five sealings of typical Susa C ('proto-Elamite') vintage were found together with proto-Elamite tablets in a building which must have functioned as storehouse or clearing house.[10] The Tepe Yahya IV C-B period is dated around 3100-2900 BC, which dates to pre-Indus period. It, therefore, implies that antiquity of the governance by authority and practice of seal impression is more than 5000 years old.

2. These seals are with a perforated boss, showing a line of pictographs and a picture. These seals were used for stamping. They were not used as amulets to be worn on the person. It is quite clear, as the seal impressions have been found. The seals may have been used as insignia or identifying the authority.

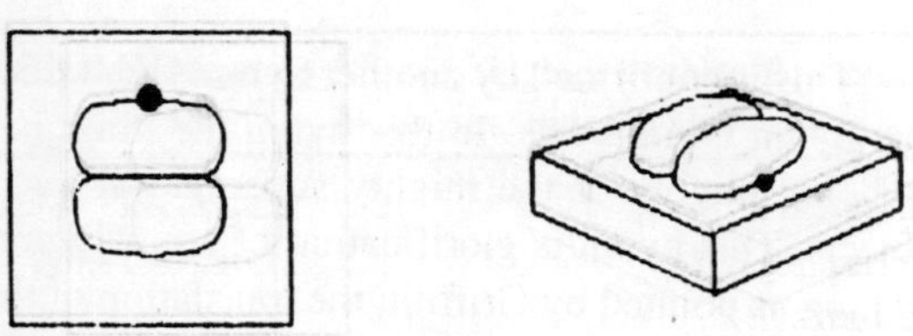

Seal moulds

3. Ratnagar has classified two functions of the sealings, namely, i) commodity sealings, and ii) message sealings. "By commodity sealings we mean the mechanism by which the contents of jars, packages, baskets or any other type of container were protected and/or guarenteed by certain authorities".[11] This is further confirmed by the excavations at Lothal. There is an abundance of commodity sealings found in the warehouse area near the dockyard. seventy five such sealings have been discovered there. Lothal with a dockyard was an export centre of the Indus culture.

4. 'Message seals' which contain only graffitti and no picture, point to these being used for storing and conveying information. It could be the identity of the sender of a certain message or a piece of merchandise, or the authority on behalf of an individual or state department to a particular agent who carried the seal impression.

The present author differs with Ratnagar on the point that all the seals were only used for stamping and not as amulets. He has shown that the famous seal, men-and-tiger-seal (No. M-1425), and seals depicting goat, man, and man under pipal canopy (Nos. M-488, M-1186, B-23, H-177) were used as amulets Here he intends to discuss the significance of the bull picture independent of the graffitti on these seals. It will be apparent from the following discussion that the bull motif was an independent symbol by itself.

Atharva Veda and the Indus Culture

The present author has earlier shown that some of the Indus culture seals are pictorial representations of the *AV* hymns. He has identified these seals as under:

1. *Pasupati* seals - 8 Nos; are pictorial representation of the *AV* hymn II. 34.[12]

2. Indus seals of three forms and seven figures and two similar seals (Nos. M-488, H-177) are the pictorial representation of the *AV* hymn IV. 37.[13]

3. The men-and-tiger seal (M-1425) is the pictorial representation of the *AV* hymn IV. 3.[14]

4. A circular seal from Lothal showing a dragon with twin goats, is the pictorial representation of twin deities attacking the dragon *VRtra* from the *RV*.

5. Apart from these seals, in the last decade Iravatham Mahadevan had done extensive and in-depth analysis of the manger-on-stand figures on the sacred bull seals. He has enumerated the various features of the manger with *Soma*-pressing and processing implements. He identified the manger as the cult object and a *Soma* juice filter. He gives a composite drawing of the sacred filter and has identified some Indus symbols being pestle and mortar signs,

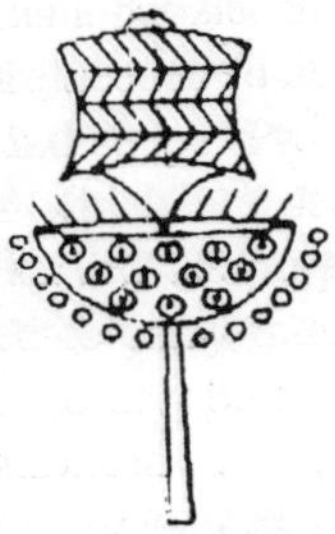

Scared Soma filter

Indra drinking Soma

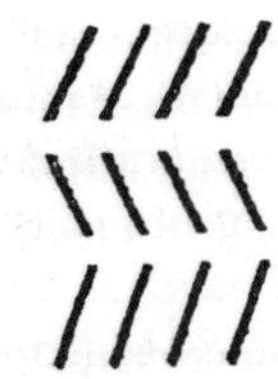

Soma drop passage

flow signs and offering signs or Indra with *Soma*-juice (Fig. 5).[15]

Bull and the Vedic Deities

Bull was considered to be sacred animal in the Vedic lore, specially in the *RV samhita.* There are several instances where the Vedic deities were called bulls. Soma is called bull in *RV* IX 64.1, IX 70.7, Agni in *RV* I. 31.1, I. 79.2 etc.; Indra in *RV* I. 33. 10, I. 54.2 etc. The famous *Rc* describing the great god appearing among the mortals -*mahadevo marty Am AviveSa* - (*RV* IV. 58.3) describes him as the bull with two heads. This particular hymn is a very famous. The words for bull i.e. *vRza* and *vRzabha* in various forms occur 195 times in the *RV samhitA*. It is to be noted here that although horse-*aSva*-is mentioned in *RV* several times, it is a carriage animal yoked to the chariots of the gods. Except in two hymns, namely, *RV* I.162 and 163, called *aSvas Ukta,* where the horse deity is praised as god, nowhere else in the *RV samhitA* any god is called the horse. This points out that bull commanded a very high respect in the Vedic society as compared to horse.

The Indus seals point to the same trend. So many of the ornamented bull figures on these seals confirm that the animal was considered sacred and commanded great respect.

AV Hymns V.16 and VI.86 and the Sacred Bull Seals

The Atharva vedic hymns V.16 and VI.86 both have presiding deity *ekavRza* —the lone or unique bull. The bull is praised to be the most powerful animal and the consecrated king is urged to possess the power of multiple bulls in *AV* V.16. The hymn has a repetitive nature.

Yadi ekavRzo S si sRjAraso S si [AV V-16.1]

Tr.: If you are with eleven bull-power, (then) you are devoid of vital water (power).

This is a very strange hymn, one of the mystic hymns from the Atharvaveda and was recited at the time of royal consecration ceremony.

An ordinary man cannot be urged to acquire oneself the power of several bulls or else remain sapless or inefficient. It was only the person with royal heritage or governing power or a consecrated king who could be urged to possess the power of several bulls, the symbol of strength and metaphor for might.

This is confirmed by another hymn *AV* VI.86. Seer of this hymn is *Atharvan.* In this hymn the king, is praised as being mighty of the mighty supernatural and natural objects. This hymn is glorification of a newly consecrated king as pointed by Griffith; the translation of the hymn by Griffith is given below.

AV VI. 86

'This is the Lord of Indra, this the Lord of Heaven, the Lord of Earth,
The Lord of all existing things; the one and only lord be thou' (*AV* VI. 86.1)

'The sea is regent of the floods; Agni is ruler of the land,
The Moon is regent of stars; the one and only lord be thou' (*AV* VI.86.2)

'Thou art the king of Asuras, the crown and summit of mankind
Thou art the partner of the Gods: The one and only lord be thou' (*AV* VI. 86.3)

Griffith opines that *asuras* referred to in the last *Rc* are the earthly lords.

The present author has shown elsewhere that Asuras in the *AV* are associated with the river Sarasvati and possibly belonged to the Sarasvati river valley which was the mainstay of the Indus culture. The time of the split between the monotheistic Indo-Iranians and the followers of the polytheistic Vedic religion occured around the time of dessication of the Sarasvati river.[16]

If an artist were to represent the concept of *ekavRza* associated with Indra, the lord of gods, the most feasible proposition becomes a bull picture with *Soma* processing set up in front. This proposition concurs with the earlier proposition about the sacred filter by Mahadevan 17.

Coming back to the hymn *AV* V. 16, if it were to be represented by an artist on the seal of the sizes as small 3 x 2 - 3 cm, he could only draw a bull-body with multiple heads.

There are seven such seals. These are listed below.

Table No. 1

Multiple-headed Bull seals from the Indus culture

No.	Seal No.	Shape of seal	No. of heads	Single-horned	Double-horned	Remarks
1.	M-298	Rectangular	2	1	1	Fish on top
2.	M-417	Circular	6	1	2	seal partly broken but could be alternately single-horned or double-horned
3.	M-1169	Rectangular	3	1	2	Graffitti on top
4.	M-1170	Rectangular	3	–	3	
5.	M-1171	Rectangular	3	1	2	
6.	A I-6	Rectangular	3	1	2	
7.	M-43	Rectangular	3	1	2	with vertical graffitti

Fig. 6 - Multiple-headed bull seal from Amri Seal No. AI-6

It is to be noted that the artists who engraved these seals did not distinguish between the image of a scared bull shown either with single horn or double horns. These could be alternately drawn as it is on the circular seal (No. M-417).

From the survey of the seals, interchangeability of bull figure with single horn and with two horns is evident from the fact that just as single-horned bull is shown with a sacred filter in front, so also, the bull figures with two horns are shown with sacred filter in their front. These seals are listed in Table 2.

Table 2

Two-horned Bulls with Sacred Filter in Front

No.	Location	No. of seals
1.	Mohenjodaro	6
2.	Lothal	3
3.	Banavali	1

The above ten seals establish interchangeability of single-horned bulls with double-horned ones. It is obvious that the incidence of royal consecration occurs once in a while and such seals could be engraved on these occasions; hence, they are so less in number. However, looking at the presence of the strong central authority and trading activity of the Indus culture society, the number of royal authority seals could outnumber all other type of seals. Over the period of centuries of existence of the Indus culture, the authorities needed a large number of scared bull seals with a sacred filter in front. These were used for sealing the merchandise with royal approval and insignia. It is confirmed by a few sealings from Lothal. Rao[18] has reported one such sealing with sacred bull motif and impression of packing material on the reverse.

Thus the bull figure was a royal symbol. The graffiti on the seal changed according to the person in authority, the location and the purpose. A parallel is to found with the tripple lion symbol of the Indian government today which is used for many purposes and by many people in authority.

The Bull-Man Seals

The most appropriate representation of these hymns is made on the seal No. M-1224 where a bull-man i.e. a figure with a human face and a body of a vertically standing bull-like figure is drawn on one face of the seal and there is sacred bull on the obverse. It, therefore, becomes evident that bull-man represented the royal person and the single horned bull represented a sacred deified bull and the royal emblem during the Indus culture period.

Conclusion

1. The unique bull symbol with manger-on-stand in front represents the *Sacred Bull and Sacred Filter* repersenting the **king of gods i.e. Indra and the *Soma* filter**.

2. Indra being the king of gods, the royal insignia was symbolically represented on majority of the seals, as bull with a single horn.

3. Two-horned bull figure with sacred filter in front on some seals point to interchangeability of the bull with single horn.

4. The single-horned sacred bulls as well as two-horned bull figures were the royal emblems of the Indus culture.

5. The consecrated king vested with supernatural power as described in the hymn *AV* VI. 86 is represented by the Indus seal of a bull-man on one face and a sacred bull on the obverse (seal No. M-1224).

6. The *AV* hymn V-16 which describes imbibing the might of several bulls by the consecrated king is represented by the Indus seals with multiple heads attached to a bull's body.

***Note:** Reference to the Indus seals given in the above article are from* 'Corpus of the Indus seals from India' and 'Corpus of the Indus seals from Pakistan', *ed. by Joshi and Parpola, and Shah and Parpola, respectively.*

Acknowledgements

The present author thanks Dr. V.N. Misra, Director, Deccan College, Pune, for making the *Corpus* volumes available, and for the discussion on the topic and Dr. S.R. Rao for stimulating discussion. He also thanks Dr. P. P. Joglekar for his help on the paleobiology and other references,discussion and suggestions on the topic.0

The present author is thankful to his friend Shri. V.V. Kumbhojkar for diligently drawing the figures.

REFERENCES

1. Roy, C.R. 1946. Unicorn in the seals of Mohenjodaro and its relation to the religion of Indus Valley Civilisation *J. Sind Historical Soc.* Vol. VIII No. ! pp39-44.
2. De vries, 1976. *A Dictionary of Symbols and Imagery,* 2nd edn.
3. Atre, Shubhangana 1985. Harappan Riddle of "UNICORN", *Bulletin of the Deccan Res. Inst. Pune.* Vol 44 pp 1-10.
4. Pathak P. V. 1991. Lady of the Beasts or the Lord of the Beasts: An Assessment, *Puratattva* Vol. X pp 57-64.
5. Zeuner, F.E. 1963. *A History of Domesticated Animals,* Hutchinson, London.
6. Grigson, Caroline, 1981. Some thoughts on Unicorns and Other Cattle depicted at Mohenjodaro and Harappa in

Bridgit Allchin (Ed.) *South Asian Archaeology.*

7. MMM, 1983 *Man, Myth and Magic encyclopedia* Ed. Richard Cavendish, Marshall Cavendish Corporation London.

8. Jetmar, Karl and Volker, Thewalt, 1987. *Between Gandhara and the Silk Roads, Rock carvings along the Karakoram high ways, Discoveries by the German-Pakistani Expeditions 1979-84* Published by Pitt Rivers Museum and Deptt. of Ethnology & Pre-history.

9. Ratnagar, Shereen, 1981. *Encounters: The Westerly Trade of the Harappa Civilization,* Oxford University Press, Mumbai.

10. Ibid p. 187.

11. Ibid p. 188.

12. Pathak 199 1op. cit.

13. *Ibid* 1992. The Indus Culture Seal of the Three forms and Seven Figures as Pictorial Representation of AV hymn IV. 37. *Puratattva* Vol. XXII Pp 59-63.

14. Ibid 1997. Geo-Cultural Scenario and Vedic and Indo-Iranian Texts, *J.K.R. Cama Oriental Institute,* Mumbai Vol. 61 pp 28-98.

15. Mahadevan, Iravatham, 1985. The Cult Object on Unicorn Seals: A Sacred Filter ? in N. Karashima, (Ed.) *Indus Valley to Mekong Delta: Explorations in Epigraphy,* Chennai pp. 219-266.

16. Pathak 1997 op. cit.

17. Mahadeven, op. cit.

18. Rao, S.R. 1985 *Lothal,* Archaeological Survey of India, New Delhi.

Further Excavations at Rakhigarhi

AMARENDRA NATH*

The excavations at Rakhigarhi have been taken up by the Institute of Archaeology, Archaeological Survey of India, New Delhi since 1997-98. A brief account of the first season's work has already appeared in the *Puratattva No.28*. Further account of the excavation carried out during the last field season (1998-99) is presented now.

During the current field season, the following four objectives set to be realised were : (i) to complete the plans of the Mature Harappan structures (ii) to continue investigation of the fortification wall and see its extension south ward i.e. on the slope of RGR-4; (iii) to lay bare more area of the Harappan settlement in the RGR-1 and RGR-2; and (iv) to locate the early and late Harappan horizons in stratified context as indications show. Besides it was also aimed at further examining the antiquity of the chambered burial in RGR-1, which ultimately turned out to be a late medieval manifestation.

In order to achieve the above objectives, trenches were laid judiciously adjacent to the previous year's diggings exposed at RGR-1 and RGR-2. For objectives Nos. (i) and (iii), a series of trenches in the west-east direction were laid in RGR-1, namely, H-5 to N-5 and W-5 to Y-5. Trench No. Y-5 could determine the eastern limit of the mound, so also, the test pit of N-13; could determine the southern limit of the mound, so also, the test pit in N-13 could determine the southern limit of the mound. However, the northern limit in test pit no. ZF-1 and the western limit in test pit no. A-5 could not be determined, both were laid on the respective extremities of the mound. In RGR-2, the trenches opened were M-19, Q-18 to Q-20, R-18 to R-20, S-18 to S-20. These trenches served the purpose noted at (i) and (iii). With regard to objective no. (ii) trenches Y24 to Y-26, Z-23 to Z-26 were for understanding the nature of the fortification wall at the south-eastern margin of RGR-2. In the same alignment trench no. D-4 was opened on the northern slope of RGR-4 with a view to see the extension of the fortification as well as sequence of culture. The objective no. (iv) was taken up for further investigation when the horizon of Early Harappa was noticed in trench nos. N-5 of RGR-1. In the sequel, trench nos. W-5, X-5, N-10 to N-13, P-11, ZF-1 and A-5 were subjected to excavation. As against the first season's sequence of culture, the current excavations at Rakhigarhi revealed the cultural horizon of Early Harappan (Period-1) succeded by Mature Harappan (Period-II). Absence of Late Harappan horizon in the stratified cuttings of RGR-1 and RGR-2 indicates their occupation of short lived nature and that too in small group possibly over the eastward extension of RGR-4 and RGR-5.

*Director, Institute of Archaeology, Archaeological Survey of India.

PERIOD -I (Early Harappan)

Period - I designated as Early Harappan was noticed in the cuttings N-10 and N-11 in the southern slope of RGR-1. Relatively limited evidence of this period was encountered in W-5 and X-5 on the eastern margin of RGR-1. Similarly test pits ZF-1 and A-5 also revealed Early Harappan occupational levels, respectively on northern and western margins of the mound. The exercise of digging on the periphery of RGR-1 could determine the extent of Early Harappan occupation extending in an area over 4.5 hectares. The deposit, nearly three metres thick, shows the beginning of occupation over the alluvium. Although the area subjected to excavation was too small yet the information gathered was of far reaching consequences. It has given a glimpse into the settlement pattern.

The structures were oriented along the cardinal directions and were with single bricks of burnt and sun dried varieties. Extensive use of kiln fired bricks produced out of mould is a unique phenomenon to be remembered; however, the proportion of 1:2:3 noted at Kailbangan-1 and Banawali-1, still remains to be determined. Some of the burnt bricks bear pre-firing mason marks; some are reminiscent to the Harappan characters.

There were three structural phases out of which Phase-1 could be studied in greater detail. The drainage system implies the emergence of a planned settlement. A burnt brick lined public drain was noticed running north to south with a house-drain from western side. The public drain and house drain were unpaved. On the eastern side of the public drain was noticed, a huge burnt brickbat floor of a courtyard sloping south-west. There were four circulars pits cut in the floor, two of bigger size were aligned north-south, while the other two of smaller diameter were aligned east-west. There were a few post-holes around these pits. The purpose of the floor is yet to be determined. But the sharp gradient in the floor towards the public drain suggests its possible use as textile dyeing courtyard. The circular pits in the floor were specially cut to the size of open mouth receptacles containing dyeing solution. An equally wide verandah was noticed on the northern side of the courtyard, which possibly served the purpose of stacking textile. The deposit of ash and shell debitage in the public drain suggested the existence of shell working in the vicinity. In Phase II immediately above the floor of courtyard were noticed two fire chambers made of lower part of a large sized vase, which was internally mud lined. Towards the western side of these fire chambers were noticed a sandstone quern. Could this be suggestive crafts area?

The ceremic industry shows all the six the Kalibangan fabrics including the technique of surface treatment, shapes and decorative elements. The ceremic handles correspond with Banawali -1. The pottery was essentially wheel-made with a few exceptions of hand-made specimens. It was relatively light and thin in fabric, red to pinkish in colour and painted in black, combined at times with white, over a self-slipped dull surface. The combination of black and white considerably increased the design-effect. The potters chose to paint the neck and shoulders. The design elements were essentially geometric. The simplest among them included horizontal bands, row of dots, latticed triangles, fish-scales etc. Motifs used as filler were radiating lines ending in solid disks, four petalled flowers, pipal leaf and circle with radiating arches. Shapes included the jar with an out turned rim, basin and dish-on-stand. A miniature vase-on-stand was reminiscent to the one reported from Kalibangan, identified as chalice. Apart from red ware, the site had yielded both plain and painted variety of grey ware. The design elements were more or less same as noted above.

Some sherds are reminiscent of 'Hakara ware' named after the Hakra river i.e. Ghaggar sites in Cholistan region. The specimens have been examined by Shri J.P. Joshi and has confirmed the presence of Hakra elements in the Early Harappan pottery found in a stratified context at the site. He also pointed out that such type of wares have already been reported from Early Harappan phase of Kalibangan. Earlier, Sothi site had reported the characteristic Hakra types like (i) incised (ii) applique, (iii) dendritic and (iv) ribbed or striated ware. The incised ware characterised by thick and thin medium sized vases, was decorated externally with groups of multiple incised lines drawn horizontally, diagonally and in wavy compositions. Applique ware is basically red, characterised by thick applique zig-zag bands occuring over big jars having pronounced out curved rim. The dendritic ware is of medium fabric and the shape met with was vases of medium size. It was first painted from neck to shoulder and subsequently treated with secondary coating of mud mixed with coarse particles. The paste is generally seen overlapping the chocolate slip applied over the out turned rim, neck and shoulder portion of a pot. The ribbed ware was both in thick and thin fabrics; the shape however, could not be determined.

Metal objects reported from this horizons were arrowhead, needle and bangle. The lithic industry was represented by chert blade as a fluted core. Characteristic segemented terracotta bangles with plano-concave section were retrieved. Other terracotta finds includes animal figurines, toy cart frames and hopscotch (Pl.1). Other important antiquities were semi-precious stones, steatite (including disc beads,) faience; stone saddle quern and sling balls.

The typical Harappan graffiti were noticed on burnt bricks and on pot sherds. Some of the graffiti signs were geometrical pattern while a few were naturalistic or in stylized forms.

PERIOD II - (Mature Harappan)

Period II was evidenced in the cuttings of RGR-1, RGR-2 and RGR-4. The evidence of the preceding period showed the beginning of Mature Harappan traits. The excavation also confirmed last year's findings. RGR-2, presumably served as the citadel. It was surrounded by mud-brick fortification wall, which was noticed eariier in the south-eastern cuttings. The core of fortification wall was of mud brick while its external and internal veenering were in burnt bricks. The north-south arm of fortification wall was exposed to a length of 70 m. Within the citadel mud-brick podiums like those at Kailbangan were found. Here, the podium had in-built oblong pit chambers, possibly for ritualistic purpose. These chambers had deposits of charcoal bits and fresh-looking cattle bones. Over the brick pavement a series of four fire altars were noticed in north-south alignment; these were brick lined with mud plaster and were found in a dilapidated condition. The middle of western fire altar had a vertical brick fixed in it, symbolizing stump-like *yashthi*. The podium was aligned east-west and had covered verandah embellished with flight of steps, suggesting entrance from western side. A brick well was also noticed at the north-western corner. The podium had a street on all the four sides suggesting its importance in terms of public utility. Apart from this, the citadel also enclosed structures of different phases. An unpaved public drain of burnt brick was noticed in trench M-19, running in north-south direction. a drain terminating from western side had a cesspool at the terminal point. From the upper level there were evidences of individual house hold drains, some discharging into the street while a few in the soakage jars and middle of the street.A potter's pit kiln in RGR-1, trench No N-5 is a unique discovery of this season (Pl.2). It is somewhat conch shape on plan, oriented east-west. In the middle, there are two semi-arch-like brick built shafts for supporting medium to miniature sized vases/jars alternatively and sandwiched between cow dung cakes. The potter used the eastern projection of the pit for arranging the pots and pans in the kiln while it was fired from western side. The vitrified plaster surface of the kiln is an indication of constant use of the kiln and the high temperature.

In addition, to the fire altars in a row noticed over the podium in RGR-2, there are a few more fire altars of distinct shapes, never reported before from the Mature Harappan levels. The courtyard in trench K-5 brought to light three different types of fire altars, oriented north-south. The one in the centre was unique on plan. It had semicircular central projection on north-south side, reminding *chiti*-like (Pl.3) configuration. In the central portion was a stump of brick over a mud plastered base. Around it, the deposit was of ash and charcoal. Towards its right flank, a small heart shaped fire altar was noticed with a stump like projection in the centre. Further to its right was noticed an oblong fire altar, which was reminiscent of Kalibangan evidence. It had two-coursed enclosure wall of brick on edge with signs of plaster. A portion of the western arm of the fire altar was found fallen in the middle portion, suggesting the practice of destroying the altar after performing the rituals. Within a good number of offerings in the form of terracotta cakes of triangular lenticular shapes and *mushtikas* were noticed. Another unique fire altar is of *yonipith* (Pl.4) type with a stump like projection in the centre in H-5.

The pottery deserves special mention. Besides, the typical Harappan wares, plain as well as painted, there also occured pots which had an unslipped dull red fabric painted over in black pigment with broad bands along the neck and shoulder. 'Reserve' slipped was also encountered. The shapes included goblets, dishes, basins, flasks, narrow necked vases, storage jars, perforated vessels, dish-on-stand and lids. The plain red ware was usually with or without a fine red slip. The painted motifs consisted of both geometrical and naturalistic elements.

Amongst the important antiquities mention may be made of terracotta animal figurines. The terracotta bulls with prominent humps, elongated body and block or joined legs were found in good number. The terracotta figurines of water buffallo could be distinguished with the help of grooved horns. Other terracota animals represented were dog, lion, leopard, rabbit and horse. As compared to animals human figurines are meagre in number. Other finds from this period including chert blades, weights, copper objects, terracotta objects, games-men, beads etc. Besides steatite seals (Pl-5) and terracotta sealings and clay tablets deserve special mention. An inscribed lead ignot of plano-convex shape was an important discovery of this season.

The results of the excavation confirmed that the Early Harappan occupation was succeded by Mature Harappan period. However, the Late Harappan occupation as indicated by the surface observation still remains elusive. The fortification of citadel mound (RGR-2) needs further probing as also its relation with RGR-3.

Chalcolithic Social Organization in Central India: A case study of Balathal

SHWETA SINHA DESHPANDE*

Introduction

"Since historical events and the essential social divisions of prehistoric peoples do not find an adequate expression in material remains, it cannot be right to arrive at a knowledge of them in archaeological interpretations".

Archaeological study into the social past of mankind was once asserted fruitless by scholars like M.A. Smith and V.G. Childe as it was thought impossible to reconstruct the social organization of the ancient societies. But 'New Archaeologist like L. Binford and C. Renfrew believed that though we have no clear knowledge about the past, we can proceed in the reconstruction of ancient societies through inferences about simple notions like diet, for example the analysis of refuse pits. More complex notions such as social hierarchy and the status of people within them can similarly be constructed on the basis of structures, burials, and the goods contained in them with the help of a systematic and sustained examination of artifacts and situations by placing them in a wider context relating to ecology, cultural contacts and availability of raw materials. Archaeology during the 1960s and 70s proved to be useful and innovative as scholars moved to interpret the scanty remains of written records or archaeological remains to reconstruct the life style, subsistence and society of the past. They worked out a model to study the increasing social complexity of past societies according to which their social systems underwent gradual process of evolution from the hunting-gathering stage to the urban civilization. These hunter-gatherer bands developed into tribal chiefdoms followed by the stratified societies or ranked societies. In line of progression evolved the proto-urban centres that then gradually developed into the civilized state organizations.

In India social archaeology saw its beginning with the discovery of the Harappan Civilization which took back the dates of a civilized culture in the country by two thousand years. A determined effort towards the development of social archaeology was made by Dhavalikar *et al* at the site of Inamgaon in Deccan India, where they identified the existence of a chiefdom society. The evidence included traces of craft specialization, public architecture, unequal distribution of wealth, social differentiation and the existence of the chief himself in the form of his house and burial. This was the only chalcolithic site in India where an effort was made to study the social rankings and status of the people within the society, until the excavation at Balathal a rural chalcolithic site in the Banas River basin belonging to the Ahar culture, was undertaken in a joint venture by the Deccan college of Pune and the Institute of Rajasthan Studies, Udaipur.

The basin of the Banas River, in Mewar, is one of those regions in India that witnessed the earliest emer-

* Deccan College, Dept. of Archaeology, Pune.

gence and local development of settled community life based on farming. The findings from the various Ahar sites show the rise and development of a distinctive regional chalcolithic culture in Mewar around 2800 BC (based on the latest carbon dates from Balathal). This culture flourished in a semi-arid region, with the settlements ranging from small hamlets of 0.8, to 1.6 hectares in area to large villages like Ahar and Gilund sprawling over an area of 5 hectares with agriculture as the main-stay of the economy. The people domesticated cattle, buffalo, sheep, goat and dog; hunted *barasingha* and caught fish, turtle and birds. The population of this culture used copper and stone tools and lived in two- or three- roomed houses built on foundations of undressed schist blocks with built-in storage bins and ovens. The ceramic industry comprised Red and Black Ware, Red Ware, Cream Slipped Ware and Gray Ware with incised and painted designs. In addition, there seems to have existed a definite relation between the Harappans of Gujarat and Rajasthan with these communities.

In this article we will try and understand the site of chalcolithic Balathal, its location, environment, artifacts and structural remains in order to reconstruct its culture and social order.

Theoretical Archaeology

According to social archaeologists, a society should be viewed as having several interconnecting parts such as subsistence, technology, contact and exchange, belief and thought; all working together within a congenial environment helping the society or culture to develop over a period of time. Hence the study of society is all about people and relations between people, about the exercise of power and the nature and scale of organization. The nature of the society is identified on the basis of: (a) scale or size of the society; (b) its dominance was the site politically autonomous; (c) internal organization were the people more or less on equal footing? Or were there prominent differences in status, rank and prestige within the society showing different social classes ?; (d) craft specialization and (e) exchange networks.

On the basis of all these factors scholars like Service, Fried and Sahalins have classified societies into four categories:

Bands: consists of members of a kin, related by descent or marriage and forming a small egalitarian society of hunters and gatherers moving seasonally to exploit wild (undomesticated) food resources. Band groups have no marked economic or status disparities and lack a formal leader.

Tribes: are larger than Bands but rarely number more than a few thousand people living in a village comprising freestanding houses. Their subsistence is based on cultivated plants and domesticated animals. They are either settled farmers or nomadic pastoralists with a mobile economy based on the intensive exploitation of livestock. These are multicommunity societies with the individual communities integrated into a larger society through kinship ties. Although some of these tribal villages have officials and even a capital and seat of government, they lack the economic base necessary for effective use of power.

Chiefdoms: operate on the principle of rank differences and social status between people. These societies are governed by a chief, have centralized power related to temples and/or a residence. Prestige and rank, is determined by how closely one is related to the chief but there is no true stratification into classes. There is often specialization in craft products and surplus of these products and agriculture are periodically paid to the chief as an obligation. The chief uses this to maintain his retainers, for public works or redistribution among his subjects in times of need. The ranking of chiefdoms is visible in settlement patterning, site hierarchy, grave goods etc.

Early States: preserve many features of a chiefdom organization but the ruler (king or queen) has explicit authority to establish laws and enforce them using a standing army. Society is viewed as a territory owned by the ruling lineage and populated by tenants with an obligation to pay taxes. State societies show a characteristic urban settlement with a pronounced settlement and class hierarchy.

The six stages of evolution of an urban civilization as put forth by Guha states that there was a continuous development from the Mesolithic Period to the State societies. Mesolithic egalitarian, hunting and gathering bands developed into the Neolithic cultures with ceramics and extended households around the fifth millenium BC. These were transformed into ranked societies with a specific pottery tradition and had a potential for evolving in stratified chiefdoms around the third-fourth millenium BC. Between 2800-2600 BC emerged proto-urban centres, which later develop into fullfledged urban states with trade and central authority.

It was the Mesolithic hunters who, due to various factors like population pressure and depleting resources, were forced to adopt an agrarian life style which would provide them with better resources. Agriculture forced them to settle near fertile arable land and water resources. Need for storing surpluses, led to the introduction of ceramics and the dwelling structures also expanded from single mud reed rooms to larger complexes. With this shift in subsistence and sedentary settlement, there was a marked change in the social organization, a part of culture that entails adaptation to economic and ecological environments. Increasing need for cooperation and organization of activities relating to subsistence led to a division of labour, more efficiency and surpluses. Surplus, needs authority to administer mechanisms of storage, allocation and redistribution. Authority also plays an important role in the administration of pastures, water sources and all other collectively held and produced goods. Surplus allows more time and the ability to support skilled and specialized crafts not possessed by all members of the society thus enhancing trade and exchange. Egalitarian bands were inadequate in dealing with these socio-economic changes that put forward the need for a central administrative authority.

The following have been regarded as the more frequent features of chiefdoms:

(a) A ranked society; (b) Redistribution of surplus organized by the central authority or chief; (c) Greater population density; (d) Greater productivity; (e) Clearly defined territorial boundaries, (f) Relation to the local environmental situations favoring specialization in production, (g) Specialization through pooling of individual skills in large cooperative endeavours, (h) Organization and deployment of labour, for agriculture and building purposes, (i) Craft specialization, (j) Potential for territorial expansion associated with the rise and fall of neighbouring societies, (k) Reduction of internal strife, (l) Pervasive inequality of persons or groups in the society associated with permanent leadership, (m) Distinctive dress or ornament for those of high status, and (n) Evidence of the chief himself.

Based on a number of excavated sites it is believed that Chalcolithic cultures worked under a chiefdom organization with clear evidence of social stratification and economic hierarchy with prominent central authority in the hands of a chief. A gradual evolutionary process culminating in the rise of just such a chiefdoms evident at the site of Balathal and is supported by archaeological evidence. As mentioned earlier, culture and environment are coterminus as culture is basically an adaptation to the local environment by a particular human community. Gradual local adaptation, development and economic prosperity contributed by prosperous agriculture, continuous water supply, specialized crafts like ceramics and beads manufacturing and contact with the contemporary chalcolithic and Pre-Harappan cultures led to the rise of a chiefdom society and increased economic, social and political complexity at the site.

Chalcolithic Balathal

The village of Balathal (24° 43' N and 73° 59' E) is located in the Vallabhanagar Tehsil of Udaipur district, 42 km east of Udaipur near the Udaipur–Chittorgarh highway. It lies about 7 km east of Vallabhanagar. The site is 3 hectares in (150 m NS and 135 m EW) with a deposit of 7m belonging to two cultural periods Chalcolithic and Early Historic.

Environment plays a very important role in the settlement and occupation of a particular region as the societies require a number of favourable factors to grow like fertile soil, water resources, moderate climate and rainfall. Hence the availability here of a large lake of sweet water and the proximity of fertile and pasture land around the site lured the early farming communities to make Balathal their home. The climate of the region is semi-arid with an average rainfall of 650.3 mm. The floral and faunal assemblage is diverse with trees like *Aam (Mangifera indica), imli (Tamarindus indica), Babul (Acacia arabica),* etc. Animals like tiger, panther, antelope; various reptiles and birds were present.

The excavations have yielded two cultural periods with a long hiatus between:

Period 1: Chalcolithic (2800 BC-1800 BC)

Period 2: Early Historic (200 BC - AD 300)with a break of 1600 years in between.

Period 1: Materials excavated at the site consist of structures, ceramics, copper objects, stone querns, hammerstones, terracotta objects, beads and an enormous quantity of animal and plant remains which will aid in reconstructing the Chalcolithic society.

Period 2: After a long occupation of thousand years the site was abandoned, and reoccupied after a gap of more than 1600 years by a new group of people using iron technology and a different material culture.

The large number of Mesolithic sites found in south-eastern Rajasthan shows that humans right from the Paleolithic period inhabited the area. Population pressure and declining resources possibly forced the people to settle down in restricted areas with congenial environments. Small settlements with an agro-pastoral economy along with hunting and gathering in the nearby forested areas developed at congenial places such as Balathal. With increasing prosperity, came developments in house construction and improved copper and ceramic technology. An exchange network seems to have existed between settlements like Ahar and Gilund, which might have facilitated the procurement of goods not available locally in exchange for products locally produced. At Balathal, large silo bases, storage bins and the structures identified as possible granaries in the living complexes give us a clear idea of the strong agricultural base in the economy. Bone analysis reveals the predominance of cattle, followed by sheep and goat supplemented by wild animals and fish.

The economy of a society forms the base and provides the means for further development. These economic benefits when exploited by a small group of people leads to the rise of socio-economic differentiation and concentration of economic power in the hands of a few. This eventually gives rise to a chiefdom society followed by organized states. Hence the economic conditions at sites such as Balathal was very congenial for an elaborate socio-political organization or stratified society to evolve come into existence.

At Balathal a chiefdom came into existence around the beginning of third millenium BC (Phase A, 2800-2500 BC). Excavations reveal an agro-pastoral economy with flimsy circular huts made of mud and reed with thatched roofs. Most domestic activities seem to have been centred outside the huts, which were probably used for storage of valuables. The discovery of two silos suggests that the inhabitants were producing surplus food-grains. Characteristic wares such as thick Red Slipped Ware, thin Red Slipped Ware and Black–and-Red Ware were being manufactured at the site. A large number of Reserved Slip Ware shards were also discovered in the lowermost levels suggesting a local origin rather than an import from the Harappan sites which seem to have borrowed and perfected the art at a later date.

The succeeding Phase B with four different structural phases (2500-1800 BC) saw marked development and prosperity of the chiefdom society. Many features emphasizing the existence of a chief with concentration of economic, political and social power are evident at the site during this Phase and shall be dealt with below.

Micro-settlement Pattern

During Phase B, there was a sudden change in the settlement pattern, with the settlement expanding to cover large areas in the central and southern parts of the mound. A fortified enclosure at the centre and an outer wall surrounding the settlement was built, which was similar to the social hierarchic planning of Harappan sites. The conspicuous use of stone for construction purposes and the rudimentary grid plan where houses were located on both sides of the bylanes and streets are features that also appear to have been borrowed from the neighboring Harappan Culture sites.

Chiefdoms are combinations of semi-nomadic and sedentary communities. Dhavalikar *et al* has correlated the circular dwellings with a nomadic component and rectangular huts with fully sedentary societies. Balathal is a combination of clustered dwellings of both types, with common courtyards, fireplaces, and storage facilities representing extended joint family units. The micro-settlement pattern at the site can also be classified into public and private architecture based on its size and ownership.

Public structures

One of the most important features of a chiefdom

society is the large number of public structures built with public funds or the surplus generated by the people. Paid labour was generated and organized with the authority of the chief from within the society itself probably in the nonagricultural season. These structures are for the benefit of the whole settlement and cannot be considered as private property or a residential area of an individual. The huge dimensions and the location of these structures all suggest against private ownership. At Balathal, at least three distinct public structures have been identified.

A domineering fortified enclosure complete with bastions and a gate has been identified in the centre of the mound. The construction of this large structure proves the existence of a strong ruler and a large economic surplus enabling the maintenance and organization of labour and funds for such public buildings. The structure was built on a pink lime floor which is absent elsewhere. This finely worked floor level, was repaired and plastered with cowdung and clay over and over again.

The exact function of the structure is yet to be decided: although most scholars consider it as the residence of the chief with a higher socio-political status and ruling the settlement from this vantage point. It is also possible that a number of families were living together within the structure and had an equal say in the administration of the settlement like the present *Panchayati* system where a number of influential individuals enjoy important status in the society. Nothing can be said with surety regarding the people or the number of families who occupied the structure but it is more than clear that the enclosure played an important role in the administration of the settlement.

It is also possible that as agriculture was the major source of livelihood and wealth, this structure protected the threshing floors or stored surplus grain along with the structures identified as granaries.

It could also have served as a place for protection of the whole population during enemy attacks or other emergencies. The walls of the structure are very thick and wide and suggest that they were built for protection. This does not seem improbable as offensive and defensive weapons like copper knives, sling balls and arrowheads have been found here. Based on this, the medieval concept of *'garhis'* or small forts can be traced to the chalcolithic period. The fortified enclosure of Balathal thus could have fulfilled a number of functions including the protection and housing of the chief as well as people in times of need as also storage for surplus grains. All these factors show the existence of the strong rule with a high economic and social status capable of organizing than impressive number of labour, finance and time required to build such a structure.

An outer fortification has been found on the northern, eastern and southern parts of the mound. This fortification is clearly an attempt to make the site completely secure from outside elements.

One of the most important features of a chiefdom is the centralized authority over agricultural surplus. The chief with his religious and divine powers along with the political and economic powers has the right to collect taxes from the people in the form of grains or other products. Structures 10 C, 10D and 10E outside the fortified enclosure are identified as granaries at Balathal. The existence of granaries clearly indicate the authority which the chief exerted over the people to collect surplus to be used in time of emergency or for public works. This economic surplus formed the subsistence base for the people and helped in concentration of economic power in chiefdoms. These public funds could also be used for the upkeep of the chief and the maintenance of an armed force to protect the settlement from external incursions. It was just such an economic base of the local chalcolithic economies that was strengthened to form a stable centralized state government during the Harappan period.

Studies of present day chiefdom–societies by ethnoarchaeologists prove beyond doubt that it is impossible to construct public architecture without central authority. It is the chief who harnesses labour for construction of buildings and ditches, fortifications, irrigation facilities, granaries, etc. The chief himself is identified on the basis of structural remains and burial goods at a site. Since the chief has a higher economic and social standing, the rules of the society do not apply to him. His house is larger than others, located in a central area, and contains prestigious goods not available to the common people. While none of these are directly evident at Balathal, the public structures do show a centralized authority and power of the chief to organize labour, allocate resources and collect taxes without which there would be no public works.

Private architecture

During Phase B, in the section south of the fortified enclosure a large number of residential and workshop complexes were established and probably belonged to different families of the influential strata of the society. Four structural phases have been recognized in Phase B, of which the second is the more prosperous. Structural Phase I was a development on the earlier circular huts found m Phase A due to economic prosperity and Harappan contact. The raw materials used were mud, mud-brick and stone. The foundations of these houses were of stone set in mud mortar and had walls of mud-bricks and small stones bound also by mud. The roofs were either thatched or of wooden beams and rafters The floors were of beaten clay plastered over with cowdung.

Three residential complexes belonging to Phase II have been identified. Complex 2 and 3 on the south-western side are separated from each other by a narrow lane and are separated from Complex 1 by a street 4.80m wide. This shows the existence of a planned, measured and thought out settlement pattern at the site.

Structural Complex 1 consists of large number of rooms (10A-K), their functions identified on the basis of objects found within them. Structure 10A with a hearth, has been identified as that of a coppersmith for repairing copper items. Structure 10B was probably a storage and dehusking area with saddle querns and stone platforms to support storage bins. Structures 10C, D and E are the public granaries and have been described earlier. Room 10F, has a mud platform and a hearth or *chulha* and hence is believed to have been a kitchen. Intensive burning activities, large amounts of charred cattle bones and potsherds indicate prolonged use. Rooms 10G, H, and I present evidence of storage and burning. Structure 10K has been identified as a poultry-keeping area.

This complex is believed to have belonged to a single family. This unplanned construction, shows that it was built and then expanded as the family grew and needed more space. Based on its dimensions and location, it can be surmised that the house belonged to a wealthy and influential family. Room 10 I, seems to be the courtyard around which all other rooms for storage, cooking and dwelling were constructed. On the basis of the available evidence from Room 10A, the structure has been interpreted as the residence and workshop of a coppersmith. The flourishing household seems to be the result of a high economic and social advantage enjoyed by the family as important craftsmen.

However, on the basis of present pattern of buildings in the village of Balathal and other villages it has been suggested that the complex is a cluster of a number of separate living complexes with continuous repairing and addition of rooms belonging to different families sharing various common walls. Rooms 10 G, F, and H, on the basis of large number of steatite beads and a hearth showing long duration of burning activity has been identified as the house lapidiary. Since the complex has not been excavated from the eastern section nothing can be said with surety.

Structural Complex 2 represented by Structure 9 is located on the western side of the main street and north of Complex 3. Structure 9 is a large enclosed rectangular area, with walls made of mud-bricks and floor plastered with clay and cowdung. The structure shows a lot of evidence of storage along with domestic activities like grinding and de-husking in the form of silos, storage bins and saddle querns. From the kind of storage facilities and the dimension of the structure it can be inferred that the complex was occupied by an economically flourishing household.

Structure 5 of Structural Phase III, is located on top of structure 9 and is identified as a potter's kiln. The section below shows a lot of burning activity leading to the assumption that even in Structural Phase II the structure was occupied by a potter's family and hence had a strong financial base.

Structural complex 3 consists of four structures, 11, 13, 14 and 15. Of these, Structure 11 is an enclosure wall with two large storage pits lined with lime and grass. One pit is at the entrance in the northern corner and the other at the south-west corner. The other structures are located within the enclosure wall. Structure 13, squarish on plan is located on the eastern half of Structure 11 with an entrance at the south-east corner. A roughly circular pit with large amounts of ash is located in the centre and the area around is heavily burnt. Scholars have identified it as the common hearth of the dwelling units within Structure 11. The function of Structure 14, rectangular, and situated on the western side is difficult to surmise in the absence of any domestic activity. Structure 15, roughly circular on plan, located to the west of Structure 14, has a thick debris deposit of burnt clay lumps suggesting that the structure was destroyed by fire. All the four structures of this complex located on the periphery of the settlement are unimpressive, lacking large stone foundations and seem to be occupied by poorer sections of the society.

This complex shows evidence of a frugal lifestyle with small rooms, including a pit-dwelling, indicating the lower economic status of the people occupying it. These could be the residences of small farmers or the people who worked and lived in the village in various humble capacities, as is the case with the present settlement of Balathal. A small group of farmers lived off the main settlement during agricultural seasons as is evident from the farmstead sites located around the main site of Balathal, and possibly occupied these scanty dwellings within the settlement in the off seasons.

To understand the relative position of this complex in relation to the others, an ethnographic study of the present village was carried out and the house of Mr. Shambhu Singh was considered for analogy. Located on the outer fringes of the village this complex consists of a long passage-*cum*-open courtyard which is the centre of domestic activities- cooking, sleeping and keeping cattle and storage of firewood. In the extreme northern corner is a small room with a single tiny entrance, which is the only source of light in the room and is used for storage of food grains in small *kotharies* or storage bins. On the whole, the structure with its wattle and daub walls, its unimpressive location suggests the poor economic standard similar to Complex 3.

Structural Phase III, is constructed mostly on top of the walls of Phase II with only a few additional structures which mostly show lack of planning. The earlier structures were replaced by rectangular or squarish single-roomed, and in few cases double-roomed build-up represented by Structures 8, 16, 24 and 25. The absence of large well built structures in this phase suggests a decline in the prosperity of the inhabitants.

Structure 8 has three rooms divided by mud-brick walls and represents a potter's workshop. The middle room is the largest of all with evidence of long duration burning and patches of dark ash on the floor and a pottery kiln. Mud-brick walls on three sides and a stone wall on the northern side enclose the pottery kiln. The deposit inside the kiln is composed of heavily burnt earth, dark ash, charcoal and and *in situ* pots and potsherds placed inside for firing. The kiln seems to be periodically repaired suggesting a long duration of occupation. The kiln consisted of seven clay containers probably for various kinds of ceramics and several elongated and interconnected channels for releasing gases. A huge stone quern is located near the kiln, probably used for pounding and kneading clay for the pots or the various slips applied on the pots for decorative purposes. Above this, a second kiln belonging to Phase IV. Observations suggest the possibility that even in Phase II this may have been a potter's residence. Finally, Structure 8 also shows clear evidence of domestic activities like storage and cooking suggesting that it was both the residence and workshop of a potter, an important artisan of the settlement.

Structure 16 consists of three rooms A, B, and C beuit over structures; 10F and G, sometimes even using the walls of the earlier structures. Though the plan and use of the rooms might have changed, the residents seem to be aware of the earlier structure suggesting that the same family continued to occupy the complex though with restricted boundaries, possibly due to declining economic conditions. Structure 16A was probably a storage room with platforms for resting storage bins and saddle quern for pounding and grinding grains. Room 16B, rectangular on plan was for dwelling purposes as no domestic activity has been noted here. The main activity-area seems to be outside with two large fireplaces, platforms for supporting storage bins, and dark burnt patches showing long duration of occupation and activity. Room 16C on the north-eastern side has not been excavated as yet hence we lack information on it.

Structures 24 and 25 are both two-roomed built over the earlier Complex 10 of Phase II. These structures indicate at least two phases of occupation with repairing of walls and floor levels; in addition, the rooms were larger in the earlier period of Phase III suggesting a decline in the lifestyle of the inhabitants of Balathal. There is evidence of cooking and storage in the rooms with potsherds spread over the area which are inferior in quality to their Phase II counter parts.

Hence Phase III on the whole shows a declining phase at the site with small structures being built over the earlier phase, using its walls opportunistically and building haphazardly without any planning. A number of repairs and support-walls were added to the existing walls of the earlier phase so that it was fit for dwelling. There is also a significant decline in the ceramics with increase of tempering materials and coarser pottery.

Attempts were made to understand this decline in Phase III with the help of an ethnoarchaeological study of the sister settlement of the present village Balathal, located on the eastern side of the archaeological site. This settlement consists of not more than 15 houses, all following the same plan with a small courtyard in the front and a single room which is an all purpose storage and dwelling structure. The courtyard is the centre of all domestic activity as mentioned earlier. This small settlement is not as prosperous as the main settlement and depicts a frugal lifestyle mainly due to low economic prosperity very similar to the Phase III at the site.

Structural Phase IV is represented by a number of broken and dilapidated walls lying in between the earlier complexes and streets. Though the present farmers trying to level the land for cultivation had destroyed the settlement of this phase at the site, a pottery kiln was excavated over the kiln of Phase III suggesting hereditary passing on of the land and craft. The small and flimsy nature of these constructions (low mud and reed walls built over the earlier existing structural remains) is nowhere close to the earlier phases suggesting a significant economic decline. The cause for this economic frugality is not evident at the site but it could possibly be related to the change in climate and other factors that also caused the decline of the Harappans during the same time period, ending around 1800 BC.

Craft Specialization

The Chalcolithic levels yield a number of artifacts that help in understanding the technological development, craft specialization and life style of the people of Balathal as it evolved gradually or in some aspects was influenced by the Harappans. The gradual evolution of technology and prosperity is suggested by the concentration of antiquities in the Layers 14-17, which contain the four structural phases of Chalcolithic B at Balathal.

Craft specialization and division of labour are important features that developed in chalcolithic societies indicating the existence of a chiefdom. Craft specialization in archaeological artifacts is evident in the presence of workshops, tool-kits, raw materials and houses of craftsmen with large storage facilities (as they were paid with produce). Various categories of artisans have been identified within the neolithic and chalcolithic societies like potters, coppersmith, mason, etc.

Crafts in the neolithic and chalcolithic societies were the result of continuous food supplies made available due to permanent settlements and stable agriculture. Surety of continuous food resources enabled the people to channelize their leisure to various specialized crafts leading to division of labour. These craftsmen occupied important economic and social standings sometimes even participating in the administration. These specialized artisans provided the people with various objects ot their requirement in return for payments in kind such as grains or finished good. Specialized craft products led to trade and exchange relations with nearby areas. A number of production workshops for crafts such as ceramics, beads and copper tools have been identified at the site of Balathal.

Ceramies

Pottery manufacture is the most common and important activity found at the site with as many as seven types of wheel-made ceramics divided into fine and coarse wares having been identified at Balathal.

The fine variety made of fine well levigated clay, has a thin and highly burnished slip on one or both surfaces and is baked at a very high temperature, giving it a sturdy reddish core with a metallic sound. This variety constitutes the de luxe pottery at the site. There are three types of fine wares, thin Red Ware, Black and Red Ware and Tan Ware. The vessel-forms comprising dishes and bowls, with or without stands and in varying sizes, were primarily used for eating and drinking. The presence of such high quality pottery suggests the presence of an elite section within the society.

Dr. Gogte's belief that Tan Ware was imported to the site has been contradicted by the recent evidences from the pottery kiln excavated in Structure 8 of Phase III and the succeeding Phase IV which seem to be especially designed for firing Tan Ware. It is, however, possible that the clay used for making this ware could have been obtained from outside. The pottery kiln seems to have continued from the earlier Phase II as patches of burnt earth continue below the excavated levels. This continuous use of one area through many generations, provides significant evidence to prove that the inhabitants not only believed in hereditary occupation of craft but also occupied the same structures for residential or workshop purposes with minute changes in the structural plan by repairing and reusing the earlier structural configuration. This idea is also justified by evidence from other structures where the inhabitants have used earlier walls and floor level, though with changes as has been discussed earlier.

Coarse Wares are made with unrefined clay with a lot of tempering material, and are poorly fired having a gray or black core. The pottery is decorated with applique and incised designs. There are four varieties of ceramics in the coarse pottery, Thick bright alipped Red Ware, Plain Red Ware, Burnished Grey Ware and Plain Grey Ware. The vessel forms include large globular pots of various sizes, and they were generally used for storage and cooking. This pottery type was used by all' sections of the society due to its utilitarian nature.

Other Terracotta objects

Excavations of chalcolithic sites often yield a number of terracotta objects, not only in form of ceramics but also toys, religious figurines, beads, etc. A number of hand-made, stylized terracotta bull figurines were excavated from the chalcolithic levels at Balathal. Similar figurines were found at Gilund and Ahar, but the largest number have come from the site of Marmi where they have been attributed to a bull-worshipping religious cult. It appears that these figurines were manufactured locally at various sites and then offered at the bull shrine in Marmi. Beside bull figurines toys like dog and perforated disks along with terracotta beads were also found. These were probably manufactured at the site itself, though conclusive evidence is lacking.

Copper technology

Copper was easily available to the people of Mewar since enough chalcopyrite deposits in the Aravalli hills west of the site were available. Though we do not have any direct evidence for locals melting and manufacturing of copper tools at the site itself, a large furnace like circular hearth found in Structure 10A could have been a small coppersmithy. Copper objects at the site include knives, razors, chisels, barbed and tanged arrowheads, axheads, and needles. These tools were made by beating copper sheets into desired shapes. The sheets could have been obtained through trade from nearby sites such as Ahar where clear evidence of copper smelting and working is present. A few copper earstuds and pendants have also been found, though they are not very common and hence could have been used by the few economically and socially influential families.

Lithic technology and objects

Equipment similar to the Mesolithic assemblages of the region have been recovered at Balathal, including blades, scrapers, points and microliths made of chert and chalcedony. In some cases a number of flaked cores of chert and chalcedony have also been found indicating that some of the tools were made at the site locally, though many may have been imported from sites such as Gilund which is known for its lithic industry.

Quartzite and granite objects like stone mullers, saddle querns, pounders, sharpeners, etc., for domestic purposes such as and grinding pounding grains, have been found in large numbers. A few locally made weapons of offens like sling balls, and birdshots have also been found. Ornaments in the form of beads and pendants of semi-precious stones have also been reported. The most common finds are the steatite paste beads manufactured locally at the site. Beads of carnelian, agate, jasper, faience and terracotta have also been found. Shell objects such as bangles and pendants seem to have been imported either as a result of exchange activities with the Mesolithic communities or from the Harappan shell-working centres.

The kind of craft specialization seen at Balathal needs not only surplus, but also a demand indicating a stratified society where people have the economic capacity and the will to pay for these commodities many of which were imported. Many of these prestigious items like fine ceramics, copper beads, carnelian and jasper beads were de lux objects catering to the higher members of the society. These objects clearly indicate social stratification amongst the people.

Social Stratification

Burials and grave goods provide important evidence to determine social stratification at any archaeological site, as the social status of the dead individual determines the treatment of his/her remains. In the absence of burials, as is the case at Balathal, other factors like structural remains, storage facilities and the materials found within them are used to identify social and economic differentiation. In chiefdoms, the social ranking of the individual is based on his relation to the chief himself. The closer the kin or blood-relation the higher will be the individual's social and polilical status. These societies are also guided by a strong sense of duty to the chief who provides for their defense, protects their cattle and redistributes the stored wealth.

The most important evidence pointing towards a stratified society at Balathal is the hierarchical settlement pattern, dominated by the fortified enclosure at the centre identified as the residence of the chief surrounded by smaller structures belonging to various craftsmen. Since the living complexes of the commoners consist of single or doubleroomed structures, the size and location of the fortified enclosure suggests that it belongs to an important individual who in this case might be the chief. On the southern part of the mound and the fortified structure are a large number of residential and workshop complexes with large storage facilities. These are identified as the houses of craftsmen, like potters, coppersmiths and lapiders who held an important position as they catered to various needs of the society. On the periphery is Complex 3 (discussed earlier) showing evidence ot a frugal lifestyle with smaller rooms and even round structures pointing towards temporary occupation. These could be the homes of small farmers or other members of the lower strata, of the society. Hence there is clear evidence of social stratification at Balathal which was probably hereditary as is suggested by the continuous occupation of space by the same families through multiple generations.

Macro-Settlement pattern

Most chiefdom societies are characterized by a kind of settlement hierarchy that is either two or multitiered with the centre exercising power and control over the smaller satellite villages settled for exploitation of raw material or arable land. In some cases, population increase at the main settlement also might lead to the formation of these smaller settlements by the order of the chief himself. As far as position of Balathal is concerned, it seems to be a specialized centre for pottery and bead production of the Ahar culture that was flourishing in the Mewar region of Rajasthan. The size of the settlement, its strategic location with a cultural occupation of more than a thousand years and the rich material evidences in the form of the fortified and residential structures, varied craft objects and their workshops corroborate this belief. The smaller satellite settlements of Balathal need to be carefully studied, as many smaller mounds with potsherds scattered on their surfaces have been located within a radius of one kilometre from the main site.

All these features point towards a well established and flourishing chiefdom society which was patriarchal and hereditary in nature and was the result of a gradual evolutionary process beginning in the Mesolithic. The increasing economic prosperity led to socio-economic differentiation giving rise to concentrated political power in the hands of the chief who was responsible for maintaining order in the community, and carrying on public utility works for the benefit of the people.

Conclusion

The evolution of the village of Balathal reflects a gradual process of transformation of the semi-nomadic Mesolithic hunter-gatherers to a completely sedentary chiefdom society around 2600 BC. Here at the beginning of Phase B we see an increase in the site's prosperity, with the flimsy wattle and daub circular huts of Phase A being replaced by rectangular stone structures with one or two rooms. During the more prosperous Phase B, structural Phase II, these evolved into huge structural complexes owned by families with specialized trades such as pottery and lapidary. Here we also see the construction of large public architecture such as the inner and outer fortification. These features suggest the presence of a central authority possibly a chief capable of managing the finance and labour required. Furthermore, the presence of specialized and de luxe craft industries and personal goods suggests the presence of a ranked society. While no direct evidence of the chief has been found at Balathal unlike Inamgaon, all the indirect evidence listed above suggests the evolution of a chietdom society at the site during Phase B.

Cord-Marked Pottery Making Tradition in Manipur

O.K. Singh*

The State of Manipur is at the extreme north-eastern corner of India and lies between 23°83' and 25°68' N. Latitudes and 93°03' and 94°78' E. Longitudes (Fig.1). It is bounded on the north by Nagaland, on the north-east and south by Myanmar, on the north-west and west by Assam and on the south-west by Mizoram. Physically Manipur can be divided into two natural divisions: (a) the flat alluvial plain "valley), covering an area of about 1,820 sq. km and (b) the hill ranges which surround the plains covering about 90 percent of the total area of 22,356 sq. km. The surrounding hills are the homeland of various tribes of Mongoloid race. These tribes have practiced shifting cultivation and till recently some of them also had practiced erection of megalithic monuments. These megalithic remains are found within the village area of the Mao Naga as well as Tangkhul Naga tribes. As such Manipur provides an exceptionally good field for ethnoarchaeological study. However, here an attempt has been made to study the cord-marked pottery mostly in its technological aspect.

Archaeological Evidence

The archaeological evidences for the cord-marked pottery in Manipur come from both the prehistoric and protohistoric sites (Fig.1). At Nongpok Keithelmanbi locality-1, Senapati district, it is found without any attendant vestiges except for a few charcoal pieces in a stratified deposit after a short break above the Hoabinhian stone artifacts. A ^{14}C date of these charcoal pieces suggests that corded ware at this site is 4460 ± 120 years old. The pottery is illfired and handmade. The cord-marks are found on the outer surface in linear and criss-cross patterns. Light red and reddish brown are the dominant colours. In thickness the sherds range from 2 mm to 8 mm, the more common being 4 mm to 5 mm. No complete pot has been recovered from the site; however, from the rim fragments the shapes appear to include shallow bowl with flat curved base and globular pot with constricted neck (Fig. 2:1-8).

The corded ware from Napachik, Bishnupur district and Laimanai, Thoubal district is characterised by the hand-made tripod wares. At these two sites the cord-marked pottery is found in association with neolithic stone artifacts. A TL-date of a cord-marked sherd from Napachik site gives the age of 1450 BC for the tripod ware Neolithic Culture in Manipur[2]. The cordmarks are present in linear and criss-cross patterns. At Laimanai site linear pattern impressions are also found on the tripod legs (Fig.2:14). Reddish brown is the dominant colour of the pottery, though there are a few grey, dark grey and whitish colours at the Napachik site. The thickness of the pottery wall is not uniform; it ranges from 2 mm to 7 mm. The tripod legs are solid, and made separately to be luted at the base of the vessel. These are of various forms long

*Anthropology Department, D.M. College of Science, Imphal.

conical, short with tapered, slanting and hollow base, and flattish etc.

At Phunan site the cord-marked pottery is found less in numbers than other forms of pottery decorated with incised marks, applique and circular impressions. The cord-marks are present in linear and criss-cross patterns (Fig 2:12). The pots are all hand-made and ill-fired. The number of cord-marked pottery from the protohistoric Sekta burial is very few.

Ethnographic Evidence

Cord-marked pottery making is a living tradition among the Oinam, a Mao Naga tribe in the Senapati district of Manipur. Till recently, they erected megalithic monuments to commemorate the individuals for their performance of social feasts of merit[3]. They are agriculturists and practice, shift subsistence cultivation and is supplemented by hunting and fishing. Besides, women weave cloth in loin tension loom of the thread extracted from the bark of wild plants. Pot-making is also the exclusive work of the women-folk. However, men-in-help firing and selling of pots. They also use beautifully carved wooden ring-footed dish and bowl (Fig.3:6&7).

Implements used in making pots by the Oinam potters.

1. **Vu:** It is a solid cylindrical wooden rod of about 50 cm in length and 5 to 8 cm in diameter. It is used in moulding, as first step of making a roughout.

2. **Titu:** It is a plain beater, made of wood. It is used in the initial shaping of the pot.

3. **Kha:** It is a cord-warped beater, used in the final shaping of the body and decoration

4. **Jane:** It is a plain piece of bamboo sliver, tapers at both the ends, with lenticular cross-section, about 30 cm in length and 1.5 cm in breadth. It is used in smoothening the surface of the pot.

5. **Tuta:** It is a stone anvil, spherical in shape, used as support, from inside, against the force of the beater in the process of shaping the pot.

6. **Ngearangde:** It is a shallow, wide opened basket, used as strainer to eliminate coarse powdered materials from the clay.

7. **Neabung:** It is a small dugout, rectangular wooden mortar, used in pounding the clay and tempering materials, as also in kneading the clay.

8. **Mee:** It is a solid cylindrical wooden pestle, about 3 metres long and 8-10 cm in diameter, used in pounding the clay and tempering materials.

9. **Platform:** It is a thick wooden plank of about 2 metre long. It is used as seat of the potter, and platform for making the pot.

Preparation of the paste

The Oinam potters quarried three kinds of paste materials from different localities within their village. They are black clay *(dongea)*, grey hill wash loam *(ngeasung)* and reddish yellow coloured detrital soil *(ngeahai)*. The clay, loam and detrital soil are dried and are again mixed in the proportion of approximately 2:2:1 respectively for pounding in a wooden mortar *(ngeabung)*; pounding is done by two to four women potters (Fig.3) in a group in a single mortar with pestles *(mee)*. When these are pounded thoroughly into powder, the mixture is strained through a basket strainer *(ngearangde)* to get rid of coarse material. Again the mixture is transferred to the mortar and wetted by pouring water; and when thoroughly wet it was kneaded by hand and pounded again with pestles in groups. After this, the paste is made into small balls of varying sizes which are kept in the Ngearangde. The suitability of the paste to make pot is tested by beating with a beater *(titu)*.

Technique of making the pot

The roughout of the pot is made by moulding on a cylindrical solid rod or on the knee of the potter. In the case of a small plain bowl with ring-foot *(ngeakoune)*, the ball paste is beaten first with *titu* into a flat surface and then again made concave by striking on the knee of the potter. After that, the wall is further pressed with the fingers to widen the opening while the palm of the other hand supports on the outside. The outer surface is again beaten with the plain beater by supporting it with the fingers of the other hand from inside, to form a roughly semispherical body. The upper edge is also made smooth by beating frequently with the plain beater and rubbing with fingers.

For other types of pots a suitable ball of the paste is taken and made into a cube by striking on the wooden platform where the potter sits. The cube is moulded on the *vu* by striking on the wooden platform several times until a desired length is obtained. The moulded paste is loosened by striking the *vu* vertically at both the ends on the platform. To make a wider hollow end in a, slightly conical shape, one end of such moulded paste is beaten with the vu on the platform by rotating after each beat along its axis. Then the *vu* is removed. To shape the shoulder and neck parts of the pot, the wider hollow end has been pressed out from inside with fingers while the palm of the other hand supports from outside. Then it is beaten lightly with the plain beater *(titu).* After this the upper end is again pressed out with the fingers to make rim while the pot is rotated by supporting with the two knees of the potter. The next step is the enlargement of the moulded paste at the middle by pressing out with fingers from inside to form the body part Then the shoulder and neck parts are smoothened by scraping with *jane* on both the surfaces. The externally beveled lip of the rim is also smoothened and levelled with *jane* but finished by rubbing with thumb and index finger.

The wall of the pot is enlarged and thinned by beating with the plain beater while a small circular flattish pebble *(tuta)* supports from inside. When the body part is enlarged by beating, additional paste is added whenever they find excessive thinness. The base of the pot is also made in the same process. After obtaining the desired shape and size, the pot is finished by beating with cord-warped wooden beater *(kha)* on the outer surface of the body and base. In the case of a small rice beer jar *(daone)* a low ringfoot is fixed at the base and a small ring in relief is also fixed as applique on the shoulder The ringfoot is generally made by fixing a roll of paste as a ring at the base and then pressing between the fingers and thumb to have a slightly tapering rounded edge all around. The whole process, right from the preparation of paste, takes about one hour. Then the finished pots are dried for a few hours in the sun and kept on the suspended platform over the family fireplace until it is completely dried and ready for baking.

Firing

Firing is done in the open, generally in the courtyard of the potter, in which both man and woman are involved. For this a round bed of straw and small branches of tree are piled over a layer of pottery which is again covered by another bed of similar materials to keep another layer of pottery and covered again with the straw and twigs. Three to four successive layers of pottery alternated by a bed of straw and twigs is made up to a height of about four feet which is finally covered with straw all over the surfaces like a small mound. Then it is lighted at one of the edges. It takes about two to three hours to get the pot completely fired. When the straw and twigs are completely burnt, it is examined by inserting a long pole whether the pots are baked well or not Then the pots are removed, if found all right, they are left to cool down after which they are gathered for disposal.

Type of pots and their uses

Fig 3.1: *Lakho–* It is a jar with outturned rim, beveled labial flanged lip, out-curved neck and convex wall and base; made by moulding and hand-beater technique; decorated with cord-marks in linear pattern. It is 26 cm in height, and 12.4 cm and 20.6 cm in diameter at mouth and body respectively It is used for cooking rice.

Fig 3.3, it is 28 cm in height, and 13.2 cm and 22.7 cm in diameter at mouth and body respectively. Decoration is done with cord marks in criss cross pattern and incised in herring bone pattern at a place on the shoulder.

Fig 3.2: *Daone–* It is a rings footed rice-beer jar, made by moulding and handbeater technique. It has outturned rim with beveled labial flanged lip, outcurved neck and convex wall. It is decorated with cord marks and a ring of applique on the shoulder It measures 23.8 cm in height, the diameters at mouth and body are 10 cm and 17.7 cm respectively. It is used for drinking rice-beer.

Fig 3.4 . *Ngeakoune–* It is a ring-footed bowl, made by hand and beater method. It has a flat lip, convex wall the body is half-spherical in shape. The height and mouth opening vary from 7.5 cm to 9 cm and 13 cm to 14.5 cm respectively. It is used as receptacle of curry.

Fig. 3.5: *Dao*– It is a jår with outturned rim, beveled labial flanged lip, long narrow and outcurved neck; the wall is convex with slightly flattened body. It is made by moulding and hand-beater technique. It is decorated with cord marks in linear pattern. It is 34 cm in height, and 10.3 cm and 24.4 cm in diameter at mouth and body respectively. It is generally used in fetching water.

The Oinam tribe also uses wooden utensils that have been carved beautifully by the menfolk. They make two kinds of utensils *Methakoune* and *Thingkung.*

Fig 3.6: *Thingkung*– It is a wooden ringfooted dish with wide open mouth (22 cm in diameter) and the total height is 5.8 cm. It is used as a rice plate.

Fig 3.7: *Methakoune*– It is a small wooden bowl on ringstand with a handle The lower edge of the stand is broadly serrated and the margin is also decorated in diamond pattern. In size it measures 9 cm in height and 14 cm in diameter at mouth. It is used as receptacle of curry.

Summary and Conclusion.

Oinam tribe is still in a very primitive technological stage. They make pottery with a very crude technique of moulding and hand-beater methods However, they can carve beautiful wooden plates and bowls with their simple tools (Fig.13.6 & 7). They practice shifting cultivation as their main economy supplemented by hunting and fishing

The pottery of the Oinam has mostly elongated body-form with outbevelled labial flanged lip; they do not make pots with large globular body, may be because of their simple technique. The work of pot-making is the exclusive task of the women folk; however, man is involved in the firing and marketing. The Oinam pottery is widely distributed among the Nagas, as far as Konyak Naga of Nagaland. The menfolk carry the pots with the help of a carrying basket *(Louman)* from village to village for sale. Their pots are decorated with cord-marks. In Manipur the corded wares are found from the Neolithic, as early as 4,460 +_120 years B P from Nongpok Keithelmanbi loc 1, Senapatí district. Bigger containers for storing water are made by scooping hollow big wooden blocks. Such hollowed true trunks are also used in the preparation of rice beer for their festivals, like feast of merit to erect megaliths (memorial stones). Considering their simple technique, Oinam pottery industry is still in the Neolithic stage But typological comparison of the pottery forms with those of the archaeological remains cannot be made, as no complete pot has so far been recovered from any prehistoric sites.

The cord-marked pottery from the archaeological sites of Manipur cannot be compared with those of the modern, except in certain process of making technology. The presence of the cord marks on the outer surface of the pottery is the clear evidence of using cord wrapped paddles in the final shaping of the pottery among both the prehistoric and modern potters. But it is not clearly understood whether the roughout of the prehistoric pottery is also made by moulding on a rod as done by the Oinam potters. The shape of the pottery, particularly the rim and lip parts of the prehistoric pottery have no similarity with those of the Oinam modem pottery. Thus it is very difficult to say whether the modern Oinam potters belong to the same ethnic group of people with those of the prehistoric cord-marked potters and continued the same pottery technology, or both have different origins; and the cord marking of the pottery is the only chance similarity. But it is clear that the village of the Oinam potters is in isolation for quite long time, which helps in the continuation of their simple technology till the present day. As stated elsewhere they still practice shift cultivation and weave cloth from the fibers extracted from the wild plants in tension loin looms. The whorl that is used in spinning thread is also made of stone. Considering the isolation and their simple technology there is reason to suppose the probability of continuing the Neolithic cord-marked pottery technology among the Oinam potters. They use the pottery for cooking, eating, fetching water, brewing and drinking rice beer etc. The Neolithic cord-marked pottery, though these do not show comparable forms with those of the Oinam pottery, might also have been used for cooking, eating and fetching water. But there is no evidence so far in Manipur for brewing of rice beer by the prehistoric corded ware people. Another aspect which is not definite, though it was probable, is that whether the prehistoric potting was the task of women alone. Because in Manipur the modern pottery making is the task of womenfolk only, except among the Nungbi Tangkhul where man is the potter. Among the Oinam tribe there is strict prohibition of the involvement of man in the process of pottery making, except in firing and marketing. This division of task between the sexes in the potter family of the Oinam tribe might also be prevalent during the prehistoric period. More research on the various aspects of the way of life of the Oinam tribe will throw more light on the relationship of technology with social and economic conditions of the prehistoric people.

REFERENCES

O.K. Singh 1986. *Prehistoric Archaeology of Nongpok keithelmanbi,* Amusana Institute of Antiquarian Studies, Manipur, Imphal .

O.K. Singh 1983. *Archaeology in Manipur (Napachik: A Stone Age Site in the Manipur Valley),* State Archaeology, Government of Manipur, Imphal. also *Stone Age Archaeology of Manipur.* Amusana Institute of Antiquarian Studies, Manipur, Imphal.

O K Singh 1985. "A Live Megalithic Culture in Manipur" in V N Misra and P Bellwood (Eds) *Recent Advances in Indo-Pacific Prehistory* p 491-496, Oxford & IBH Publishing Co., New Delhi .

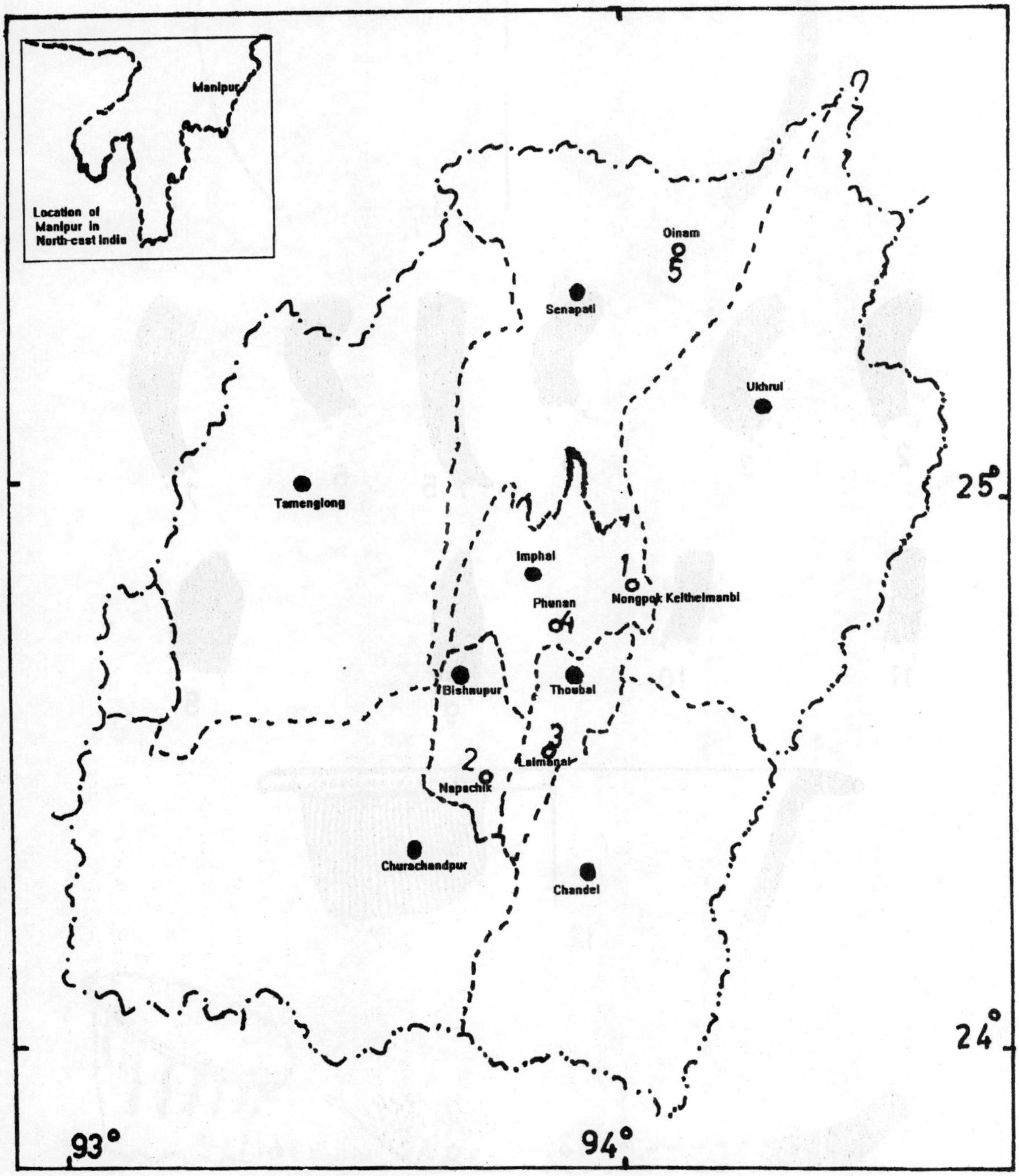

Fig. 1 Map of Manipur showing distribution of cord-marked pottery sites: 1-4, Archaeological sites; 5, Modern Potter village site.

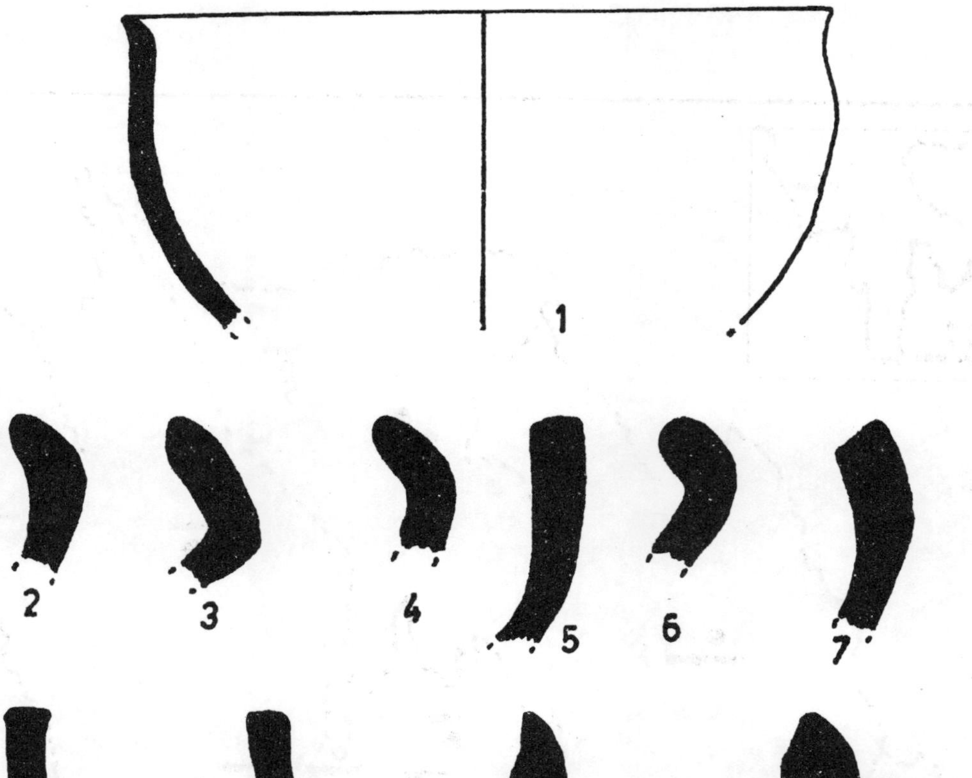

Fig. 2 Cord-marked pottery types from the archaeological sites of Manipur: 1, 10-13, bowls; 2-9, jars; 14, tripod leg.

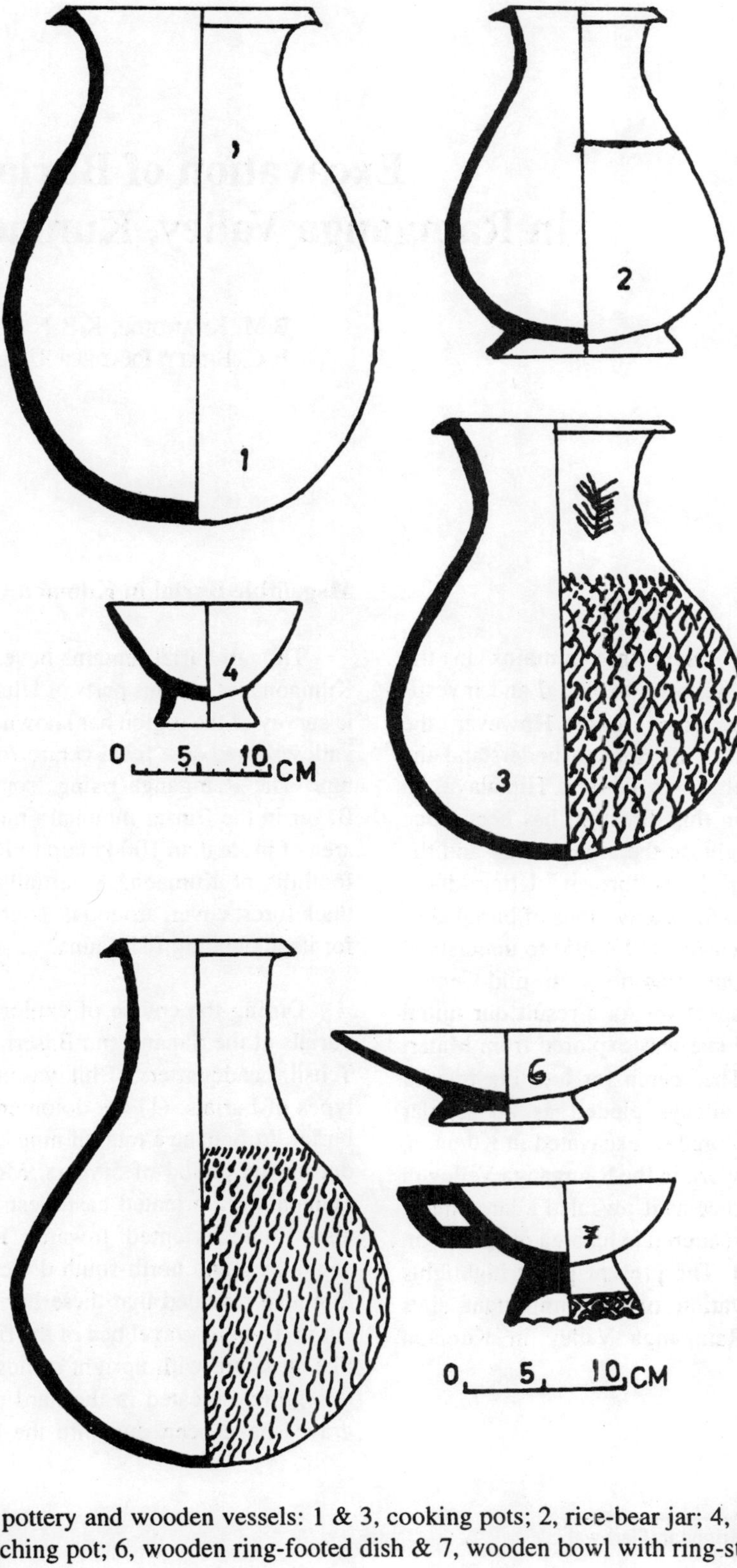

Fig. 3. Oinam pottery and wooden vessels: 1 & 3, cooking pots; 2, rice-bear jar; 4, ring-footed bowl; 5, water fetching pot; 6, wooden ring-footed dish & 7, wooden bowl with ring-stand and a lug,

Excavation of Burial Complexes in Ramganga Valley, Kumaon Himalaya

B.M. Khanduri, K.P. Nautiyal, Vinod Nautiyal,
R.C. Bhatt, Pradeep Saklani and Y.S. Farswan*

Introduction

A large number of megalithic remains in the Uttarakhand, Himalaya have been explored and investigated by various workers since long[1]. However, the description available is not sufficient to understand the archaeology of burial culture in Central Himalaya. In recent years some work in this direction has been done systematically to throw light on the archaeology and the chronology of the 'burial' culture in Uttarakhand ,Himalaya[2]. As a follow up the excavations of burial sites were conducted for five seasons (1992-95) to understand archaeology of the 'burial' traditions in mid-Central Himalaya in a larger perspective. As a result our initial field survey, a cave-burial site was explored from Malari in Garhwal ,Himalaya[3]. The search for locating regular human burial sites had always eluded as no regular human burial site was explored or excavated in Kumaon, Himalaya. Therefore, the work in the Ramganga Valley in Kumaon assumes importance as it revealed a large number of human burial sites scattered in an area of 32 sq. km from Ganai to Bhikyasen. The present paper highlights the results of the excavation of two important sites Sanana and Baseri–in Ramganga Valley in Kumaon Himalaya (Fig.-1).

Megalithic Burial in Kumaon

Though burial remains have been found scattered in Kumaon and various parts of Uttarakhand yet a systematic survey of the region has shown that the Ramganga river valley served as a focal centre for the spread of this culture. The Ramganga rising from the forests of Kodiya Bagar in the Binsar mountain ranges covers a catchment area of more than 100 km up to Ramanagar, a town at the foothills of Kumaon. A partially snow-fed river with a thick forest cover, around its source region, is still famous for its abounding fish fauna.

During the course of exploration a large number of burials at the Sanana and Baseri, 10 km north of a small Tehsil headquarters, Bhikiyasen brought to light two types of burials: (1) the dolomenoid-cist and (2) the urn burial. At Sanana a total of nine cist burials were exposed during the period of 5 years. Most of the cist burials at Sanana were oriented east-west but some of them were also found oriented towards north-north-east,–south-south-west and north-south direction (Pl.1). The excavation also revealed that these burials wẹre after a pit was cut in the hard gravel bed of the river. The rectengulr box-like structure with upright orthostats, were fixed with in this groove created in the hard constructed bed. All the graves have been dug into the alluvial terrace up to a

*HN Bahuguna University, ·Srinagar, Garhwal

depth of 1.0 m to 1.50 m below the surface. The exposed section shows only loose deposit of gravel, sand and matrix and no habitational material was encountered. The burials were away from habitation and after exposure elsewhere bones were collected and buried. The Megalithic people used various types of stones–shale, schist and quartizite–for the construction of their burials. A notable aspect revealed was that almost every cist-chamber was bounded all around by boulders arranged in rectangular or semi-oval shape. In general the urn burials were laid outside the periphery of this boulder circle or boundary (Pl.2)

The site of Baseri is located on the lowermost Terrace of the river Ramganga which is about one km south of the site of Sanana. At Baseri, six cist burials were excavated which are designated as BSR-1 to BSR-6. Regarding the layout of these burials: here the river Terrace being a steep gradient of 30m height makes almost all the cists virtually hang on the river section suggesting that the burials might have been invariably laid on the bank of the river. The study of the exposed deposit of the burial at the site of excavation indicates that the river has eroded the eastern terrace continuously for centuries.

Architectural features

At both the sites the chambers consist of three or six shale orthostats placed vertically according to the need and size of the body or the funerary objects. They measured variously from 1.28x0.40m, to 2.32x0.50m. These box-like rectangular chambers were covered with a required number of capstones. Particularly, for instance in the case of a cist burial, at least seven capstone slabs were used as a covering. On the bottom of the chamber there were shale stone slabs on which the remains of the dead body and the funerary materials were placed. Another interesting point recorded in the excavation is the discovery of twin-cist burials. These burials are at Baseri, BSR-1, BSR-3 and BSR-6. In such cases small cist measuring 30x22cm to 53x32cm were found adjacent to the main burial. These small burials also yielded few pottery sherds.

At Baseri BSR-3 a 11.3cm long femur and a tooth were found in a dish placed over the flat shale stone slab (Pl.3). Similarly in SNA-3 (Cist-1), human teeth along with a bead of banded and small pots agate were are discovered. The nature of the human remains undoubtedly suggests that before internment of the mortal remains were first exposed for excarnation and the remainder was then given the ritual of a burial.

Urn Burials

Urn burials have been excavated both from Sanana and Baseri. The urn burials were discovered from BSR-2, BSR-5 and BSR-9. The Megalithic people had also constructed stone walls for the protection of the urn burials. The contained a large size hand made jars ranging in size from 48cm to 56cm diameter. The jars were found to have borne mat impressions or ripple marks. Another type of pot burials were of a sturdy or coarse red ware and black ware. The urn burials were also found near the cist burials as recorded from BSR-1, BSR-5, BSR-7 and SNA-3; but in most of the cases such burials were outside the periphery of the bounding wall of the cist burials.

Human Skeletons

A large number of disarticulated skeletal remains were found from most of the cist burials excavated from Baseri in Ramganga valley. Most of these were found in highly degenerate state, because of the high acidic nature of the soil. As it was difficult to carry out a detailed analysis of each and individual skeletal and tooth remains, some preliminary observations were made on the human remains to know the general characteristic features about the age and state of health of the individual buried at Ramganga Valley. Most of the burials contained tiny fragments of human bones and teeth but the discovery of disarticulated bones of two skulls, femur, tibia-fibula, parts of upper jaw (maxilla) and lower jaw (mandible) and a few stray jaw, skulls, etc. buried systematically inside the chamber were worth noting from Baseri BSR-5 (Pl.4). Interestingly, both the skulls were found place together side-by-side suggesting the practice of multiple burials. A detailed examination of the skeltal remains brought to light some interesting facts. The skull-1 is a part of posterio-lateral side in which parieto-temporal suture is present and temporal bone is missing. The sutures of the skull indicate that it belongs to a person of more than 60 years of age indicative while the other skull-II belongs to a person less than 40 years of age as the coronal suture is not fused and the upper jaw shows all the 32 teeth intact with firmly grounded molars. A pre-molar in this jaw is missing. The first and second molar shows cavity indicative of either some disease or the effect of heavy flesh or hard chewing. The three molars on right side also cavities on the buccal side indicating heavy flesh chewing. The femur shows ridge like structure *(linea aspara)* which again confirms that it belongs to a human being. The lower part of left fibula, a fibula portion close to ankle, is also variable.

Similarly, again two skulls and teeth were also discovered from SNA-3, cist-7 during 1994-95 excavation. Due to an acidic soil most of teh bone remains are found highly disintegrated[5].

The grave goods consist of pots and a few beads either of agate or carnelian. The presence of iron is represented only by two fragmentary iron pins and a nail along with a broken piece of a sickle. This was a lone evidence from one of the burials at Baseri (BSR-3) and rest of the excavated ones both at Sanana and Baseri did not furnish any evidence of iron at all.

Pottery

A large variety of pottery is another characteristic feature of these burials as at least some eighty pots of various sizes, shapes and fabrics were discovered from the burials. The pottery belongs to a catagory of red, grey and black ware. The main assemblage consist of dishes, miniature bowls, vases, globular goblets, bowls with pedestal base and bowl with flat base. It was noticed in the excavation that they were placed towards the western side of the burial. The fabric ranges from the coarse red to a fine wheel-made red and grey ware. Significantly the Urn-burials of red ware have ripple marks on the outer surface. The typical Black-and-Red ware generally associated with mainstream megalithic culture is totally absent from these two sites. Instead, it shows strong affinity with the Painted Grey Ware of the Ganga-Yamuna *doab* region (Fig.-2).

The shapes in dishes and bowls mostly are akin to those of the Painted Grey Ware, comparable with the shapes found earlier at Hastinapur, Ahichchhatra, Thapli, Kakher and a few other PGW sites in the Ganga-Yamuna *doab*[6]. A few common features in the form of ripple marks, variety and shapes of those at Jakhera, a PGW site in Aligarh district. Sahi reported ripple marked pottery and the PGWpaintings from period IIA of Kakhera which has been assigned to Proto-PG ware or forerunner of the PGW culture. Though geographically these two are far away from each other yet the theory propounded by Sahi designating the ware as a proto-PG ware holds good and brings us to put the Sanana-Baseri ware anterior to the matured PGW types (Fig.-3). Apart from this another type of pots which were discovered in the graves are Red ware having various shapes like bowl with pedesatal base, globulr goblet, flat-based bowl with incurved rim, concave sided bowl etc.

Chronology

Some radiocarbon and thermolminescence dates are available for such burials from Kumaon. From Ganai in the Ramganga valley a T.L. date of 2680 B.C. was provided by Agarwal. Similarly from Gagrigol, Almora district a radiocarbon date of 2666-2562 B.C. was given for such burial site[7]. On this basis Agarwal concluded that the cist-burial tradition in this area continued for more than 1500 years from 2600 B.C. onward[8].

On the basis of the above evidences, it can be concluded that the excavated grave pottery of Kumaon which very well compare with the Painted Grey Ware tradition of the Ganga-Yamuna *doab* coupled with a recently available radiocarbon and thermoluminescence dates provided by Agarwal, suggests that these burials from Kumaon can be tentatively placed in between the middle of the 3rd millennium BC and 1st millennium BC But this may have to be finally confirmed by some more supporting data in the near future through our own sample which ware now under process of examination.

Acknowledgements

The authors thankfully acknowledge the financial support received from Museum of Himalayan Archaeology and Ethnography, HNB Garhwal University and University Grants Commission under the SAP-DSA Programme for conducting the Archaeological Research. We also extend our sincere thanks to Dr. (Mrs.) Rekha Thapliyal, Sri A.K. Sharma, Late D.L. Rajput of the Department. Thanks are also due to R.S. Rawat, V.P. Chatwal, G.P. Nautiyal, K.S. Negi, J.S. Rawat, J.S. Negi and Mastan Singh of the Museum for assisting in the field. We are specially thankful to Mohan Naithani for line drawings on AutoCad.

REFERENCES

1. Dabral, S.P. 1968, *Uttarakhand Ka Itihas*, part II, pp. 223-35; Henwood, W.J. 1856, Notice of the Rock Basins at Devidhoora near Almora in Upper India, *New Philosophical Journal*, New Series 4 : 204-206; Joshi, M.P. 1985-86, "Dots, Cup-marks and pits vis-a-vis the Megalithic New Evidences from Kumaon", Puratattva No. 16: 26-28; and Wheeler, R.E.M. 1951, Early India and Pakistan, London, pp. 150-160;

2. Agarwal, D.P., Bhatt, Diva, Malaya, Sudha and Kharkwal, Jeevan 1991, "Archaeology of Kumaon: Problems and Prospects", *Man and Environment,* Vol. XVI, No.1, pp. 59-63; Agarwal, D.P., Kharkwal, Jeevan, Kusumgar, Sheela and Yadav M.G. (1995), "Cist Burials of the Kumaon Himalayas", *Antiquity*, Vol. 69, No. 264, pp. 550-54; Rivett–Carnac (1977), "Rough Notes on some Ancient Sculptures on Rock in Kumaon Similar to those found in Monoliths and rock in Europe", *Journal of Asiatic Society of Bengal*, XLVI(1), 1-15; Mathpal, Y. 1986, Uttarakhand Ke Intijar Mein Ramganga Ghati, *Pahar,* Vol. 2, 20-22; and Sharma, A.K. 1990-91, Excavation at Ladyura, Almora, U.P. *Puratattva* 21: 77-79

3. Bhatt, R.C. & Nautiyal, K.P., 1987-88. "Trans Himalayan Burials vis-a-vis Malari: An Assessment". *JOSHARD,* Vol. 11 & 12, pp. 95-101; and Nautiyal, K.P. and Khanduri, B.M. 1991, *Emergence of Early Culture in Garhwal, Central Himalaya,* University Museum of Himalayan Archaeology and ethnography, HNB Garhwal University, Srinagar, Garhwal;

4. Farswan, Y.S. and Nautiyal, Vinod 1997, "Investigation of Phosphorus Enrichment In The Burial Soil of Kumaon, Mid-Central Himalaya, India", *Journal of Archaeological Science,* 4, 251-258.

5. Ibid.

6. Ghosh, A. and Panigrahi, K.C. (1946), "The Pottery of Ahichchhatra, District Bareilly, U.P.", *Ancient India,* No. 1, pp. 36-59; Lal, B.B. 1954-55, "Excavations of Hastinapur and other Explorations in the Uppar ganga and Sutlej Basins, 1950-52: New Light on the Dark Age between the end of the Harappan Culture and the Early Historical Period" *Ancient India* No. 10-11; Nautiyal and Khanduri 1991; and Sahi, M.D.N. (1994), *Aspects of Indian Archaeology* op cit.

7. Agarwal, 1995 op cit.

8. Ibid.

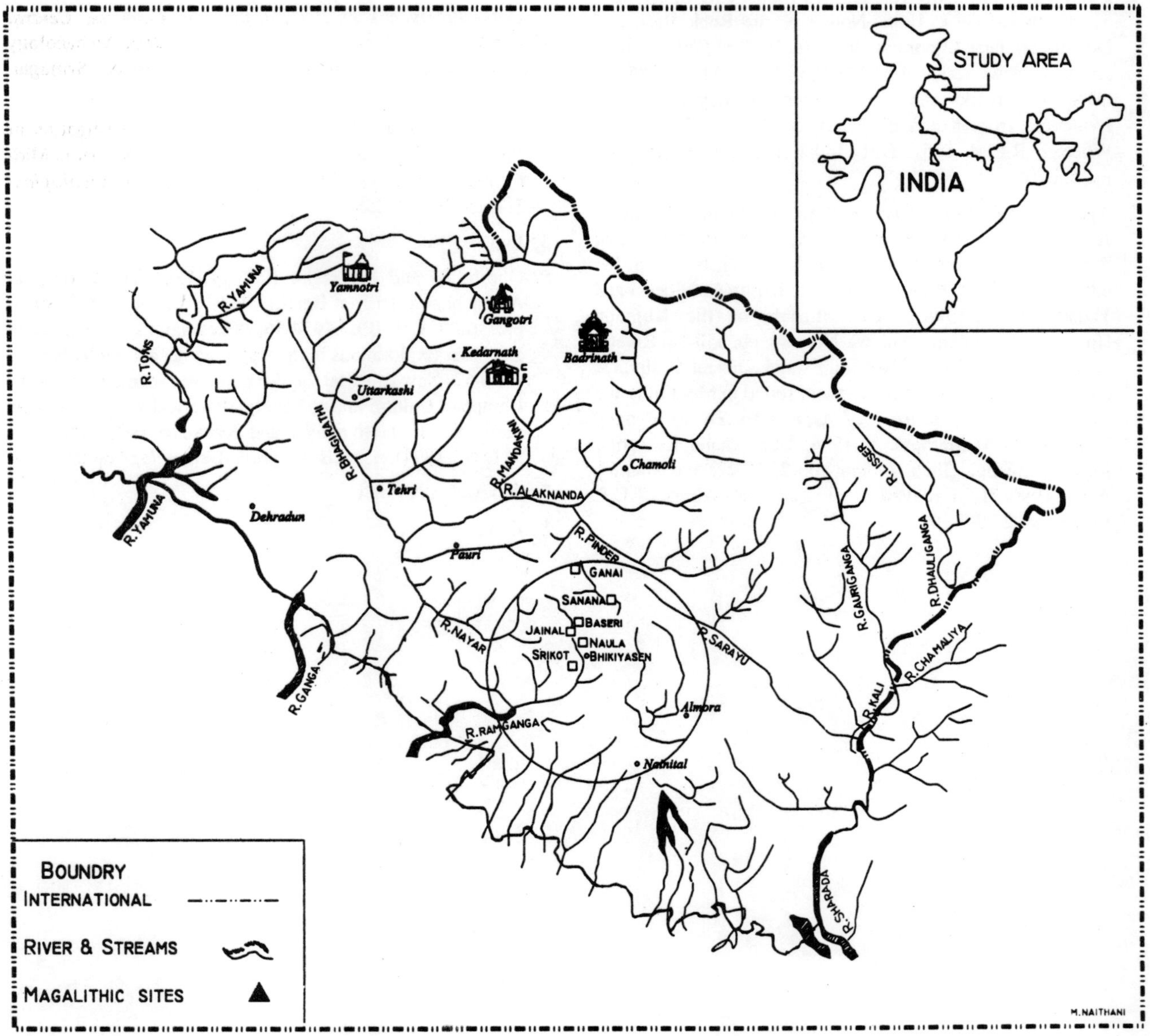

Fig. 1. Map Showing Sites of Megalithic Burials in Ramganga Valley, Kumaun Himalaya

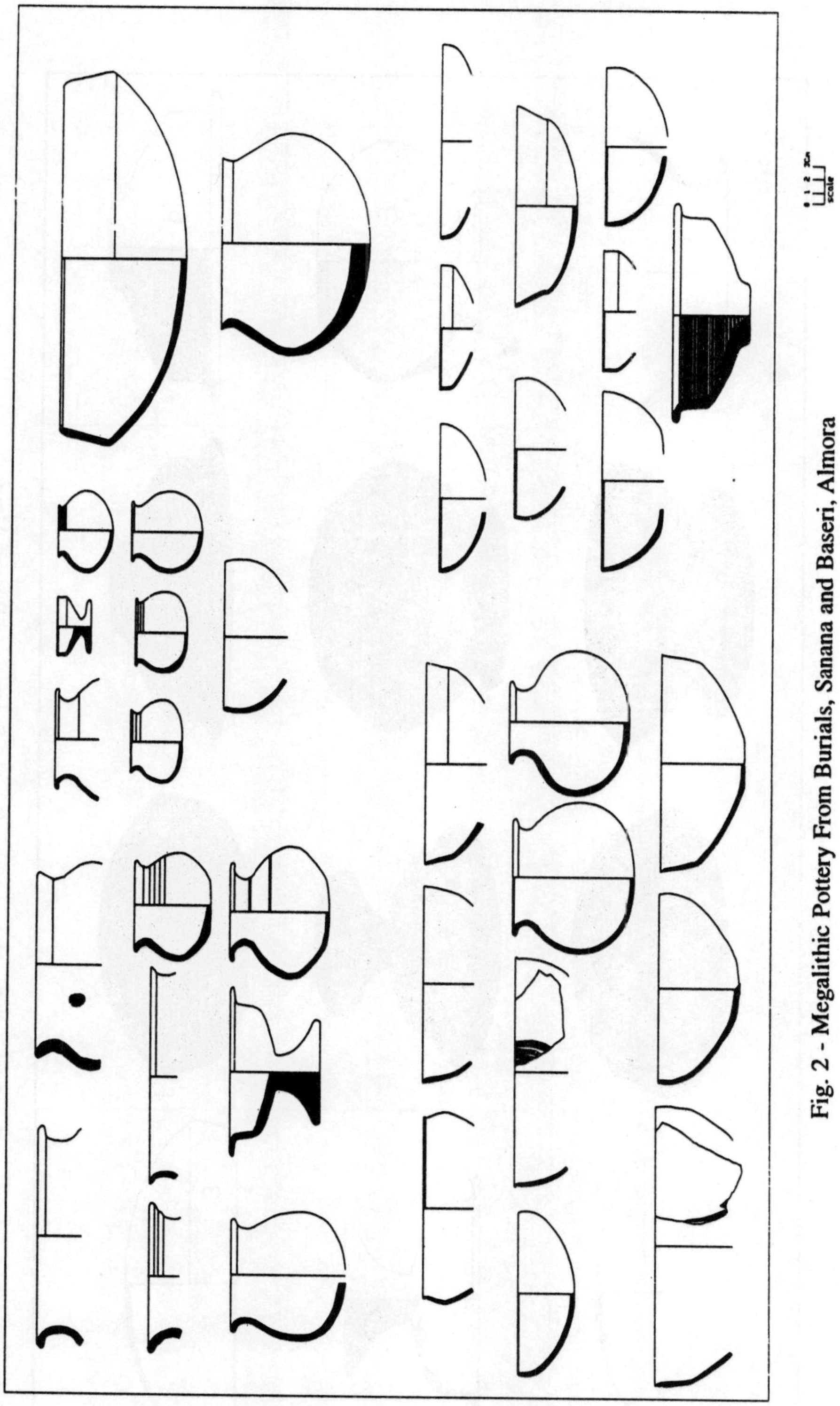

Fig. 2 - Megalithic Pottery From Burials, Sanana and Baseri, Almora

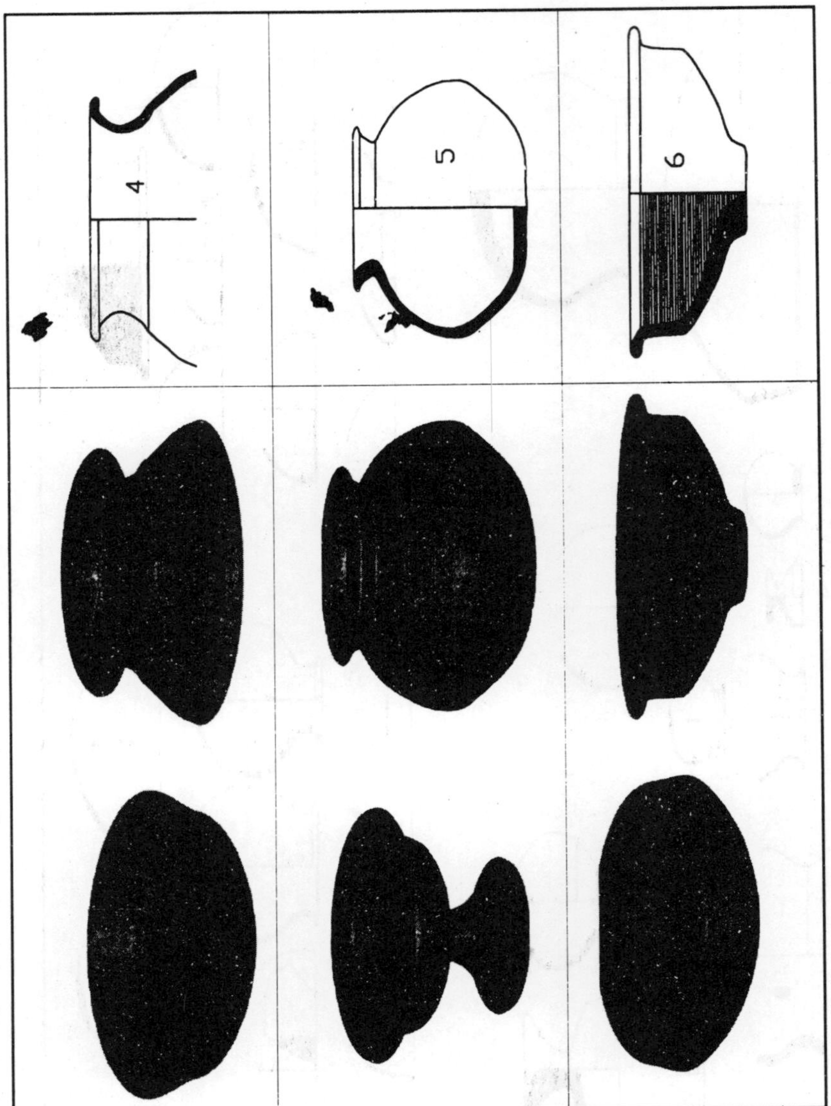

Fig. 3 Megalithic Pottery from Burials, Sanana and Baseri, Almora

The Ratna-Chankrama Chaitya (The Shrine of Jewel-Walk),Bodhgaya: A Reappraisal

ARVIND MAHAJAN*

More or less parallel to the northern wall of the Mahabodhi temple stands a raised brick platform–53 feet long, 3 feet 6 inches broad, a little more than 3 feet in height; distance between the platform and the northern wall of the temple being 1 foot 11 inches at the eastern end and 2 feet 11 inches at the western end. On this raised platform are positioned 19 lotus emblems to indicate the places where the wonderful flowers sprang up under the foot-prints of the Buddha, which are said to have been 18 in number, during a meditative walk for seven days from the eighth or fifteenth day of his enlightenment[1]. The site came to be known as the 'Chankrama Chaitya' or 'the shrine of the slow or meditative walk'. It was also called 'the covered and cloistered walk' and later on as 'the Jewelled Cloister'. Chinese traveller Hiuen-tsang reports this shrine as, "To the north of the Bodhi tree is the spot where Buddha walked up and down. When he attained Enlightenment, he did not rise from his throne but remained perfectly quiet for seven days lost in contemplation. Then rising he walked up and down during seven days to the north of the tree; he walked there east and west for a distance of 10 paces or so. Miraculously flowers (lotus) sprang under his foot, traces to the number of eighteen. Afterwards this space was covered in by a brick wall about 3 feet high"[2]. Fa-hian also makes mention of it. "On all these spots (where Buddha suffered mortification for six years) men of after ages have built pagodas and set up images, all of which are still in existence. Where Buddha, having attained perfect wisdom, contemplated the tree for seven days experiencing the joy of emancipation; where Buddha walked backwards and forwards under the Pei-to tree for seven days"[3].

There seems to have been a superstructure, as inferred from a depiction on an oblong panel of one of the comparatively longer pillars of the vedika at Bharhut, over the shrine of the Buddha's Jewel-walk[4]. The depiction presents the front view of the covered walk, consisting of a long platform in the open pillared hall of a two storeyed building, which has a vaulted roof with small pinnacles and two gabled ends. The platform bears on its upper face certain ornamental impressions which are symbolical flowers and other offerings made thereon, and on its front side representations of human palms. Each floor has perambulatory within a stone structure. The upper floor is provided with three doorways from which three garlands are hanging. Each pillar of this structure has an octagonal shaft with a lotus ornament and a bracket[5].

What is visible today of this superstructure is only a row of pillar bases *in situ* along the northern stretch of the platform. However, according to Cuningham, on each side of the platform there was a row of eleven

*Patna Museum, Patna-800 001.

Persipolitan pillar bases, of the well known pattern of a vase placed above three or four steps and surmounted by parabolic moulding with an octagonal top for the reception of an octagonal shaft[6]. Cuningham further says that , "each of these bases was marked with a separate letter of the Aśoka alphabet, the eleven bases on the south side bearing the eleven vowels, i.e. from *a* to *ah* and the northern bases, the first eleven consonants from *k* to *t*"[7]. "The *that* southern row of these bases was partly hidden under the basement of the Great temple which had been built over them, on a slightly different alignment, part of the two most westerly bases alone appearing seven inches outside the wall, while all the easterly bases were completely covered"[8].

But in the light of the report of G.A. Griers on to the Secretary, General Department, Govt. of Bengal, dated November 29th, 1895[9], Cuningham's observation, regarding the alphabets appear a mere hypothesis. Grierson reports, "The row of the pillar bases on the south side, mentioned by Cuningham is no longer visible. In the process of repairing the Great temple most of them have been left buried within the wall of its foundation. This may be presumed from Cuningham's description, and is borne out by the statement of Jagannath Singh, the custodian of the temple on behalf of the Mahanth, who was there when repairs were going on. It is stated by him that only base was unearthed from the foundations, and remaining bases on that side were never seen by Cuningham"[10]. Grierson further writes, "The Mahanth and his people assure me that no one has ever seen the pillar bases on the south side, except the first one, which Sir Cuningham says was marked *a*. They say, 'Cuningham Sahib read his books and took measurements, and then dug into the wall of the temple and found the a̲ base. He never dug into the wall for the others, but as Cuningham Sahib says they were there. Cuningham Sahib could read book and know everything, and when he said anything was in any place, he was always right'. This probably meant that General Cuningham did not venture to dig into the walls for the last eight bases which his account shows were entirely within the foundations. He (Cuningham) certainly removed the No. 1, and probably the plinths of Nos. 2 and 3, which were partly visible and could be removed without injury to the main building (?)"[11].

Grierson sums up the report : There were eleven bases on each side, the first (western) base was marked with letter *a*. There is no evidence as what letters the other bases on each side, the first (western) base was marked with letter *a*.

"On the north side the first (western) base has *ka*, and the seventh has *cha*; *cha* is the seventh consonant of the Sanskrit alphabet and the sixth of the Aśoka alphabet. If, therefore, the pillars are in their original order, as Jagannath Singh states, this tends to prove that Sanskrit was a written language when the masons made the marks.

On the other hand, the letter which Cuningham appears to have read as *ga,* and which he says he saw in its right alphabetical place on the third base, is really on the fifth base, and, if it is *ga*, is not in correct alphabetical order. If, therefore the reading is correct, the bases were either not originally set up in alphabetical order, or have since been interchanged. In either case their values as regards the history of the Indian alphabet is very small.

The letters *ja* and *ta* seen by Cuningham are no longer visible. The importance of these bases rests on the correct reading of the mark on No. 5. If it is read as ña̲, they go to prove that Sanskrit was written in the 2nd cen. BC when the mason's mark were made, or, at least, add a hitherto unknown letter to the Pali alphabet[12].

However, the contribution of Cuningham to Bodhgaya can not be undermined. What is in the Mahabodhi campus today in the form of art and artitecture of antiquity in a solid state of preservation is the contribution of Cuningham and his colleagues.

Cuningham contends with certainty that the canopied roof over the Jewel-walk shrine was of wood. he says, "From the small ends of the longitudinal beams, as seen in the gables, I gather that the roof must almost certainly have been of wood"[13].

It is quite interesting that Hiuen-tsang, though refers to the shrine of Jewel-walk, does not make mention of the canopied roof over it. It indicates to that the shrine did not have it in his time. Reason behind it may be that it might have been removed during the construction of the Great temple, as the southern row of its pillar bases lie buried in the foundation of the temple, or would have been razed to ground in course of the catastrophe, made by Śaśānka, the Gauda King.

A close scrutiny of the *Ratna Chankrama* episode in the Buddhist literatures, of the contemporary religio-cultural settings of the land as well as of the other contemporary literary sources and of the architecture and art motifs in the depiction of the shrine at Bharhut, put a big question mark and a challenge for its affiliation as an exclusive Buddhist monument. It appears to be a shrine of folk tradition and cult of an earlier antiquity than Buddha. The foremost of the notable lacunae is the lack of coherence in Buddhist literature, so far as the Jewel-walk episode of Buddha is concerned. In the earliest set of Buddhist literature, i.e. the *Pitakes,* the *Lalitvistara* etc. the episode of Jewel-walk is wanting. The account of *Lord's* stations in the first five weeks after the *Enl*ightenment, according to the *Mahāvagga*[14], are viz. Bodhi tree, the goatherd's Banyan tree. In the *Lalitvistara*[15] the sequel is *Bodhi maṇda,* the long walk extending over the whole universe, Buddha looks with unblenching eyes to the *Bodhi maṇda,* he goes for a short walk from eastern to the western ocean, Muchalinda, the Goatherd's Banyan tree and the Tārāyana tree. The episode of Jewel-walk appears in the *Mahāvāstu* and the *Mahāvamsa,* but in a totally different context i.e. on occasion of Buddha's first return to his native town of Kapilvastu[16] which, according to Fouche, is depicted on the inner face of the right jamb of the eatern gate at Sanchi.[17] How and when this episode got interpolated into post-Enligh tenment activities of the Buddha at Bodhgayā and gained a place in the Buddhist literatures, is still a riddle. In the light of conflicting traditions it is very difficult to precisely set the time of Buddhist affiliation of this monument; however, some inferences may be drawn.

Its depiction at Bharut and row of inscribed pillar bases *in situ* at the site establish beyond doubt that it was there in the 2nd cenț BC. Aśoka is known to have undertaken constructional activities at Sambodhi (Bodhgayā) An open air, flat-roofed pavilion over the Vajrasana is evidently credited to him which has got a duly labelled depiction at Bharhut[18]. Here it may be opined that the superstructure over the Jewel-walk shrine might have been erected by him, in spite of whatever be its religious affliation as Ashoka's tolerance towards other faiths is well known. But a close comparison of its depicted architecture with the other pre-Aśokan, which are per-Buddha as well like the *agnisala* of Uruvela (depicted at Sanchi)[19], palaces and buildings of Kapilvastu[20], Rājgriha, Srāsti and other places, and Asokan architecture which have are depicted at Sānchī, Bharhut, Bhodhgayā, Amrāvatī etc., place it in the pre-Asokan time bracket. As for material wood dominated the pre–Asokan architecture where as Asoka utilized chiefly stone for the same. It is evident from the literary traditions, excavated materials, as well as by the comparison of depicted architectural examples at various sites. Excavations at Bodhgaya have not yielded any remains of the superstructure over the Jewel–walk shrine and Cunningham also inferred that the canopy or superstructure over the shrine was of wood[21]. So far as the lithic columns supporting the canopy are concerned, they might have been replaced for the wooden columns during Aśoka or the period following him. The wooden canopy, thus, makes its antiquity at least pre-Asokan which may go even earlier, as the palace of the Bumbisāra who was contemporary of Buddha, the palace of Siddhārtha Gautama at Kapilvastu, the palace of Chandragupta Maurya — to which Megasthenes refers to and which Chandragupta got from the Nandas, were built chiefly of wood.

An analysis of the personality traits of the Buddha, gleaned from literature, may be of some help in solving the aforesaid riddle. In the *Mahāvagga,* the depiction of Buddha is as a human being and not deified personage. *Lalitvistara,* though more or less a Sanskrit version of the early *Pitakas*, depicts Buddha as a deifed person with various dogmatic fictions woven round him. *Lalitvistara* is supposed to have been composed in 1st –2nd cen. AD[22] and Buddha is not known to have performed Jewel–walk a Bodhgaya till this date. *Mahāvāstu* and *Mahāvaṃsa* were written around 3rd–4th cen. AD[23] and they refer to the Jewel–walk, but at Kapilvastu during the first visit of the Lord to his native place[24]. The Jewel–walk episode of Buddha at Bodhgaya appears for the first time in the *Jātaka Nidāna kathā* which has been dated in the 5th cen. AD.[25]

Fa–hien (A.D. 399-414) in his travelogue mentions the Jewel–walk episode and the shrine at Bodhgaya [26]. It indicates to that in this period such a story was prevalent at Bodhgaya. In the subsequent period Bodhgaya gained importance as one the four Bauddha Mahātīrthas which is evidenced by the erection of the Great Mahabodhi Temple and the abrupt rise in frequency of inscriptions at Bodhgaya. *Raison d'etre* for all these developments was the changing nature of the religion. Whatever was styled as religious-rites, sites or rituals at or around Bodhgaya got Buddhism over the land. The example of the Prāg–Bodhi hill episode may be cited in this context which does not occur in any of the Buddhist religious texts till 7th cen. AD, but Hiuen–tsang refers to it in very glowing terms[27]. After interpolation of such sites or rites into Buddhism, justification were made by composition of literatures in their favour. As for example–*Bhaya–bherava Sutta* for the Prāg Bodhi hill episode, the *Mettā Sutta* and the *Peta–vathu* for the *Srāddha* ries, Jewel–walk at Bodhgaya for the Ratna Chankram Chaitya.

Ancient Buddhist and Jaina text and the early Budhist monuments reveal the existence of a primitive religion in eastern India, particularly in Videha, Aṇga and Magadha. This was more favourable to the development of plastic art than the Vedic religion and the form of this art was purely folkart[28].

The most important feature of this primitive religion was worship of the *chaitya.* In a short dialogue of the *Aṇguttara Nikāya,* Buddha explains to the *Lichhavi–Vajjis* of Vaishali the seven conditions of welfare. Two of these, that relate to religion are:

(i) "So long as the *Lichhavi-Vajjis* honour and esteem and revere and support the Vajjian *chetiyas (chaityas)* in the city or outside it, and allow not proper offerings and rites as formerly given and performed to fall into desuetude, so long may the *Lichhavi–Vajjis* be expected not to decline but to prosper."

(ii) "So long as the rightful protection, defence and support shall be fully provided for the *Arhants* among them, so that *Arhants* from a distance may enter the real and the *Arhants* therein may live at ease, so long may the *Lichhavi–Vajjis........*"[29].

In the *Mahāparinibbāna Sutta,* Buddha repeats the same seven conditions of welfare of Lichhavis when speaking to the minister of the king Ajātsatru of the Magadh[30]. The same *Sutta* refers to the six *chaityas* of Vaishali, viz. *Udena, Gotamaka, Sattambaka (chaityas* of the seven mangoes), *Bahaputta (chaityas* of many sons), Sārandada and *Chapāla*[31]. Some Pali texts to another *Bahuputta chaitya* between Rajgṛiha and Nālanda. In the commentary on the *Theragāthā,* that *chaitya* has been called *Bahuputraka* Banyan, that is to say it was a holy Banyan tree (Ficus religiosa)[32]. In the *Mahāparinnibbāna Sutta* the chaitya of the Mallas has been called the *Makutbandhana* (the tying of the diadem) *chaitya*[33]. In a stanza uttered by Buddha in the *Divyāvandāna*[34] *chaitya* tree is distinctly mentioned. It relates, "Men without fear take refuge in mountains, forests, gardens and *chaitya* trees; such refuge is not good, such refuge is not the best; by taking such refuge (one does) not escape from all miseries". In the *Bhaya–Bherava Sutta* of *Majjhima Nikāya,* Buddha says that before his full enlightment he took shelter in the wilds (near Uruvela according to the other sources) and visited *ārāmachetiyānī* (the *chaityas* in the parks), *vanachetiyānī* (the chaityas in the forests) and *rukkhachetiyānī* (tree *chaityas)* in order to discover fear and dread[35]. In the *Samyutta Nikāya*[36], the *Maṇimala chaitya* in Magadha is said to be the haunt of Yaksha Manibhadra[37]. *Sūrya Prajñapti,* an ancient Jaina text, tells us that a Manibhadra *chaitya* stood to the north–east of the city named Mithila, the capital of ancient Videha[38].

Not exactly these, but some such *chaityas* have got depictions at Sānchī, Bharhut, Bodh–Gayā etc. Some such depictions from Bharhut are: (i) a holy tree with an altar underneath surrounded by lions and antelopes assembled in a friendly spirit. Above the relief is engraved in Brahmi— *mig samadak chet(i)ya,* i.e.'the *chetiya* that gladens the heart of animals[39] (ii) A tree with altar to which three elephants are evidently offering worship. The inscription above is— *abode chatiyam,* ie.'the *chaitya* on the *Arbuda* (Mount Abu)[40] (iii) Another bas relief on a coping, though not so named, undoubtedly represents a *chaitya* tree. The inscription it reads *jabu Nadode pavate,* i.e. 'the *jambu* tree on mount *Nadoda* (the Naro range about 6 miles to the north of Bharhut). This bas–relief shows a tree out of which come out two human hands, the one holding a bowl and the other pouring water with a pitcher on the hands of man seated on a basket[41]. In the outstretched hands we recognize a tree *spirit* or *deva.* The story of a tree spirit or deva who supplied food and drink to the travellers, has been told in the *Dhammapada commentary*[42]. A bas relief, very similar this, on a pillar of the old railing of Bodhgayā has been described by Cunningham[43].

The Jaina *Aupapatika Sutra* gives the stereotyped jain account of a *chaitya* in connection of the Purnabhdra *chaitya* near Champā, the capital of Aṅga; Some extracts of which are: "Outside the city of Champā, to the north

–east thereof, was a sanctuary named Pūṛṇabhadra. It as of ancient origin, told by men of former days, old, renonwned, rich and well known......... It had diases built in it, and was reverentially adorned with a coating of dry cowdung bore figures of five fingured hands painted in gosīrsha sandal, fresh red sandal, dardarā sandal. There was in it great store ritual pitchers. On its doorways were rituals jars and well fashioned arches........ This sanctuary of Purn Qabhadra was encompassed round about by great wood....... In this wood was a broad mid–space.Therein, it is related, was a great and fine Asoka tree (of holy nature)......... with dias of earthern block, eight cornered and figured with wolves, bulls, horses, elephants etc.[44] This description of Purnabhadrachaiya of Champā offers a striking similarity to that of the jewel–walk of Bodhgayā, depicted at Bharhut. The Asoka tree with diases below reminds us of the Bodhi tree and the Vajrāsana. During Buddha's time Anga and Magadha were a cultural unit which is evidnced by the participation of Anga people in the Mahāyajña of the Jatilas[45].

Actually the Ratna–Chankramachaitya appears to be the site of Vasu worship during *sraddha* at the *Asvattha* tree which is definitely a pre-Buddha phenomena at Bodhgayā[46]. The palm (five fingured hand) prints over the shrine leads us to think on this line. The Vasu worship is a tradition of hoary antiquity having its roots in the primitive cult of worship of earth godess. It is practiced even today in every walk of the society with rites and rituals of its own on almost all the major ceremonies like birth, marriage, *sraddha* etc. In each and every village or about the temples in cities there happens to be diases (low height platforms) upon which lie simple, small lumps earth which in modern times may be of cement also. Females during worship use to bemsear these lumps with *ghee* (clarified butter) or with paste of yellow vermillian (dardarā sandal) in *ghee.* Them they put their palm prints numbering five seven, eight or two rows of eight according to the occasion on the wall of the dias; medium for the prints happen to be either the paste of wheat or rice flour in water with a bit of turmeric powder or paste in it or the paste of yellow vermillian in *ghee*. Only, thereafter worship takes place which are of very simple nature and without any priest. The worship comprises offering of flowers and garlands, burning of incense and lamps, offering of fruits and finally pouring milk or ghee over the lump. On certain occasions these rituals (those after the putting the palm prints) are performed with an officiating priest who utters certain *mantras* in praise of Vasu, specially during pouring of milk or *ghee*. But more often these rites are exclusively done by the females without priest help on each and every, minor or major ritualistic functions. The palm prints over the depiction of shrine at Barhut leave no doubt that from the time of Buddha till the depiction of the chapel, this platform was undoutedly used for the Vasu worship.

B.M. Barua presents three possible explanations for the palm prints: (i) that these indicate that the platform is set up as an extended alter for worship; (ii) that these are to keep visitors at a respectable distance from it and (iii) that these signify the merit of worship whereby the worshippers might secure *(abhaya)*[47]. But the way the palm prints are put on the ceremonials occasions and the places where they are put, i.e. on the wall of the houses, with pre–historic paintings, over the clothes of ceremonial nature, the explanations of Barua does not hold water.

The putting of palm printers appear to be the earliest and most primitive form of signing, as the palm prints differ from person to person in the same way as the signatures do. The motive of puting behind palm prints during ceremonial rituals. Since all the major ceremonies like birth, marriage and even death are celebrated with such pomp and gaity particularly birth and marriage ceremonies are called *janmotsava* and *vivāhotsava* respectively. Involvement of more than one is quite apparent on such occasions and in ritualistic acts. Religious acts which have become individualistic today were not in olden times. And it may be the explanation for presence of more than one palm print. With passage of time putting of palm prints before ceremonial rites became a ritual.

In modern times also, particularly in Indian subcontinent, two sets of rituals go side by side irrespective of caste, creed or religious affiliation. After the priestly rituals which happen to be of very primitive nature and need no priest or any such personality. The rituals of the household ladies appear to be the carry forward of the same when the tribal matriarch dominated the society and rituals were part and parcel of their duties. With the Aryan influence over the land, the nature of the society changed and it became patriarchal. Sons came to be known by the name of their father. In this changed society, the rituals became the duty of the male head of the family. But the ladies did not give up their rituals and continued as before. In subsequent periods with the switch over of the family head to any other religion of his choice, the religion of the entire family used to get changed. The other members of the family were forced to follow the new religion. Rites, rituals, customs or major ceremonies also accordingly changed but the females, however, continued to carry over their traditionally old rites and customs. Vasu worship which is actually the worship of earth, is one of them. It is purely a primitive folk–cult which got Brahminical sanction in later period with incorporation of saga. It is interesting to now that in Brahmical laegends a male deity or hero–Vasu Uparichara replaced the earth godess–Vasumati or Vasudharā.

As a personage of Brahmical legends 'Vasu' appears to be amysterious figure. In one place in the Mahābharatā he is described as following the *ahimsa* doctrine. He is further described as a devotee of Hari, worshipper of Vishnu and of the pitrs and so on[48]. In the next chapter[49], he said to have performed as *Ashvamedha* sacrifice, in which the chief priest Bṛhaspati could not see *Narayana* or *Puraana Deva* when he had come to accept obaltions. But Uparichara (Vasu) saw him.In the next chapter[50], am Vasu is said to have decided a feud between the *devas* and the rishis regarding whether animals should be sacrificed or not. Vasu, though an advocate of *ahimsa* gave verdict in favour of the *devas* that animals should be sacrificed. As consequence Vasu had to enter the earth through the curse of the rishis. But the devas gave him the boon that even while living in the earth, Vasu would get as his food 'the *Vasudhara*, given by people during the sacrifices. The ***Matsya Puram***[51] relates the beginning of the bloody sacrifices in the *Treta yuga* when Indra first started it. But the Brahmins refused to accept them and a quarrel followed between the Brahmins (rishis) and the *devas*. The whole matter was reffered for decision to king Vasu Upari chara. The Brahmins advocated the bloodless sacrifices (with ghee and grains) By saying that it was started by Brahāma, and that *tapasyā* (penance) was the chief religion. These legends clearly reflect the struggle between the sacrifice cult of the *devas* and the *ahimsā* cult of the rishis.

The above legend of Vasu Upari chara in a slightly different form may be traced in the *Chetiya* of *Chaidya Jātaka*[52] which mentions the king as Upachara. He had through supernatural faculties the priest was Kapila. He had promised Kapila to make the latter's son his priest after the father. But later on the king wanted to make another favourite his priest by telling a lie. All his supernatural powers thus vanished and unable to stay and longer in the air, he fell on the earth. He began then to tell further lies to his family priest and began to sink into the earth upto the ankle after the second lie, upto the knee after the third, upto the hips after the fourth, upto the naval after the fifth and upto the breast after the sixth lie. He told the seventh lie, the earth opened and the flames of the *Avīchi* leapt up and seized him. Thus by reviling sage Kapila, Upachara was swallowed by the earth on the seventh day.

Purānik legend and Jataka both agree in saying that the king was at first very pious, but for telling a lie he had to enter the earth. The legends thus indicate that Vasu had some relation with 'earth', i.e. Earth goddess, '*Vasudhara*' and some relations of Siddhārtha Gautama– the Bodhisattva with Vasudharā, the Earth goddess for favour when Māra– the Great Temptor and the Evil tendency of mind attacked him during his effort of getting the Supreme Knowledge. The Buddhist literature vividly depict this episode[53]. This episode of Earth goddess shows the existence of worship mother goddess; perhaps even a shrine at that site dedicated to that goddess may be called for. This episode is of such importance that images of Buddha in earth touching posture came into being at Bodhgayā.

Since time immemorial, Gaya is known for the ***sraddha*** i.e. offering for the departed ancestors. During *śrāddha*, offerings are made for each and every flora and all major or minor deities and divinities. As other than the sacred Bo-tree at Bodh-Gayā, there is no site for offering in favour of *Aśvattha* which is the holies of holies in flora; other than the Ratna-chankrama chaitya, there is no other site of Vasu in the sacred ambit of Gayā. The worship of Vasus was essential at Dharmāraṇya (Bodh -Gayā) for the Vasus were the pitrs[54].

Mpreover, *'Ratna'* is a synonym of 'Vasu'[55] and *'chankrama'* has been often applied for *'pradakashinā'*[56]. The name is suggestive or people at the shrine of Ratna-chankrama form a pradakshiṇā (circumanbution) perhaps round an altar on which people used to worship *Vasu* and perform *Vasudhārā*, prior to *śrāddha* rituals at Bodh-Gaya¯. The same has been enjoined by the White Yajur Veda[57] and the Sraut Sūtras[58]. Moreover, depiction of the shrine of Jewel-walk at Bharhut displays provisions for circumbulation within a stone structure[59].

Epilogue

In the light of above evidences it appears that the shrine of jewel-walk actually was the site of *Vasu* worship in the sacred ambit of Gayā. Vasu worship, which is evidently the worship of Earth, is one of the earliest and primitive rituals. The mode of worship, is purely a folk-cult which is practiced even today by the folk and tribal people with rites and rituals of the own. The depiction of the shrine at Bharhut too substantiates its folk affiliation.

The superstructure over the shrine also followed the contemporary folk tradition of architecture because when it was erected, there was nothing like royal or cout at Bodh-Gayā. There were similar other examples of the same tradition, which were pre-Buddha, at Bodh-Gaya and have depictions as embellishments at various sites. Though, these depictions belong to the Sungas time (2nd cen. BC), they amptly exhibit contemporary folkart tradition. During the Sungas, the folk–art traditions made a spurt. Actually the Sungan time was the time of the revival of the folk–art tradition, which was in to oblivion during the Mauryas, but in a different fashion. The executors of the new art form were the scions of the Mauryas, that is why the elite touch in the art forms was inevitable, in spite of the subject matter being purely folk.

Concluding it may be held that the shrine of Jewel-walk was monument of the cult and tradition which was inbibi into the Buddhist stream when the tide of Buddhism pervade the region. B.M. Barua rightly says, "The folk is folk every where and in all stages of human civilization. History bears a clear testimony to the fact that whatever the real character of a religion and its tenents, the rise of each religion serves only to supply fresh excuses and opportunities through its legends for its followers to make public demonstrations of the glory of their faith and to associate certain supernatural phenomena with some of their sanctuaries (so called). And Buddhism and its followers (later champions) were not an exception to this rule"[60].

REFERENCE

1. *Cuningham A. Mahabodhi or The Great Buddhist Temple under the Bodhi Tree at Bodhgayā* Reprint, Varanasi (1962), pp.8 and n, 35 and n. Kern H. *Manual of Indian Buddhism,* Strassburg (1896), P.21.
2. Beal S. *Si-yu-Ki; Buddhist Records of the Western World,* Trans. from the Chinese of Hiuen–tsang (A.D. 629), Reprint, two volumes bound in one, New Delhi (1969), vol. II, p. 123.
3. Giles H.A. 1972, *Record of the Buddhistic Kingdoms,* Reprint Varanasi, p.76
4. Barua, B.M. *Bharhut,* 1979 Reprint, Patna, Book–I, p.23
5. Ibid. p.75, pl. XLIV, Scene–42
6. Cuningham A. *Mahabodhi,* p. 8
7. Ibid.
8. Ibid. p. 9
9. Grierson 1895, Report to Secretary, General Deptt. courtsey Govt. of Bengal Dr. M.R.Kazimi, New Pataliputra, Patna.
10. Ibid p. 2
11. Ibid p. 5
12. Ibid.
13. Cuningham: op cit, p.10
14. Rhys Davids, TW and Glendberg, H (Tr), *Mahavagga, I. 1-5,* in F Maxmuller (ed.) *Sacred Books of the East Series* Vol. XIII, Reprint Delhi (1982)
15. *Ed. R.L. Mitra, Lalitvistara,* Calcutta (1863), p. 488ff
16. Ed. E. Senart, *Mahavastu,* 3 Vols., Paris (1882-1897), III, p.113 *Mahāvamsa,* XXX. st. 81 etc., Ed.W. Geiger, Pali Text Society (PTS), London (1908); Eng. Tr. W. Geiger, assisted by Mabel Haynes Bode, PTS, London (1912).
17. Foucher A. *Beginings of Buddhist Art,* Tr. by L.A. Thomas and F.W. Thomas, Paris/London (MCMXVII–1917), pp. 19, 93–95, pl.IX.2
18. Cuningham A. : op.cit pp. 4–7
19. A. Foucher: op.cit., pl. IX.1

20. Ibid. pl. IX.2
21. Cuningham : op.cit, pp.8-10
22. Kern H. : op.cit, pp 1–8s
23. Ibid. pp. 1–11
24. *Mahāvāstu,* op.cit; *Mahā vaṃsa,* op.cit.
25. Barua B.M. 1934 *Gayā and Buddha–Gayā,* Culcutta Vol. II, Book II, p. 25 and notes.
26. Giles, H.A. op.cit
27. Beal, S. : *Si–yu–ki,* Vol. pp. lxi–lxii;Vol II, pp. 114-1
28. Chanda, R.P. *The Beginning of Art in Eastern India with special Reference to the Sculputures in Indian Museum,* Memoirs of Archaeological Survey of India,. No. 30, Calcutta (1927), pp. 3-4.
29. Morris T. and Hardy E. (Ed) *Anguttata Nika¯ya,* PTS, Vol. IV, London (1899), pp. 16-17,
30. T.W. Rhys Davids Tr., *Mahāparinibbāna Sutta,* SBE, Vol. XI, Reprint Delhi (1980), pp.
31. Ibid.
32. Rhys Davids: 1913 *Psalms of the Bretheren* (Eng. Tr. of the Theragatha), PTS, London), p. 361
33. *Mahāparinibbāna* Sutta, op.cit, p.
34. Cowell E.B. and R.A. Neil, *Divyāvadāna,* (Ed) Cambridge (1886), p. 164
35. Lord Chalmers: 1926 *Further Dialogues of the Buddha,* Vol. I, London, p. 13.
36. *Sayutta Nikāya,* I. 10.4, Ed. Tr. T.W. Rhys Davids and K.F.L. Woodwards, pts, London (191-30)
37. Leon F.M. 1884-88 - RhysDavids and K FL Wood wards (Tr.) 1917-30. *Sayutta Nikāya,* London
38. Chanda: op.cit. p.7
39. Barua op.cit, pp. 113–14, pl. LXXX, Scene–108
40. Ibid. pp. 133-35, pl. LXXXIV, scene-124(a)
41. Ibid. pp. 162-64, pl. XCI, scene-140
42. 2.1.6, *Dhammapada Commentary,* H.C. Norman, (Dhammapadaṭṭhakathā), 5 Vols, op.cit PTS, London (1906-1915)
43. Cuningham: op.cit, p. 13, pl. VIII,
44. Dr. Ernest Leumann (Ed.) Leipzig (1833), *Aupapatika Sūtra,* pp. 22-24; Eng. Trans. by L.D. Barnett, The *Antagada–Dasao and Anuttarovavaiya–Dasao,* London1907.
45. T.W.Rhys Davids and J. Estlin Carpenter Ed., *Dīgha Nikāya,*Vol. I, London (1889), pp. 135ff. ; *Anguttara Nikaya,* op. cit. Vol. II, p. 207
45. Mahajan Arvind *"Srāddha, Ecology and Buddhism",* The Hindustan Times, Patna Edn.dated 22.09.1998
46. *Mahābhārata,* Eng. Trans. op.cit, Vol. II, Book–II, p.26
47. M.N.Dutt, *Barua Gaya and Buddha Gaya II,* Calcutta, (1895–1905), Shantiparvan, Chapter 335
48. Ibid. Ch. 336
50. Ibid. Ch.337
51. Taluqdar of Oudh A. Eng Traans., *Matsya Purāṇa,* 2 Vols, Sacred Book of the Hindus (SBH), Allahabad (1916-17)
52. *Chetiya Jātaka,* V. Fausboll, Ed., London (1877-97), No. 422

    Mahāvagga, op.cit.
53. *Suttanipāta,* SBE, Vol. X, V. Fausboll, Tr. Reprint Delhi (1973), pp. 69-71

    Beal S., Tr. into English from chinese SBE, *Fo–Sho–Hing–Tsan–King,* Vol. XIX, Reprint Delhi (1975. pp. 147–156.*Lalitivistara,* op.cit., pp. 404ff
54. T.W. Rhys Davids: *Buddhism,* London (1878), pp. 36–39

    Matsya Purāna, op.cit. 19.3 *The Laws of Manu,* SBE, Vol. XXC, Tr. Buhler G., Ed. Reprint Delhi (1982), III. 82
55. Monieṛ–Williams: *A Sanskrit–English Dictionary,*

    London (1899), Edn. 1963 from Delhi, pp. 930–31
56. *"idam Vishnur vichkrame",* Rg Veda, I. 22. 17, (Rg Veda, with Sayana's commentary, ed. Poona, 1933; Sripada Sarma, Aundha Nagar, Bombay, 1940; Tr. R.T.F. Grifith, Banaras, 1896–97)
57. *White Yajur Veda,* Book–XVIII
58. W. Caland, Ed., *Baudhāyana Sraut Sūtra,* 17.24–26, Calcutta (1904–23)
59. Barua B.M. Bharhut, op. cit. p. 75
60. Barua B.M. , *Gayā and Buddha–Gayā,* op.cit. Vol. II, Book–II, p.60

Archaeology of Calcutta: Evidence from Bethune College

Uttara Chakraborty*
Swati Biswas**

The rapid growth of cities in the last few decades had led to the fast disappearence of archaeological evidence thereby losing many vital information in understanding the urban archaeology. It is a fact that most cities had a long history, but unfortunately this has not been properly understood from archaeological point of view. This is because, very little attention has so far been paid to the understanding of the archaeology of urban setting. Hence it has become necessary to retrieve every bit of archaeological record from urban areas for the reconstruction of the history of a city.

The early history of Calcutta is known mainly from literature and early British records. This is not enough to understand the evolution of the city of Calcutta from a rural setting to a metropolis. We have to collate the archaeological evidence not only from Calcutta but from neighbouring areas for the reconstruction of the early history of the city.

Fortunately, some fresh archaeological evidence have come from the Bethune College campus which would certainly throw light on the early history of the city.

Bethune School and College are two very old institutions founded in 1849 and 1879 respectively and are situated in the same campus. Very recently the buildings of both the institutions have been declared heritage buildings. In April 1997, while digging foundation for a proposed auditorium in the College campus, several terra cotta figurines, lamps, *chulums*, glass and porcelain pieces besides pottery were found which are now housed in the College Museum. Besides, a number of bricks were also found from the digging. Meanwhile, the Directorate of State Archaeology carried out excavations in two phases (i) 15th Nov. 1997-6th Jan 1998 and (ii) 10th Dec. 1998-2nd Feb. 1999. From the excavation similar objects and a large number of potsherds have been collected. The excavation has also revealed structures belonging to several phases.

Location of Bethune College and history of locality

Bethune College is located in the northern part of the city of Calcutta. It falls in ward no. 26 of Borough 4 of the Calcutta Corporation. The College and the School campus is bounded by Maniktola Street, now known as Ramdulal Sarkar Street in the south. Bethune Row in the west, Bidhan Sarani (former Cornwallis Street) in the east and Beadon Street in the north. In front of the College the otherside of Bidhan Sarani is a very old tank now con-

*Lecturer, Bethune College, Calcutta
** Part time lecturer and Research Scholar, Bethune College Calcutta.

verted into a swimming pool and park, known as Azad Hind Bag.

This part of Calcutta is considered to be very old. The area was known as Simulia in the past because of abundant growth of *Simul (Bambox Ceiba (sc)* Red Silk Cotton trees. Other was an extensive and popular market place called Simulia Bazaar on the site of Bethune College. This bazaar was very old. Earliest mention of this bazaar is found in archival documents dating back to 1773 and 1774[1].

The origin of the market could be earlier. However, this is very difficult to prove since, the documents preserved in the State Archives do not go beyond the eighteenth century.

Part of the bazaar was taken over in 1850 by the East India Company's Government in Bengal on the request of J.E.D. Bethune, the founder of the School and the Law member of the Governor General's Council,[2] for the building of his School. The bazaar continued to exist on the western side of the College campus till the beginning of the twentieth century (The bazaar is shown in a 1901 map of Calcutta drawn by the Survey of India). It was finally demolished in 1904. In 1916 A.L. Janau, the then Principal of the College sought permission from the Govt. of Bengal to construct a boundary wall to incorporate the vacated land into the College campus[3]. The newly acquired land formed the western side of the campus of Bethune School and College. It is here where antiquities were found while digging for the foundation of the auditorium. This was also the same place where the State Archaeology Department carried out its excavations.

History of Sutanuti: Origin of Calcutta

In the eighties of the 17th century, the East India Company was searching for a new site to establish their factory and warehouses. They preferred a place further south of Hooghly, and were close to the Sea. Job Charnock the Company's Agent had made frequent tours down the river Ganga (Hooghly). In 1686 his choice fell upon Sutanuti hat on the east side of the river. This was a cotton weavers market where bales of cotton piece goods and threads were bought and sold; hence the name Sutanuti[4]. In 1690, he decided to have the permanent residence of the Company's Agent at Sutanuti. Eight years later, his son-in-law, Eyre got the permission to rent the three villages of Sutanuti, Govindapur and Calcutta from Azim-ush-Shah, the Moghul Subedar of Bengal.[5] These three villages formed the nuclei of the later colonial city of Calcutta. However, the fact that there were already existing revenue yielding zamindaries is an indication of the existence of busy settlements in this area long before the English actually arrived.

Of the three villages, Sutanuti now forms the northern part of the city and this is where Bethune College is situated. In the area behind Bethune College, live the Nans, Seths and Basaks. They are weavers by caste and profession. Now, of course, they have given up their age old profession. Their ancestors came to Sutanuti leaving Saptagram, then a dying market town, attracted by the lucrative business at Sutanuti hat. In fact the Seths and Basaks are considered to be the earliest settlers of the new city of calcutta. According to Gourdas Basak, a nineteenth century scholar, and brilliant student of Hindoo College, the Seths and Basaks came here even before the Moghuls arrived in India[6] (1466-the date given by G.D. Basak).

On interviewing Mr. Sachhidananda Nan or Badal Babu, as he is popularly known, resident of Bethune Row (former Simulia) we come to know that his family came to Sutanuti in 1660, leaving their ancestral home at Rajbolhat near Saptagram. Later on they built their house and a temple on the site beyond Bethune College. Simulia was a part of Sutanuti, perhaps the heart of the cotton market. Could it be possible that Bethune College stands on the earlier Sutanuti hat site ?

In medieval Bengali literature, particularly in the two *mangal kavyas 'Manasa Mangal'* and *'Chandi Mangal'*-there are references to Calcutta as 'Kolkata'. The earliest *Manasa Mangal* (1495) was written by Bipra Das Pipalai who lived in Baduria in North 24-Parganas, very near the present city. Whereas Mukundaram poet of *Chandi-Mangal* belonged to the 16th century and lived in Burdwan, during the time of Akbar. Both the poets while describing the travels of their protagonists (Chand Saudagar of *Manasa Mangal* and Dhanapati of *Chandi-Mangal*) down along the river to the sea, mention how they passed Calcutta and arrived at Betor, on the west side of Ganga. Betor was situated further down the river, south of Calcutta or 'Kolkata'. It's present location is in Howrah.

During 15th and 16th centuries. Betor became very important as an anchorage. Early Italian and Portuguese writers like, Caesar Frederick and De Barros give a vivid account of the River, and all the market places on both sides of it C.R. Wilson (*Annals of the English in Bengal*) mentions the Adi Ganga, also known as Tolly's nullah and settlement on its side. It was at one time (upto 13th century), the main stream of Ganga. Incidentally the Tolly's nullah or Adi Ganga, flows right across Calcutta.

Many ancient archaeological sites like Boral, Harinarayanpur, Deolpota belonging to early historical period have been discovered on its both sides.[7]

The 19th and early 20th century British historians like W.W. Hunter, C.R. Wilson, O'Malley, and H.E. Cotton believed that Calcutta and the regions around it have a history of many centuries. "The Portuguese anchored their ships at Betor and took their goods in shallow boats to Saptagram or Satgaon. Soon they were transacting business with the Setts and Basaks at Sutanuti"[8]. Wilson says the third and final stage of the early growth of the city happended only later when Job Charnock set up the Bengal factory at Calcutta.[9] The first and second stages being the coming of the Portuguese at Betor and the setting up of the Cotton market at Sutanuti.

Rev. James Long writing in the mid-19th Century[10] explains why the English chose the left bank instead of the more healthy right bank of the Ganga. This was because the weavers lived on the left bank.

The name Calcutta is found in Todarmall's rent roll preserved in the *Ain-i-Akbari.*[11] Though no mention of Sutanuti is found, Calcutta has been mentioned as a *pargana* of "Sarkar Saptagram". It would also be relevant to mention the existence of Tanna a Moghul Fort, on the opposite bank of Sutanuti at the site of the present Botanical gardens. Tanna[12] posed a threat to the English in the initial years.

Early Medieval and Ancient times

Deltaic Bengal has always been important in history and had been frequently mentioned in ancient literature.

The whole of Bengal was perhaps a part of Gupta Empire Pundra-vardhana Bhukti was perhaps the eastern most province. It extended from North Bengal to probably Khari in the Sunderbans region. A hoard of Gupta coins of different types had been found in Kalighat in 1783 during the time of Warren Hastings. These are now kept in the British Museum.[13]

In the Mahabharata and in the Buddhist text *Samyukta Nikaya* and later on, in *Raghuvamsam* of Kalidasa, in Dhoyi's *Pavanadutam* and *Dasakumara Charitam* of Dandin, we come across the name of Sumha and Sumhadesa. In all the texts, Sumha Desa is described as a prosperous and well populated country. Dhoyi the court poet of Lakshmana Sena gives a vivid account of the palaces, markets, and people of Sumha Desa which was always "washed by the waves of Ganga" (*Pavanadutam*)[14].

Rakhaldas Banerjee had identified Sumha Desa with the present Tribeni, Saptagram, Pandua and the Hooghly Districts.[15] D.K. Chakraborty on the other hand associates Sumha Desa with coastal Midnapur and the associated area in the north.[16]

Since all these regions are very close to Calcutta we may just as well ponder upon the question whether present Calcutta and its surrounding regions were parts of Sumha Desa once upon a time.

We know that Khari was a *vishaya* of the Gupta Empire. Khari is now in Diamond Harbour division of 24-Parganas.[17]

Bengal was the core of the Pala Empire between 8th and 11th centuries, while its periphery extended upto northern U.P. Relics of Pala period in the form of stone sculpture, Buddhist *stupas,* terracotta figures and other artfacts have been found from different corners of Bengal. Remains of Pala period had been found at Chandraketugarh at specific stratified layers of excavations. Incidentally Calcutta is only 37 kilometres from the excavated site of Chandraketugarh.

At the time of Bakhtyar Khalji's invasion of Bengal (1204-05) Lakshmana Sena, the last great Sena ruler was residing at Nadia (100 km from Calcutta). Writing in 1260 Minhaj-us-Siraj has described Nadia as a big and crowded town. It seems that Nadia was important as a residential town of the royalty in the 12th century. In the 15th century Nadia was an university town. Detailed description of the town is found in contemporary Vaishnava literature. In the century that followed Nadia was fast becoming a commercial town, once more proving the viability of South Bengal from an economic point of view (Aniruddha Roy, *Madhyayuger Bharatiya Sahar*).

Saptagram was a port of eminence in the 15th century. In the 16th century Saptagram was one of the 19 *sarkars* of the Bengal *Subah* (*Ain-i-Akbari*). There were 53 *mahals* in Saptagram. Most of these were on the eastern side of the River and they extended from south-west Murshidabad to Hatiagarh. Hatiagarh is now situated near Diamond harbour. Incidentally 'Kolkata' was a *pargana* of Saptagram. This has been mentioned earlier.

Materials of the second-half of the sixteenth century also speak of rural markets along the Hooghly River where all sorts of commodities produced by local farmers and artisans were sold.

Lastly there are references to 'Ganga', the famous market town of the ancient times as mentioned in Ptolemy's account and also in *The Periplus of the Erythrea Sea.*[18]

Where was Ganga? The question provides a lively debate. While P.C. Dasgupta identified the excavated site at Chandraketugarh with Gange. Dr. D. K. Chakraborty hesitates to accept this view. He would rather have Gange and Gangaridai placed on parts of coastal Bengal.

D.K. Chakraborty thinks that there was no gap in the historical settlements in lower Ganga region. "There was a major arterial route in West Bengal which linked the entire area from the Barind tract in the North as modern Maldah and Western Dinajpur to the Rupnarayan Delta and Coastal Midnapur in the south.... we feel that the major early historic towns and cities of West bengal were linked in various ways with these arterial lines of communication".[19]

Ibn Batuta who travelled along the Hooghly River in the mid–14th century seemed to have noticed the same thing six centuries ago, "a chain of villages lay on the banks of the river; it was as if we are going through a ma rket."[19a]

Archaeological Findings

As mentioned earlier, several antiquities have been found the Bethune College Campus while digging the foundation for the auditorium. This might throw light on the antiquity of Calcutta. These antiquities are being described below with historical background and perspective to substantiate our hypothesis that the existence of Calcutta would certainly go beyond British colonization.

Terracottas

The terracottas mainly comprise both male and female figurines besides an animal figure. On the basis of style most of these figurines belong to early medieval, period; while a few might belong to late medieval period.

Besides a number of other terracotta objects have also been collected which comprise inkpot, varieties of *chelums* both plain and decorated, balls, canee-shaped earthen lamps, hopscotch, a round terracotta ornamental object with floral design on the obverse. One of the important findings is the portion of a terracotta toy cart. It has two projected knobs which might represent the axle. The object has been badly damaged.

Pottery

The ceramics from the site mainly comprised red ware, red slipped ware, red ware with dark brown slip, grey ware with grey slip etc. These potteries are prepared out of well levigated clay and are well fired. These are mostly of fine texture and vary between thin to thick fabric. The incised designs, noticed on some of the potteries include concentric lines, notches, vertical strokes etc. Some of these pottery types are comparable to those of early medieval period as found in other places of West Bengal. The shapes of the pottery include *handi, lota,* vase with a narrow mouth, miniature votive pots, lids, lamps etc. of these mention may be made of a vase-shaped pot with narrow mouth which is very similar to a miniature amphorae. This elongated pot has similarity with a piece kept in the section from Tamluk, Midnapur (dated 2nd c. BC-1st c. AD) at the State Museum of Archaeology in Behala. The potsherds collected from the college site also seem to have similarities with those kept in the Museum. Besides other terracotta objects are found which are similar to certain terrcotta objects kept at this particular museum in texture, colour and shape; particularly with items from Mathurapur, Deolpur, Tamluk and Chandraketugarh.

Bricks of different sizes and shapes have been collected, which include both *"lakhori"* bricks and bricks of early British period. Three particular types need to be mentioned. The first is of triangular shape with semicircular upper section possibly used in columns. The second type is rectangular in shape. The third type includes round shapes ones with jutting tangs which probably formed part of pillars. It may be noted these sort of bricks were in use in some of the late medieval temples as cornice elements.

Glass and Porcelain

Varieties of glass pieces mostly, of broken bottles, have been collected which belong to late medieval period. The colours are black, olive green, green and blue. Certain pieces are translucent with mica shine finish. Porcelain pieces are mostly of Chinese origin. One of the pieces is of very high quality whereas rest are of usual types. Some of these pieces can be dated to late medieval period.

Apart from the evidence from Bethune College few objects have also been recovered from the area in North Calcutta near Narendra Krishna Dev Park, while digging the tunnel for the Metro Rail. These are presently displayed at the Metro Station at Shovabazar. Of these the terracotta figures of an ascetic deserves special mention. It is a good example of syncretic cultural traits of two different pantheons. This monk-like figure seems to have certain Central Asian traits. This male figure was unearthed in mid-1992 from the region around N.K. Dev. Park. The pot and the lamp displayed at Shovabazar Metro Station look similar to those desciibed in this article both in texture and shape. The pot was recovered in early 1993. The above fact is revealed by the Metro Railway authorities.

Other Archaeological Sites near Calcutta

The site (Bethune College campus, Calcutta) from where these items are collected is surrounded by almost six archaeological sites–Mahanad in dist Hooghly, Chandra Ketugarh in dist. North 24-Parganas, Harinarayanpur, Deolpota, and Boral in South 24-parganas within a radius of 32 km to 40 km. Apart from these a large number of archaeological sites belonging to early historical period such as Haroa, Tamluk, Tilda, Bahiri, Panna etc. have been reported from South Bengal. Some of these site can even be pushed back to the chalcolithic phase.

Certain expansion did take place in different phases, and settlements must have reached near Calcutta to some extent. At least the settlement might have extended 5 km in each phase and thus settlement is possible in and around Calcutta in the early Medieval times. Dilip K. Chakraborty's statement in this context is relevant. "The Bhagirathi of course never witnessed a gap in the sequence of historical occupation from the early historical phase onwards".[20]

One should keep in mind that lower Bengal had been in the past devastated periodically by tidal floods. Such a coastal flood occurred in the 16th century. There was yet another in 1737[21]. In that year a terrible hurricane along with an earthquake wrought havoc in Calcutta. Vivid descriptions of the disaster are to the found in C.R. Wilson's *Early Annals of the English in Bengal* and in *Calcutta Past and Present* by Kathleen Blechynden. Wilson quoted from a letter written by Francis Russell, a member of the Calcutta Council and an eye-witness of the cyclone, and also from the *Gentleman's Magazine* "On September 30th last, happended a furious hurricane in the Bay of Bengal attended with a very heavy rain which raised 15 inches of water in 5 hours and a violent earthquake which threw down abundance of houses ... the storm reached 60 leagues up the river". Another contemporary, Archdeacon Hyde had mentioned (quoted by Wilson), "deluge of mud and wreckage washed over the settlement by the 40 ft. tide, when the ebb of the Hooghly had been forced back". We may, therefore, surmise that settlements with their necessary material evidence must have got buried, time to time under the alluvium, due to such floods. This may be a possible reason why ample archaelogical evidence are yet untraceable in Calcutta.

Moreover, Calcutta had never been exposed to any kind of archaeological excavation. Though there was large scale digging during the construction of the Metro Railways, historical findings could not be recovered, partly due to ignorance and mostly because entirely different method of digging by technical devices which prevented any kind of recovery of materials.

We have already seen that there are ample literary and historical evidence to suggest that lower Bengal had always been a prosperous and well-populated region. The navigability of the river Ganga (both the Hooghly and Adi-Ganga in the past) and nearness of the sea made this area socially and economically important.

ACKNOWLEDGEMENT

We are grateful to Sarvashi S.B. Ota, S. Maiti, and others of the Archaeological Survey of India for their valuable help and guidance and for cooperation to Shri S. Nan. Thanks are also due to Dr. N. Goswami of Ashutosh Museum Calcutta, Dr. R. Chatterjee of Calcutta University, Shri T. Ghatak of C.M.D.A., and Shri S.C. Banerjee and his colleagues from Metro Railway, Calcutta.

REFERENCE

1. Chakraborty, Adhir. Director of Archieves, Govt. of West Bengal: List of Documents on Calcutta Vol-1 1764-1800.
2. Letter from J.E.D. Bethune to Major General Sir J. Littler, Deputy Governor of Bengal: West Bengal State Archives, General, Education, Consultation 16/20.
3. Bethune College File No. VII serial no. 659 date 21st Nov. 1916.
4. Wilson, C.R. *The Early Annals of English in Bengal.*
5. Ibid.
6. Basak, G.D. Kalighat and Calcutta. *Calcutta Review* Vol. 92 No. 184, April 1891.
7. Wilson, op cit
8. Basak, op cit
9. Wilson op cit
10. Long: Rev. James, *Peeps into Social Life of Calcutta.*
11. Banerjee R.D. *Bangalar Ithihas.*
12. Hunter: W.W. *History of British India,* Vol. II.
13. Banerjee op cit *Journal of Asiatic Society of Bengal 1884.* Part-II, also Archaeological Survey Reports Vol-III.
14. Majumdar: R.C. *Ancient History of Bengal.*
15. Banerjee, R.D. J.A.S.B. 1909, and N.L.Dey: *The Geographical Dictionary of Anciant and Mediaval times.* Bhattacharya A. *Historical Geography.*
16. Chakraborty D.K. *Archaeology of Eastern India: Chotanagpur* West Bengal.
17. Majumdar. op cit
18. Ibid.
19. Chakraborty: op cit

19(a) Tchitcharov A. India: *Changing Economic Structure in the sixteenth to eightenth century.*

20. Chakraborty: op cit.
21. Blychynden, K. *Calcutta Past and Present.*

Traditional Practice and Knowledge of Wild Plants among the Ethnic Communities of Garhwal Himalaya

PRADEEP MOHAN SAKLANI*

Introduction

The basic instinct for obtaining food resources from the immediate environment developed with the evolution of prehistoric man and gradually with the time the exploitative strategies changed for expanding and enlarging the food spectrum during the prehistoric period itself. It has been shown that man—animal and man—plant relationship is similar to modern domestication and it must have tended to occur throughout the Pleistocene, wherever this was the most profitable economic strategy in the prevailing circumstances[1]. These observations definitely suggest that despite the transition from hunting-gathering to agriculture and domestication, the practice of collecting wild edible and the medicinal plants and the hunting of animals still provided a most viable and a nutritive food base. In recent years with the advancement of archaeobotany and archaeozoology, the prehistoric and ancient plant and animal economy has been well documented and reconstructed fairly well and a vast body of literature is available on these aspects[2].

The plant and animal economy which assumed importance in ancient India can be judged from the fact that a whole section of Vedic and Later Vedic text is devoted to plants and animals.

In the Rigveda there are references to 99 species of *aushadhi* (herbs or plants). The Yajursamhita refers to a large number of plants of sacrificial and medicinal use. The *Kalpa sutra* of Atharvaveda refers to an exhaustive list of 288 varieties of plants and 579 plants respectively and mentions their botanical characteristic and ingredient. The Brahamanas also rafers to the plants of sacrificial use. Besides this we get an exhaustive and minutest details about the anatomical parts of plants, their classification, life cycle, medicinal and aromatic value etc. These above references suggest that the flora and fauna attained great economic importance for an early man and during the ancient period it became an integral part of his daily life and even entered into ritual and religious life. In this context, it may not be out of place to mention that the Ayurvedic system is entirely based on the folk experimentation on medicinal plants and there are several other type of folk utilization[3].

In recent years, however, due to the rapid loss of a rich biodiversity of the country, particularly of the Himalaya, some of the most important wild and the medicinal plants have gradually vanished from the surface of the earth. This alarming situation has drawn the attention of scientists. Therefore, in view of this state of affair some very exhaustive studies have been done to document the

* Department of History, Ancient Indian History including Culture and Archaeology, HNB Garhwal University, Srinagar, Garhwal, 246 174 (U.P.)

taxonomic and the biological worth of the wild plants.[4] As a result of such studies, attention has been focussed to conduct an ethnobotanical survey. Based on the ethnobotanical studies in various parts of the country including Himalayan part, it has been observed that the basic subsistence economy of the tribal and ethnic communities living in the marginal areas in the Himalayas is still based on the use of wild plants which supplement their various other food requirements[5]. In an another important study, the role and utility of wild plants in the tribal communities of North East Himalayas have also been conducted. Based on this particular study it has been shown that the tribal communities besides practicing agriculture still prefer to procure the wild plants because, they not only provide an additional and nutritive food base, but also meet the diverse human needs of taste, ritual, medicine etc.[6]

In this respect the exploratory survey in recent years in Garhwal Himalaya have also highlighted some of the most valuable unknown species of wild and medicinal plants. Similarly the ethnomedicinal plants of Himachal Pradesh have also been explored[7].

Therefore, following the ethnobotanical work done by Gaur and others, the present paper has also attempted to expand the scope of ethnobotanical work by studying the traditional practices associated with the exploitation of wild plants prevailing amongst the present day ethnic communities of Yamuna valley.

Study Area

The Yamuna valley (Long.78° 74′ to 78° 31′ E. Lat. E. 30° 31′ to 30° 01′N) covering an area of 8280 sq.km forms the westernmost flank of the Garhwal Himalaya (Fig.1). Administratively, the entire region of Yamuna valley comprises three districts of Uttarkashi, Tehri and Dehradun in U.P. Himalaya. This valley right from the high altitude region to the foothills is inhabited by three distinct ethnic groups belonging to the areas of Rawain called Ranwalta, Jaunsar-Bawar called Jaunsaries and Jaunpur known as Jaunpuria respectively.

Methodology

The present study-survey of the wild plants has been-carried out in the interior parts of the Yamuna valley of Garhwal Himalaya. The traditional use of wild and medicinal plant were identified following the usual methods adopted by others. Simultaneously the older people living in the area, the shepherds and the local medicinal men called *vaidyas* and others who had the knowledge of plants, were consulted for their use by villagers. During the field trips locals were also employed in order to get acquainted with the traditional prescription, the use and vernacular names of plant species etc. First hand information was obtained from them about the plants and were subsequently identified with the help of taxonomist.

Uses of Medicinal Plants

It has been recorded during the field study that the ethnic communities of Yamuna valley has learnt and developed a traditional knowledge of identifying and using the wild plants for the edible and medicinal purposes from their ancestors.

The investigation has shown that the vegetation around the village or nearby forest is rich in medicinally important taxa. The knowledge of the village-folk in the traditional medicine practices is a unique combination of folklore and superstitions As a normal practice the traditional knowledge of the medicinal value of the plant species is kept as a guarded secret. It has been observed that natives of this area can identify the plants used for medicinal purpose. But the practice of traditional medicine is only by the local *vaidya* in the village who is well versed with the identification, extraction of medicinally rich organic compounds from the different parts of the plant and its application to particular disease or disorder. Therefore, owing to the great utility of the plants in providing them not only sustenance but cure also, most of the plants species have assumed a special importance and they have entered into their rituals and religious ceremonies.

The following are the details of the plants used for various purpose.The vernacular name is given in the parenthesis(Table 1).

Aesculus indica–vern. : ***Panger***

The seed paste is applied in case or rheumatic pains; flower of seed is given as an antidote for intestinal worms.

Aconitum atrox–vern.: ***Mithu or Kidya Moru***

It is found throughout in the subalpine and Alpine zone. The tubers are roasted in ash and smoked with tobacco at bed time to relieve asthma. The root paste is fried in 'ghee' (clarified butter) and rubbed on the skin for the treatment rheumatism, neuralgia and paralysis. The inhabitants of the upper Yamuna valley also use the roots in cauterishing snake bites. Reference to the use of this plant has also been found in a hundred year-old document (written in Garhwali dialect) showing that purified roots were used for several diseases like phthisis, dyspepsia, rheumatic fever and purpeural fever[7] (Fig.2). Interestingly, the use of this plant is also refferred to in the Adiparva of Mahabharata.

Acacia catechu–vern.: ***Khair***

The decoction of wood and bark is given in coryza, cough and inflamation of throat. It is given in diarrhoea and applied externally on the mouth in stomatitis. Reference to *Acacia suma* is also found in Adiparva and Anusasanaparva of the Mahabharata.

Aconitum violaceum–vern.: ***Dhudi Attes***

The root paste is applied externally in case or rheumatic joint pain.

Anemone polyanthes–vern.: ***Ratanjot***

The decoction of seeds is used for inducing vomiting in case of food poisoning and the root paste is applied externally in the treatment of eczema.

Adhatoda vasica–vern.: ***Bansu***

The root bark of *Adhatoda vasica* is given in fever. Warmed leaves are applied for relieving rheumatic pains and in inflammatory swellings. The extracts of root is given in epistaxis, cough and asthama. It is given to check blood in cough and asthama with honey. The application of this plant is mentioned in Dronaparva and Karanaparva of the Mahabharata.

Anogeissus latifolia–vern.: ***Bakala***

The root of this plant is burnt to ash and given to women in purpueral fever. Decoction of bark is given as an antidote of diarrhoea.

Reference of this plant is also found in Adiparva the Mahabharata.

Azadirachta indica–vern.: ***Neem***

The bark paste is applied to wounds in scabies and urticaria. Decoction of bark is given in fever. Leaf of juice mixed with salt is taken as antidote for cannabis poisoning. Reference to this plant is also found in Anusasanaparva of the Mahabharata.

Angelica glauca–vern.: ***Choru***

The leaves are is used in the treatment of sore tonsils. The root decoction is given to the cattle along with water to relive severe cases of poisoning.

Zanthoxyl um alatum–vern.: ***Timru***

For the medicinal purpose various parts of this plants are widely used in day–to–day life by the inhabitants of this area. The seeds are used in abdominal trouble and eyes, ear ailments and also in leucoderma. The juice obtained from the fruit is frequently employed to relieve severe toothache, twigs are used as tooth brush. The most interesting use of the bark of this plant is for intoxicating fishes. The detailed use of this plant in fishing practice has been given in the following pages.

Berberis aristata–vern.: ***Kasmoi or Kingor***

An extract obtained from the root bark is used in the treatment of the infection of the eyes. The root decoction is given internally in fever menorrhagia and jaundice.

Bupleurum falcatum–vern.: ***Janglee Jeera***

The root is used in liver trouble and also usc daiphoratic.

Buchanania lanzan–vern.: ***Piyal***

The kernel paste is applied in skin diseases and also given in causes of cough.

The reference to this plant is also found in Aranyakaparva of the Mahabharata.

Callicarpa macrophylla–vern.: ***Daiyya***

The fruits are chewed in apthea and the warmed leaves are applied on body swellings and rheumatic arthritis.

The use of this plant is also mentioned in Aranyakaparva of Mahabharata.

Coriaria nepalensis–vern.: ***Gangeru***

The major concentration of this plant is confined to the Tons valley bordering Himachal and Yamuna valley. The leaf–juice is applied to cuts and wounds. The fruit is given as anema. The seeds of this plant are also considered narcotic in character.

Corydalis govaniana–vern.:***Bhutkeshri***

The decoction of roots is an efficient remedy for fever, liver trouble and suppressed urination. Root paste is applied in causes of syphilis . The dried leaves are used as an insecticide.

Holarrhena antidysentrica–vern.: ***Kuri or Kurchi***

The bark of this plant after mixing with the bark of another plant, *Myrica esculenta*, is given to children in case of fever and diarrhoea. The bark is also used in dysentery. Seeds are given to children suffering from gastroenteritis. Decoction of seeds is given in case of cholera.

The charcoal remains of this plant have been reported from period III at Hastinapur belonging to the second half of the 5th century BC.[8]

It is not possible to say whether the barks were kept by the inhabitants as charcoal or firewood which turned into charcoal in course of time[9]. The wood of *kurchi* is reported to have been used mainly for carving and toy making in and around Hastinapur[10]. This tree is well known for the special property of its bark which is used as a tonic and febri, fuge and in dysentery[11]. Beads made of this wood are worn around the neck as a medicinal charm[12].

Lychnis indica–vern.: ***Bacrolya***

The juice of leaves and young shoots is applied in eye infections.

Megacarpaea polyandra–vern.: ***Barmoola***

The decoction of roots is given in the treatment of and dyspepsia.

Podophyllum hexandrumvern.: ***Bankakhri***

The root paste is applied in urticaria on ulcers and in hoof and mouth diseases of cattle.

Prinsepia utilis–vern.: ***Bhekal***

Root decoction is used to check stomach disorders. The seed oil is taken in bowel complaints and applied externally on burns.

Rhododendron hypenanthum–vern.: ***Bhotiachai***

Ersatz tea is made from the leaves of this plant by the *Jaad* (Bhotiya) tribes, which is also considered useful in general cold headache and fever.

Rhus javanica–vern.: ***Arkhoi***

The bark paste is applied on the body swelling; seeds are given in bowel complaints and in colic disorder.

Saussurea obvallata–vern.: ***Brahma Kamal***

This is one of the rare plant identified under the endangered category of plants. Locally the flowers are fried with butter and filled in the bottles which are applied for massage at the time of rheumatic arthritis.

Semecarpus anacardium–vern.: ***Bhilao***

The black resin of pericarp is applied on the burns. The inhabitant of lower Yamuna valley used the fried fruit with the oil of *Sesamum orientale* and applied in wounds and abscesses.

The smoke of the nut is considered benefecial in haemorrhoids. The nut is rubbed with water and rheumatic arthritis.

The reference of this plant is found in Aranyakaparva of Mahabharata.

Stephania glabra–vern.: ***Ghindaru***

The juice of the roots of this plant is given to children in fever and dysentery. Roots are put under running water for 10 to 12 hours and cooked. This preparation is given as a curative for asthma.

Viola pilosa–vern.: ***Vanapsa***

The leaves are boiled in the same manner as tea and the decoction is used as a remedy for cold, malaria and lung troubles. Infusion of leaves is also given in suppressed urination.

Ziziphus mauritiana–vern.: ***Ber***

The decoction of root bark is given in diarrhoea. Infusion of root bark is given in fever. The fruit is given as a remedy for cough.

The use of this plant is mentioned in Adiparva of Mahabharata.

Consumption of Wild Food Plants

The following are the most common wild species from different altitudes of Yamuna valley. Wild plants supplement the food requirments of the inhabitants. The following is a brief description of the use of wild plant as revealed by the local informant consulted during the field work (Table 2).

Angelica glauca–vern.: ***Choru***

The wild fruits and aromatic root of this plant are added to food to give flavour. It is further believed that when the roots are used as seasoning agent for curry, it provides good strength and vigour to women after delivery.

Allium humile–vern.: ***Jimboo***

The young aromatic leaves are used as green vegetable and after drying it is used as a condiment.

Ceropegia bulbosa–vern.: ***Gilothi***

The fleshy leaves are eaten raw and the tuberous roots which are sweet in taste are taken after boiling in water. It is considered to be a good digestive tonic.

Commelina benghalensis–vern.: ***Kansura***

Tender shoots and leaves are cooked as vegetable. The tender leaves are cooked with gram flour, spices and fried in the mustard oil.

Cichorium inlybus–vern.: ***Dudhelu***

The young leaves are eaten raw as a salad and the leaves are also cooked as vegetable.

Gonatanthus pumilus–vern.: ***Jangli Pindalu***

The tuberous roots and leaves after thoroughly washing and prolonged boiling are used as a vegetable. Leaves are coated with gram flour and cooked in oil.

Ipomoea hederacea–vern.: ***Beduli***

The ripe fruits of this plants are eaten.

Indigofera heterantha–vern.: **Sakina**

The flowers of this plant are thoroughly washed, boiled and cooked as vegetable. The pulverized flowers are sandwiched with chapaties.

Meqacarpaea polyandra–vern.: ***Barmoola***

The tender leaves are used as vegetable. Stem is also eaten raw as a salad.

Nasturtium palustre–vern.: ***Gaderi***

The tender leaves of the plant are eaten as a pot herb increase appetite. In remote part of the Yamuna valley where the fresh vegetables are scarce or are not available fresh leaves of Gaderi are picked and eaten with potato, *dal* or with meat soup.

Paeonia emodi–vern.: ***Chandrain***

The young shoots and leaves are very tasty This is usually taken after it is throughly washed, boiled and roasted. It serves to the natives as the most nutritive food–vegetable and is considered very useful after child birth. The leaves are generally stored by the inhabitants for the winter season. After washing and boiling the paste preparation is sandwiched between chapatis.

Podchyllum hexandrum–vern.: ***Bankakhari***

Raw fruits are eaten. The fruits and seeds are used in fermenting local liquor *(Sur)* by the inhabitant of Yamuna valley.

Pueraria tuberosa–vern.: ***Saral***

The large tuberous roots are sweetish, when young and eaten raw. The older ones are thorougly washed, boiled and cooked as vegetable. The tender shoots are also edible.

Rhododendron arboreum–vern.: ***Burans***

The tree of Burans is widespeard in the entire region of Uttarakhand. The flowers are eaten raw as salad or ground to prepare sauce. If flowers are taken in a large amount it causes intoxication. It is also one of the most economic plant for the preparation of cold drinks which has a slightly acrid *cum* sweet taste.

Sorbaria tomentosa–vern.: ***Ban Tamakhoo***

Flowers, spikes are used to flavour the tobacco.

Silene vulgaris–vern.: ***Bakrolya***

Young shoots and leaves are cooked as vegetable by shepherds and by the pastoralist.

Taraxacum officinale–vern.: ***Dudhee***

The leaves are thoroughly washed, boiled and cooked with salt and used as vegetable. The roots are often eaten raw as a salad or boiled and eaten as vegetable. The leaves and flowers used in preparing alcoholic drinks by the inhabitants.

Typhonium diversifoliumvern.: ***Nakdoon***

The use of this plant is very interesting and useful. The parts of the roots are used as energetic by the inhabitants of upper part of the Yamuna valley. A small quantity of the root powder is mixed with honey for avoiding the feeling of hunger for a prolonged period. Presently the wild plant of *nakdoon* is found primarily in the high altitude zone of the Yamuna valley.

Polygonatum verticillatum–vern.: ***Devringal***

The fleshy white tuberous roots which are sweet in taste and eaten raw. Sometime young shoots are cooked as vegetable.

Allum wallichii–vern.: ***Ladu***

The young leaves are cooked as a green vegetable and in dried condition, they are used as condiments. The detailed ethnobotanical description shows that these very natural plant provides a most vital source of energy and as well as medicinal purpose. The use of wild edible and medicinal plants have became compimentary to the basic necessity of the ethnic community in such a manner that they have almost become a life sustaining system for them and therefore, have almost become a part of their rituals and worship.

Conclusion

So far as their use in past we do not have direct records of these plants from any excavated archaeological sites in Garhwal, due to unavailability of plant remains. However, the reference of a few above mentioned plants in ancient literature is an indicator of their great importance during ancient periods and similarly the direct evidence of a few plant remains from an early levels of an excavated site elsewhere in India as pointed above substantiate the literary references. Similarly the continued widespread use of these species of wild and edible and medicinal plants by the present day community in the Yamuna vallev confirms the archaeological evidence and the literary reference regarding their specific use and utility.

Based on this observation it may be stated that the rich biotic community of wild plants must have provided an important source of sustenance to the ancient tribal groups inhabiting these mountainous tract from the earlist time and to the other nomadic tribes of Khasas who ventured into these inaccessible and most tough terrains of Himalaya. Therefore, it may be said that during protohistoric and historic times the inhabitants must have had experimented with the wild plants and might have substantially substituted their food requirement with the available nutritative wild plants. growing in this region. In this regard the use of *Typhonium diversifolium (Nakdoon)* seems interesting since the intake of such plant avoids hunger for considerable period and because of its unique properties it must have been exploited and used even during the ancient times very frequently by the pastoral nomads who had to move a long distance along with their livestocks.

Table 1 Use Of Medicinal Plants By The Inhabitants Of Yamuna Valley

S.No	Plant species	Name	Altitude	Plant part used	Used in Disease
1	2	3	4	5	6
1.	*Aescuisus indica*	Panger	1500–3000 Mt.	Seed	Rheumatic pain
2.	*Aconitum atrox*	Mithu or Kidiva Mom	32004200Mt.	Root	Astama and Snake bites
3.	*Acacia catechu*	Khair	Uptp 600 Mt.	Bark	Diarrhoea
4.	*Aconitum violacem*	Dhudi Atees	32004200 Mt.	Root	Rnumatic pain
5.	*Anemone polyantnes*	Ratanjot	30OO 4200 Mt.	Seeds	Inducing vomiting
6.	*Adhatodavasica*	Bansu	Up to 1500 Mt.	Root Bark	Fever
7.	*Anogeissus latifolia*	Bakala	Upto l000 Mt.	Root	Puerperal Fever
8.	*Azardirachta indica*	Neem	Upto 800 Mt.	Bark and Leaves	Fever
9.	*Angelica glauca*	Chonu	25003500 Mt.	Fruits	Dvspepsia
10.	*Zanthoxyium alatum*	Timru	Upto 600 Mt.	Seeds/Leaves	Eye and Ear ailments
11.	*Berberis aristata*	IKashmoi Kingor	600–2000 Mt.	Root	Leas,es used for Fishing, Fever and Jaundice
12.	*Bupleurum falatum*	Janglee Jeera	1200–4000 Mt.	Root	Liver trouble
13.	*Buchanania lanzo:ı*	Piyal	Upto 1600 Mt.	Kernel	Skin diseases
14.	*Callicarpa Macrophylla*	Daiyya	600–1500 Mt.	Leaves	Body Swelling
15.	*Coriaria Nepalensis*	Gangeru	?000–3000 Mt.	Leaves	Cuts and wounds
16.	*Corydalis Govanisana*	Bhulkeshri	30004500 Mt.	Root	Fever and Liver Truble
17.	*Holarrhena Antidysentrica*	KuriKurchi	Upto 1000 Mt.	Seeds/Bark	Cholera. dysentery
18.	*Lychnis Indica*	Bacroly	16003300 Mt.	Leaves and Youn Shoots	Eyes Intectery
19.	*Megacarpea polyandra*	Barmoola	2500–3500 Mt.	Root	Fever
20.	*Podophyliun Hexandrum*	Bankakhri	28004500 Mt.	Root	Cattle Diaese (Hoop)
21.	*Prinsepia Utilis*	Bhekal	12002500 Mt.	Root/Seed	Stomach Disorders/Burns
22.	*Rhododendoron Hypenathum*	Bhotiachai	3000–4500 Mt.	Leaves	Colds and Fever

1	2	3	4	5	6
24.	*Saussurea Obvallata*	Brahma Kamal	37004900 Mt.	Flowers	Urinary Truble
25.	*Semecarpus*	Bhilao	Up to 1200 Mt.	Fuuits	Wounds
26.	*Stephania Glabra*	Ghindar	Up tŏ 200 Mt.	Root	Fever and Dysentery
27.	*Viola Pilosa*	Vanapsa	1800–3000 Mt.	Leaves	Cold/Maleria
28.	*Zizphus mauritiana*	Ber	Up to 600 Mt.	Root Bark	Diarrohea

Table 2 Composition Pattern of Wild Plants by Inhabitants of Valley

S.No	Plant species	Name	Altitude	Plant part used	Used in Disease
1	2	3	4	5	6
1.	*Angelica glauca*	Choru	2500–3500 Mt.	Friuts and Aromatic Roots	food
2.	*Allium humile*	jimboo	3000–4000 Mt.	Leavs	Vegetable
3.	*Ceropegia bulbosa*	Gilothi	1200–1600 Mt.	Leaves	Boiling in water take as a to nic
4.	*Commelina benghalensis*	Kansura	Up to 800 Mt.	Shoot and Keaves	Cooked Vegetable
5.	*Cichorium inlybus*	Dudhelu	Up to 2400 Mt.	Leaves	Salad/Cooked Vegetable
6.	*Gonatanthus pumilus*	Jangli Pindalu	1500–2500 Mt.	Tuberous roots/ Leaves	Cooked Vegetable
7.	*Impomopa hederacea*	Beduli	Up to 2000 Mt.	Fruit	Food
8	*Indigofera heterantha*	Sakina	1500–2700 Mt.	Flowers	Cooked Vegetable
9	*Meqacarpaea polyandra*	Barmoola	2500–3500 Mt.	Leaves/Stem	Cooked Vegetable/ Salad
10	*Nasturtium palustre*	Gaderi	Up to 3000 Mt.	Leaves	Cooked Vegetable with potato
11	*Paeonia emodi*	Chandrian	1500–2700 Mt.	Young shoots/ Leaves	Roasted as Food
12	*Podohyllum hexandruim*	Bankakhri	3000–4500 Mt.	Fruits/Seeds	Food/Fermentation for local liquor
13	*Pueraria tuberosa*	Saral	Up to 1200 Mt.	Tuber	Cooked Vegetable
14	*Rhododendron arboreium*	Burans	1500–3000 Mt.	Flowers	Salad/Sauce
15	*Sorbaria tomentosa*	Ban Tamakhoo	2000–3000 Mt.	Flowers	Smoke
16	*Silene vulgaris*	Bakrolya	1500–4000 Mt.	Shoots and Leaves	Cooked vegetable
17	*Taraxacum officinals*	Dhundhee	2000–3500 Mt.	Leaves, Roots/ leaves and Flowers	Coocked Vegetable/ Preparing local Liquor
18	*Typhonium diversifolium*	Nakdoon	2300–3600 Mt.	Roots swollen	Food
19	*Polygontium verticillatum*	Devringal	2000–4000 Mt.	Tuberous roots/shoots	Food/cooked vegetable
20	*Allum Wallichii*	Ladu	2500–4000 Mt.	Leaves	Cookes vegetable

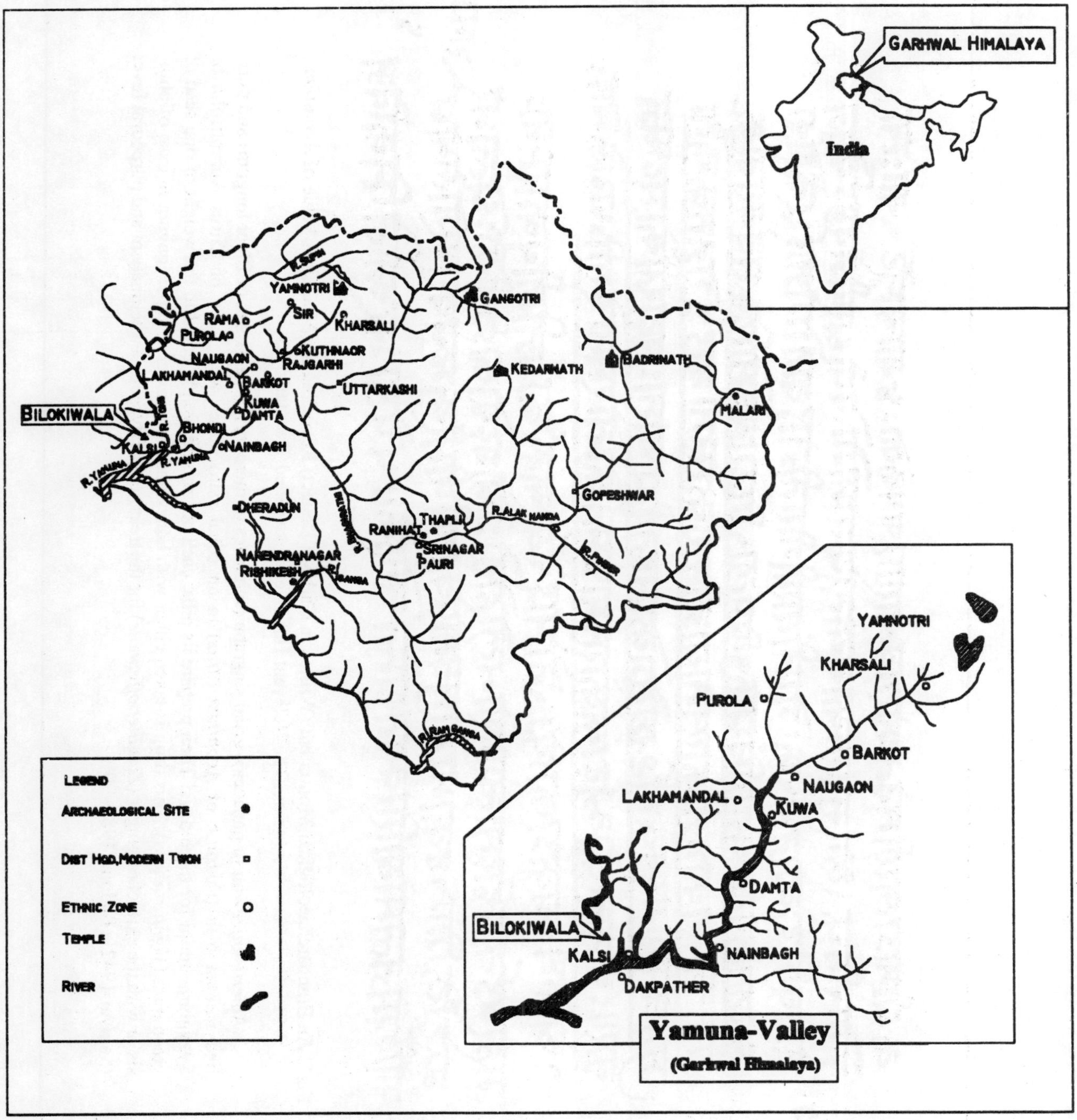

Fig 1 Prinsipal Archaeological Sites With Ethnic Zone In Yamuna Valley

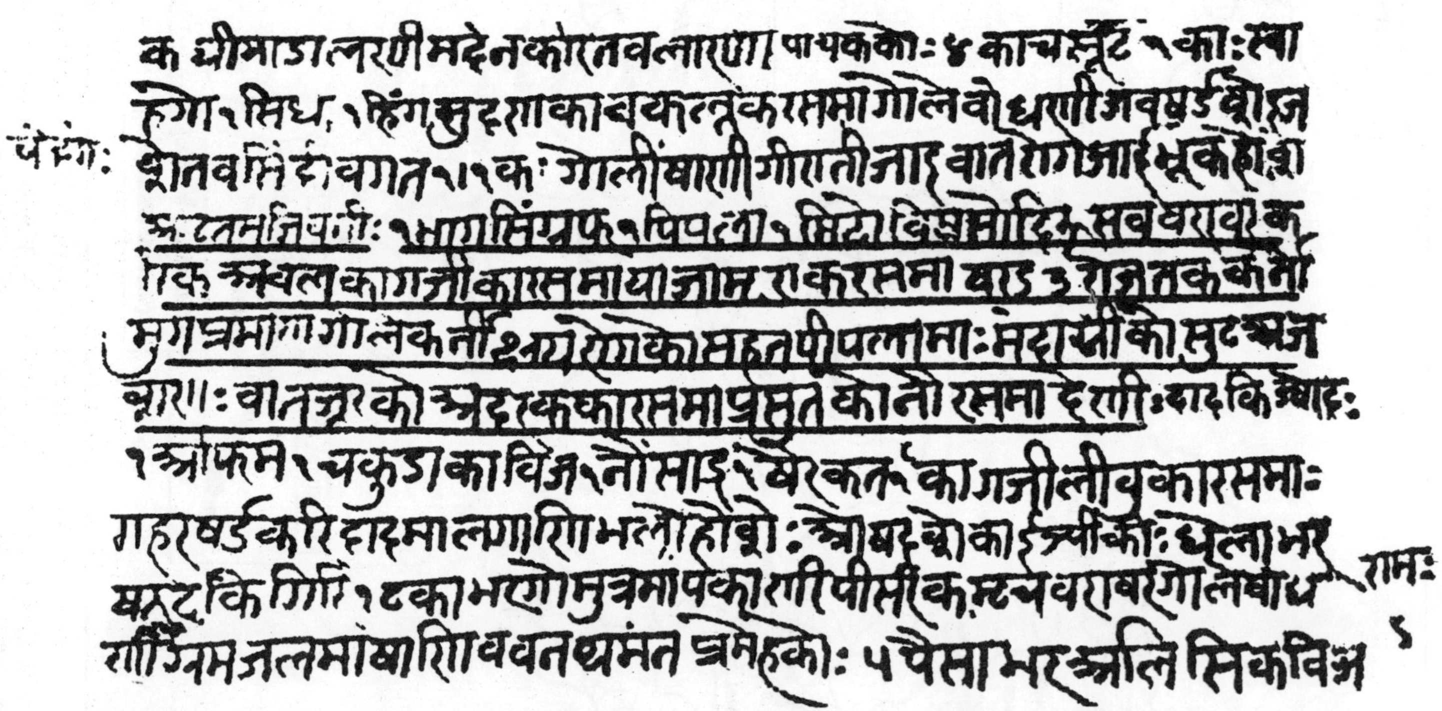

Fig 2 An Ethnoarchaeological Monument (Written in Garhwal Dialect) Revealing the Medicinal Value of *Aconitum Atrox*. The Relevant Has Been Underlined Translated As:

'*Ameritsanjeevani* (a panacea): grind singraph (sulphates of mercury), pipal (roots of PIper longum) and purified meetha bish (rhizome of *Aconitum atrox*) in an equal ratio either with juice of Citrus Aurantifolia or Syzygiumcumini for three days. Then prepare its pills, each pill should weight equal to the weight of one seed of greengram (*Vigna radiata*). This drug is taken either with honey and root power of piper longum in case of phthsis or with the extract of ginger (*Zingiber officinale*) for the treatment of dyspepsia; rheumatism and purpeural fever (Samvat 1942) (Badoni, 1989–90).

REFERENCE

1. Higgs, E.S. and M.R. Jarman 1969. The origins of agricul ture: a reconsideration. *Antiquity* 43. pp. 31-41.
2. Alur. K.R. 1990. *Studies in Indian Archaeology and Palaeontology,* Dharwad. Shrihans Prakashana; Badam G.L. 1986. *Preliminary Report on the Faunal Remains from Chalcolithic Daimabad, Maharashtra* Archaeological studies, Varanasi, pp. 93-100; Buth, G.M. 1986. SEM. Study as an Aid in identifications of caryopses of Triticum, *Journal Economic Taxonomic Botany*, 3, pp. 537-540; Chanchala, 1984. Wild Plant Remains from Arehaeological sites A Palaeobotanical Palaeological and Palaeoethnobotanical study. Ph.D. Dissertation, Lucknow University. Clason; A.T. 1974. Archaeological study in India in *J.E. Lohuizenode Leeuw and J. M. M. ubaghas* Sourth Asian Archeaeology 1973 *(Eds.) pp. 78-89, Leiden:* E. J. Brill. Harlan, J.R.1977.The Origins of Cereal Agriculture in A.Reed. Charles (ed). *Origens of Agriculture,* Mouton Publishers.
3. Chopra, R.N., Nayar, S.L. and Chopra, I.C. 1956. *Glossary of Indian Medicinal Plants.* CSIR, New Delhi.
4. Gaur,R.D.1987. A Contribution to the Flora of Srinagar Garhwal. *J. Econ. Tax Bot*, 9: 31 pp. 63. Gaur. R.D. and P.B. Singh 1994. Ethnomedicinal Plants of Mandi District. Himachal Pradesh. (in Press), Kirtikar, K.R. and B.D. Basu 1918. *Indian Medicinal Plants* Pt II (Allahabad); Maikhuri, R.K. 1991. EcoEnergetic Analysis of Animal Husbundry in Traditional Societies of India, *Energy* Vol. 17. No. 10, 959 967. Badoni, A.K. 1989-90. Remarks on the High Altitudinal Medicinal Plants of Garhwal Himalaya. *Journal of Himalayan Studies And Regional Development.* Vol. 13-14. pp, 37-45. Bhatt, K.C. and Gaur, R.D. 1992. A contribution to the ethnobotany of Rajis of Pithoragarh district of Uttar Pradesh, *Himalaya Acta, Bot. India,* 20, pp. 76-83. Gaur, R.D., Semwal, J.K. and Tiwari, J.K. 1984. A Survey of High Altitude Medicinal Plants of Garhwal Himalaya. *B.M.E.B.R.* 4: 102 116. Gaur, R.D. and Tiwari, J.K. 1987. Some little known Medicinal plants of Garhwal Himalaya An ethnobotanical Study. in *Medicinal and poisnous plants of the tropics* Leewenberg (ed.) Netherland pp. 139-192. Kajale, op cit. Kapoor, S.K. and Sarin, Y.K. 1977. Useful medicinal ferns of Jammu and Kashmir, *Indian Drugs.* 14 pp. 136-140. Murty, M.L.K. 1985. The use of Plant Food by some Hunter Gatherer Communities in Andhra Pradesh in *Recent Advances in Indo Pacific Prehistory* pp. 329-336, New Delhi: Oxfcrd IBH, Uniyal, M.R. 1977. *Uttarakhand Vanaushadhi Digdarshi Ka Cerimh,* New Delhi.
6. Maikhuri, op. cit.
7. Badoni 1989-90 op. cit.
8. Lal, B.B. 1954. Excavation of Hastinapur and other Explorations in the upper Ganga and Sutlej Basins New Light on the dark Age Between the end of the Harappa culture and the Early Historical, period' *Ancient India,* No. 10 and 11, pp. 4–151.
9. Ibid
10. Trotter,H. 1944. *The Common Commercial Timber of India and their Uses.* Dehra Dun.
11. Kartikar and Basu op. cit.
12. Gupta, B.L. 1928. *Forest Flora of Chakrata Dehra Dun and Saharanpur Forest Division*, United Provinces 3rd ed. Calcutta. p. 316.

Identification of Archaeological Sites From Space

P. V. SATHE AND A.S. GAUR*

Introduction

Though the word remote sensing literally means detection of objects from a distance, it is usually used in a restricted sense to mean the study of the earth from space using satellites and aircrafts with the help of electromagnetic radiation. Before the 1970s remote sensing was largely confined to the study of aerial photographs while satellites were considered useful only for astronomy and communication purposes. The technique of aerial photography was known to man from the last century but it became popular only during the Second World War when infrared photographic films were developed. World War II also ushered total photographing of Western Europe which later became an important tool of archaeological exploration since it showed many deserted villages of the 11th, 12th and 14th centuries[1]. Full potential of remote sensing was, however, realized only after satellites started sending digital images of earth in different spectral channels especially in infrared and microwave parts of electromagnetic radiation. Remote sensing has already become an indispensable part of most disciplines of the earth sciences such as meteorology, geology, forestry, agriculture, town planning and a host of other pure and applied branches. Its use in archaeology has been restricted mainly to the study of simple aerial photographs. Infrared False Colour Photography is yet not used extensively. The aim of the present paper is to familiarize archaeologists with new trends in remote sensing with their possible implications for archaeological exploration. We shall not dwell on details on the applications of aerial photography except to enlist its obvious advantages in this section because they are by now well known to the archaelogists. We shall concentrate more on satellite-based remote-sensing application where an 'image' rather than a 'photograph' of a terrain is studied.

It is well known that remote sensing is the only non-destructive method of earth's exploration. Archaeologists in particular, cannot preserve a site as well as study it through ground-based methods. The study implies removing objects and material piece by piece, taking them to the laboratory and ultimately leaving the site without any rudiments of its history. Though remote sensing cannot completely replace ground-based exploration, it can do away with a lot of laborious and destructive ground work by the methods to be discussed later in the paper. In some ways, it even surpasses ground-based exploration since the study of a site through an aerial photograph displays not only the site but it also represents the spatial, economic, agricultural, social and political patterns that surround the area of study. Ground-based vision does not encompass such a large field. There are several large features of archaeological importance which can be seen only through remote sensing such as Anasazi roadwork in New Mexico, or raised field complexes outlining

* National Institute of Oceanography, Dona Paula, Goa 403004

buried ancient structures[2] etc. Ground surveys cannot notice these features because their signs are too faint to be visible over a small area.

Culturally significant objects also have a 'context' of their existence at a place in a site such as their orientation, the surrounding material, type of terrain where they are found, the geographic peculiarities in their immediate neighborhood, etc. Similarly, every site also has a context of its own in terms of its vicinity from the nearest water-body, the surrounding plateau, vegetation types found around and its geographic set-up with respect to the land-mass where it is located. While all objects including the soil material can be removed from the site and studied in the laboratory, the context cannot. Aerial photography of the site before removing the objects remains the only way to preserve their context. Archaeological sites often lie in not well-travelled and inaccessible areas where ground maps are not available. Ground surveys in such areas can be aided by aerial photographs to make pre-field logistic estimates. Besides, other extraneous details such as trees, rocks, specific landforms etc. help the surveyor in fixing his position. Aerial photographs are also known to be used for mitigation purposes, i.e., to preserve the unknown cultural resources before earmarking a land for development or other purpose. In several instances, aerial photographs are taken of a vast landmass before it is acquired for some other purpose. This helps archaelogists to infer at a later date how a given landscape looked years before its appearance was changed by man.

Infra Red False Colour Photography (IFCP)

The colours in an ordinary true-colour photograph are generated by suitably mixing three primary colours namely, the red, the green and the blue. There are three separate pigments in a colour film to record the three components for every colour emanating from a coloured object. In False Colour Photography the blue component is not recorded at all. Hence all natural objects coloured blue, indigo and violet are not seen in IFCP. This is done through a yellow filter since yellow cuts blue completely. This is because in natural landscapes, there is little information available through the blue colour except the atmospheric haze. Removal of blue improves clarity of photographs significantly because of its haze penetration capacity. Instead of the normal red, green and blue, the IFCP records infrared radiation (besides the red and the green colours). Thus, the IFCP records infrared, red and green components instead of the normal red, green and blues in case of true colour photography. The infrared radiation emanating from an object is recorded as red, the red is recorded as green while the green radiation is recorded as blue in IFCP. Thus, objects reflecting infrared appear as red in IFCP, the blue objects are not recorded at all and the red and green objects appear in misplaced colours.

The technique is found to be more useful in earth sciences as it possesses some advantages of infrared photography and yet retains some features from true colour photography (through in misplaced colours). All vegetation appears red, the red soil appears green and man-made objects appear steel grey. Its application in archaeology is not yet fully explored. It is recommended that a few known sites in India should be studied using IFCP, since this promises to emphasize many unexpected features giving a completely new perspective to the archaeological sites.

Underwater Photography

A large number of archaeological sites lie buried underwater. Underwater photography is the only way for preliminary assessment of such sites. One cannot resort to infrared photography in this case because light is the only radiation to which water is slightly transparent. Such photographs whether taken with submerged or airborne cameras lack clarity. This is because of extensive scattering of blue light by water molecules and turbidity caused by suspended sediments. Remote sensing in visible channels also has exactly the same drawback though on a different scale. The atmosphere also scatters blue light and aerosols cause lack of transmissivity. Techniques used in remote sensing to overcome these drawbacks can also be applied to underwater photographs. One of them is to use the 'minus blue' filter. This is to cut off most of the blue caused by scattering of blue light. Second method is to digitize the photographs and apply what are called the 'haze removal' techniques (filtering) in image processing. Effect of turbidity can be largely reduced if digitized underwater photographs are filtered by an image processing system.

Laser-Based underwater Scanning

This is a new and emerging area in remote sensing having tremendous potential for underwater archaeologists. Light does not penetrate water significantly beyond the upper few metres because of its high attention. Even when one carries a flood light below the sea, the radiation quickly attenuates. The only way to overcome this setback is to resort to laser-based techniques. Laser is a strong beam of light of just one wavelength (or centered around one wavelength). It has a very high intensity because the energy which is normally spread over several wavelengths in normal light is accumulated in just one wavelength. Its penetration in water is remarkably higher than ordinary light. There is sufficient energy in a laser beam to penetrate water from air reach several metres down to the bottom, get reflected upwards and leave the water surface back to the detector[3]. Laser-based sensor either submerged or air-borne can actually scan the bottom just as a satellite scans the earth and give true underwater images of high resolution This is an upcoming technique and once developed, marine archaeologists can expect to be the direct beneficiaries.

Thermal Imagery(TI)

Interpretation of thermal imagery follows the simple principle that hotter objects emit more infrared radiation than cooler ones. The brighter shades in the Tl relate to warmer objects while lighter shades are given by cooler objects. Thermal imageries are found to be very useful for defense purposes because a man made strategic object such as a tank, aeroplane and even supply vehicles like trucks and buses which can be camouflaged in the ordinary photograph by covering them in green vegetation carpets reveal themselves in TI by virtue of their higher temperatures. Even submarines which are not seen in ordinary photograph of the sea can be clearly seen in Tl because the heat generated by submarines warms the sea surface.

TI promises to be very useful in archaeological explorations. Archaeologists always consider vicinity of fresh water source as a prerequisite for any archaeological site since civilizations cannot thrive without water. It is here that Tl reigns supreme because it instantly locates water bodies on land (or islets in water). This is because water and land are never at the same temperatures Water has a higher specific heat capacity than land and hence water takes longer to cool and heat. Thus, water will be either hotter or cooler than land depending upon whether it is night or day. In any thermal imagery of a landscape, presence of water is most easily discernible as having either darker or brighter shade. Thus, delineation of exact coastline, small islands, small water bodies, springs, streams, lakes, ponds etc. stand out very clearly in Tl.

The technique is also useful to detect caves hidden in the shrubs, metal objects buried in the sediment because metals are at higher temperatures than the surrounding while the caves are at low temperatures. The temperature of an object is decided by specific heat capacity which is unique for each material. Objects seen by human eye are often at different temperatures but since the eye is not sensitive to infrared it does not notice any contrast.

The most important advantage of TI is that such imageries can be collected even during night when ordinary photograph will show nothing. This is because thermal infrared radiation is emitted by objects unlike light which is just reflected. Thermal imageries can also be taken through fog, smoke dust haze etc. because infrared radiation passes through such media. During evenings and early mornings when the ambient temperature begins to change, each material on a site begins to cool (or heat) at different rates depending upon its specific heat capacity. Thermal imageries obtained at such times will show a variety of diverse materials at a site which are not normally discernible to the eyes even in normal day light. This is because their contrast for visible light is much less than that for infrared radiation.

Satellite Image

A satellite looks at a scene on the earth in a way very different from a human eye. Firstly, satellites give an aerial view like an aerial photograph while human eye is rarely oriented to give such a view. Human eye is sensitive only to the light (visible channels) while satellites receive radiation from both infrared and microwave part of the spectrum besides 'light'. All types of radiation are differentiated from one another in terms of their wavelengths. For example, wavelength of light varies from 400 to 700 nanometres, while infrared varies from 700 nanometre to 1 millimetre and microwaves vary from one millimetre to one metre. Thus, light has a smaller wavelength than infrared while microwaves are known by their large wavelengths. Human eye receives all wavelengths of light and gives a picture averaged over the wavelengths. Satellites do not do so. They restrict their view to a certain small range of wavelengths such as from 440 to

460 nanometres or 510 to 530 nanometres etc. and ignore radiation coming in other wavelengths. Even while looking at the earth in infrared or microwave channels, satellites look at the earth only through a small range of their respective wavelengths. This small range is called channel. There are many channels on board a satellite and satellite looks at a scene on the earth simultaneously through all its channels[5]. Thus! if a satellite has 7 channels it gives 7 independent images of the same scene, one for each channel. Each of these images can be used for different type study of the scene; either separately or in combination with other channels.

This unique way of looking at the earth enables one to detect presence of different materials on the earth based on their specific spectral properties. This is so because each material on the earth absorbs and reflects radiation in a special characteristic way[6]. Besides, most processes on the earth are such that they are affected by only certain wave-lengths of radiation Thus, satellite image contains enormous information both about a site and the various processes that affect a site on the earth. This is the basis of remote sensing. We shall discuss some of the techniques used to extract the information from an image which have a tremendous potential for archaeological exploration

A. Detection of Sites

Archaeological sites are characterised by presence of specific material depending upon the period, location on the earth and the cultural parameters. Material found is unique to each location. Material may be exposed or buried under alluvial deposits and rocks of granite or any other suitable material which was possibly used for construction works. These features make it easy for detection of sites based on spectral signatures.

Spectral signature is unique and characteristic distribution of reflected radiation from an object. Although the radiation incident on all objects is the same (usually sunlight or skylight) each object absorbs different wavelengths and reflects the remaining radiation. Since spectral signatures of objects span across several wavelengths, multichannel satellite images are very useful for their detection. When spectral signature of objects are known, it is easy for the computer to find out whether those objects exist from the satellite image and if so, what is their location. If this technique is to be used to detect the archaeological sites, it is necessary that spectral signature of all archaeologically significant material should be measured. This can be done by an instrument called the spectro-radiometer.

B. Geolocation

A large number of archaeological sites lie in remote inaccessible areas whose presence is known to local tribal communities. One of the major exercises is to register all such sites with correct latitude and longitude on known maps. This enables archaeologists to know their distances from the nearby townships and also the most convenient access to them. This process is called geolocation. If aerial photographs or satellite image of the place is available, geo location becomes very easy.

There are several image processing packages available with built in geolocation algorithms. All an archaeologist has to do is to identify the site on the image and the package instantly registers it on a gridded map with all known reference points, besides giving its geographic location in terms of latitude and longitude

C. Measurment

Measurement of total area occupied by archaeologically significant sites by ground-based methods is difficult, laborious, time consuming and often inaccurate. The problems are compounded specially when the site includes hills, valleys, forests or water bodies. However, when location of such sites on a satellite image is known measurement becomes very easy and straightforward with the help of remote sensing techniques. When images are displayed on TV monitors, area occupied by the cursor is exactly equal to one 'pixel' on the image. Dimension of one 'pixel' equals resolution of the satellite image. Resolution for different satellite images are well-known.

One can easily count the number of pixels covering a given area with the help of the cursor manually or through using suitable image processing package. Thus, one knows exact area of an archaeologically significant site. The geometry of the pixels and the cursor does not change with the topography on the ground. Hence this method works well in all different kind of terrains.

D. False Colour Composite

Colour in the colour photographs are reproduced by mixing three primary components, viz, red, green and blue. In case of digital photograph, the three components are stored separately and mixed only when the picture is viewed on a colour TV monitor (or white printing). A colour TV monitor has three independent guns, the red, the green and the blue. A digital photograph is viewed on a TV screen by sending red component to red gun, green to green gun and blue to blue gun. The three guns simultaneously illuminate the TV screen in proportion to the respective component and each point on the screen gets illuminated by all the three guns. Thus, three components mix at each point on the screen creating the original colour. This is known as true colour composite (TCC). TCC gives only as much information of the terrain as seen by human eyes.

In case of false colour composite (FCC) red component can be sent to either green or blue gun just as green or blue component can as well be sent to any other gun. One may even drop one of the components and get a picture using just two guns. Such a picture generated on the TV screen has all colour misplaced and some lacking. FCC thus emphasizes different set of objects on the ground than what the eye is commonly used to seeing. Many unexpected features become bolder which are often overlooked by the human eye in the normal view. This gives an entirely different perspective to the site. FCC has been found to be more useful then TCC in such diverse disciplines as agriculture, geology, botany, geography etc. Their application potential in archaeology is not yet fully explored partly because of non-availability of digital photographs and partly due to archaeologists exposure to image processing facilities. It is recommended that a few well known aerial colour photographs of important sites may be converted to "digital pictures" using available image processing facilities and FCC may be studied in the first instance by expert archaeologists.

Such a study promises to offer a completely new look to their known sites with several new and unexpected features enhanced. Expertise obtained from observing known sites may then be utilized for exploration of new sites.

FCC of a satellite image has more potential than that of a digital photograph because a satellite image has more components of the same view (channels) unlike a digital photograph, which has just three. Moreover channels can extend into the infrared and microwave regions also. Any three of the channels can be sent to the three guns of a TV screen to get a false colour composite. Thus there can be 210 possible FCCs for a seven channel scene FCCs are known for many serendipitous discoveries in remote sensing because emissive and reflective properties of different materials on the earth through visible, infrared and microwave part of the radiation combine in a unique way in each possible FCC and give a myriad of colour pictures of a site. Features not visible to the human eye show themselves through different colours. This technique will certainly give a new dimension to archaeological studies specially with regard to their spatial patterns.

E. Stereoscopic Effects

Some satellites such as SPOT view the earth in such a way as to give stereoscopic effect to the image[7]. This is done by viewing the same scene twice during the successive orbits through different look angles. When the two images of the same scene thus obtained are viewed through a stereoscope it shows elevations and depressions on the terrain. Though such views are not very suitable for measurements of topography, they display the valleys, slopes and hilltops clearly. Archaeological sites are often found on the foot of hills with slopes varying between 0 to 5 degrees with adjoining areas locally flat; stereo-images easily bring out such features.

Image Processing

Image processing is a computer science which deals with making pictures more meaningful and pleasant to the human eye using a computer. Before a computer can process a picture, it needs to be converted into an image by a process called scanning. Scanning involves converting every point in the picture into a number which is proportional to its brightness. Computer processes these numbers so as to bring about changes in the image with respect to its tone, brightness, contrast, colours and performs many other useful transformations[8].

Satellite images are directly accepted by computers for processing because each point in the image is in fact, a number which is proportional to the amount of radiation received from the corresponding ground element. Processed images are very useful for a trust of applications. Some of the applications useful for archaeological explorations are given below:

1. Searching for a given feature in images of unknown sites.
2. Suppression of unwanted details on a site.
3. Enhancement of certain hidden features including edges of desired objects.
4. Stretching of contrast for better resolution of finer details.
5 Colour coding of similar features.
6. Transferring archaeological site locations onto geographical maps.
7 Reducing several sites on the same scale for comparison.
8. Contouring of landscape.
9. Rectification of oblique photographs into "nadir-view" photos.

These are but a few of the applications of image processing. There are many more complex transformations which are difficult to cover within the scope of this paper

Microwave Radar–Based Techniques

Part of remote sensing involves generating microwaves of a certain wavelength and sending them to the terrain from the satellite or an aircraft and measuring the back–scattered microwave radiation[9]. This is very similar to the principle of ground–based radars except that radars use radio waves and not microwaves. The back–scattered microwaves are shown to contain a diverse type of information about the terrain such as elevation and depressions on the land, vegetation type, moisture, slopes, hardness/softness and a host of other parameters of special interest. The physical shape and size of the things on the terrain plays an equally important in deciding the kind of back–scattered radiation besides the nature of the material that comprise them.

Over the water surface such images have revealed bottom topography and even the signatures of submerged objects such as sunken ships. There are also efforts to detect the presence of buried objects on the land from such images. The technique is new and has always given serendipitous results. Objects of archaeological interests are small and present resolution obtainable from this technique can be as large as 6 x 6 m. Images obtained by low–flying aircrafts irradiating a given terrain in microwaves of different wavelengths need to be made available to trained archaeologists to study what clues they hold for detection of sites. Archaeologists need to work in close collaboration with remote sensing community who study signatures of underwater and underground objects from microwave images.

The net advantage of microwave imaging is that microwave images do not require any atmospheric correction. They are known as all weather sensors because microwaves pass through all atmospheric constituents, including thick clouds.

Limitations Of Remote Sensing Techniques

Contrary to common belief, remote sensing does not replace ground–based exploration. It is complementary to *in situ* observations. Remote sensing is also limited to its resolution. Using short waves improves the resolution but also adds to the atmospheric correction problems. Although remote sensing is said to be cheaper in the long run, it is not so in the short run.

Satellite images are expensive and require extensive computer installations to process and study them. The subject itself is in developing stage and has given incorrect estimates of many geophysical parameters due to lack of complete understanding of the interaction of radiation with the earth, ocean and atmosphere. Despite these limitations, archaeologist will find this new tool very useful and interesting in their exploration.

Acknowledgements

The authors are thankful to the Director, National Institute of Oceanography, Goa for providing facilities during this study. We are extremely grateful to Dr S R Rao, Adviser, Marine Archaeology Centre for continuous encouragement. We are thankful to Dr. L.V.G. Rao, Head, Physical Oceanography Division for providing facilities in this study. Authors are also thankful to Shri. K.H Vora

REFERENCES

1. St. Joseph, J.K.S 1966. *The use of air photography in nature and man in a new perspective*, London, John Baker
2. Ebert, J.I. 1983. Archaeology, Anthropology and Cultural Resources Management, in Colwell, R.N. (ed) *Manual of Remote Sensing*, Vol. II
3. Measures, R.M. 1984. *Laser Remote Sensing and Image Interpretation,* John Wiley & sons, New York, pp. 442-487.
4. Rinker, R.J. 1973. *Infrared thermal detection of Caves;* US Army Engr. Topo Labs Ft. Belvoir p. 10.
5. Lillesond T.M. & Kiefer, R.W. 197.9 *Remote Sensing and Image Interpolation,* John Wiley & Sons, New York, p. 442-487.
6. Hoffer, R.M. 1978. In Swain P.H. and Davis S.M. (Ed.) *Remote Sensing: The Quantitative Approach,* Mcgraw-Hill Int. Boon Co. New york, p.228-86.
7. Simonett D.S. 1983. The Development and Principle of Remote Sensing, Manual on Report Sensing, Vol.1 *in* Colwell, R.N. (Ed.) p.11
8. Sabins Jr. F.F. 1978. op cit. Vol I p. 11 *Remote Sensing, Principles and Interpretation.* W.F. Freeman & Co; San Francisco, p. 233-75.
9. Ulaby, F.T., Moore, R.K. and Fung, A.K. 1981. *Microwave Remote Sensing Active and Passive* Vol. 1, Addison-Wesley Pub. Co. London, pp. 5-12

Conservation and Sustainable Development for the Historic Town of "Amber" (Jaipur, Rajasthan)

D.P. KAMBO*

Overview

Most of the Historic towns in India are engulfed by new developments and have lost their identity over a period of time. Alternatively they have emerged as commercial centres. Several Historical towns also have lost their economic potential, because there had been no attempt by the state or professionals to seek their economic benefit through any planned and equitable strategy.

A review of Amber has thus been conducted to see and explore how the role of this historic town could be rejuviated in a rational manner in the present context.

Amber is strategically located on one of the important touristic route linking Delhi, Jaipur and Agra and has several important historical precincts possessing many antiquities. The growth of this town over the last two decades have been phenomenal, in spite of the limited land, undulated topography, surrounded by reserve forest and devoid of basic existence of adequate infrastructure. However, the potential and opportunities of the town is rich. Historical setting, important historical structures such as fort and palaces, draw domestic and foreign tourists throughout the year. Several religious festivals are held around the year. Amber draws most of the needful resources from the city of Jaipur. The adjoining area of the town and the surroundings of Amber has a few large water bodies which offer many opportunities for its potential development.

Amber was a small settlement in the 16th century and its location and linkages with Agra and Ajmer was recognised by the rulers of the times. The town's antiquities and the state of its neglect can be seen through several abandoned buildings of social and cultural values.

The city stands out as a landmark for the acceptance of Mughals as Indians. The contribution of artisans and craftmen and their recognition by Akbar, Mansingh and later by Mirja Raja Jaisingh testifies to the synthesis of two cultures as seen in early 17th and 18th century, which is reflected in the art of building tradition of the period.

The Present status

Amber is a tehsil of Jaipur district in Rajasthan state. It is designated as Class-IV medium town having a population of (Approx. 16,000) according to 1981 census. The town is administered by an Executive Officer who is assisted by the Notified Area Committee (NAC). NAC has little funds at their disposal and no development work is taken except some maintenance of roads and culverts. The question of maintenance or restoration of historic

*Formerly Prof. School of Planning & Architecture, New Delhi.

buildings do not arise. Because of the absence of any planned development and no control over landgrabbing encroachment has been continuing during the last two three decades. The neglect of this historic town thus continues.

Settlement Pattern

The settlement pattern follows the gradient of the hilly terrain. The fort, palace and the houses of chiefs are located at defensible and strategic locations. Places of worship for the people and public places are generally located near the palaces, gates are at primary places where directional routes meet in the town. The drainage pattern in and around the town had helped the vegetal growth and development of afforestation. However, there is no conscious effort of planting of trees, shrubs or even to create distinct features for landscape as an aid to soften the town's barren topographical features. However, in the planning of palace complex, Royal gardens and around lakes there had been very conscious efforts plants and trees have been carefully selected.

Erosion of soil over the centuries have made certain slopes of the hills quite barren and do not help in retaining moisture for the growth of plants which did not allow any vegetation.

Social Structure of the Town

The population in the fortified towns is generally of poor and middle class and are mostly engaged in Government services. Certain section of the population is engaged in agriculture as labourers and others in constructions and household industry. A small section of people have been engaged in stone cutting, polishing and carpet making. Some social institutions have also set up training centre for teaching vocational crafts to handicapped and poor sections of the society.

Amber also provides educational facilities up to high School level to the students drawn from the adjoining villages. There is a whole sale vegetable market close to Amber which serves Jaipur city.

Commercial Facilites

The commercial activities of the town is limited to a stretch of the road linking Gandhi Chowk and Royal Chowk at the entry point to Amber palace complex. Notified Area Committee had taken up some paving work and provided drains in certain section of the town. The town is well connected to the walled city and the present bus service is adequate to the needs of the inhabitants. Private taxi, scootors are generally used by tourists.

Future Prospect

(i) To provide stable and sustainable economic base for the town, a policy for remunerative land uses could be followed. The development of flower valley and "Kanak garden" has already given the area a new look and there is need to retain the values that could not only enhance the town but could add to the economic uplift of the area. Development of orchards and fruit growing trees be planted for such remunerative land uses. Such areas need to be earmarked for such social actions.

(ii) The existing gardens of Kesar Bagh and Ram Bagh, have gradually deteriorated because of the absence of any policy and guidelines. Afforestation and steps towards development of social forestry could further help in providing even firewood for the local population for which voluntary and public participation must be encouraged under the experts advice. Public ownership of such areas for such development works must be earmarked.

(iii) All water bodies, tanks, wells should be maintained by cooperative efforts under the Department of Culture and Tourism, and conservation plan, should be drawn up with the help of experts.

Tourism Potential

Amber town has not fully exploited its potentials; , its links with Delhi, Agra and Ajmer which could have promoted the movement of tourists, pilgrims trading and resource mobilizations of skilled professionals but the town attracts the passers by only for a short stop over i.e. just to see the Fort and Amber palace.

There are several areas rich in character which are neither visited nor known to people, due to the absence of any available material on the Town's historicity. There are several architectural buildings depicting the facets of buildings of the previous era which are a source of information for the present day.

There are several tanks, wells lying abandoned, which could be improved and become parts of the town and could further add to its resources. Development of Sagar talao, Dharmshala could be undertaken to bring economic benefit to the town.

The town has potential to develop household and craft oriented industry. At present there are various items like manufacturing of bangles, stone cutting and polishing of gems and precious stones manufacturing of plastic utensils and art works. It is possible to provide technical know-how and to upgrade their quality. This will improve the employment prospects for the local population.

Most of these activities such as manufacturing, production or even teaching institutions are inadequately housed in poor buildings. The poorly paid craftsmen cannot afford to move or build new structures or in addition to their present ones. On the other hand several buildings historical or otherwise are either abandoned or purchased by people for speculations and locked for ever.

The revenues generated from tourism or from taxes in the city is limited The present form of development is carried on only by unauthorized means. It is rather difficult for the Notified Area Committee Area to bring any subtantial change. It is therefore, suggested that conservation strategy and actions should be such that it can embrace all levels of activities in the town. The following points are proposed as guidelines to achieve the conservation objectives:–

1. Improvement of basic infrastructure pertaining to hygiene and sanitation in the town.

2. All forms of building activities such as reconstruction or new buildings should be controlled in the historic, religious and cultural zones in the fortified town. The proposed activites, to be housed in the listed structures are fully examined for appropriate functions as far as possible.

3. Public ownership of the common land, purchase of structures which are either in a derelict state, unsafe, or abandoned, could be adopted for required facilities.

4. Raising resources and to channelise conservation activities through incentives and public donations for training artisans and craftmen; and

5. Setting up a vocational centre to promote arts and crafts of the region.

NOTES AND NEWS

A Preliminary Study of Marine Molluscan shell Remains from Bagasra: A Harappan Site in Gujrat

This report deals with the preliminary observations carried out on the marine shells recovered from the Harrapan site of Bagasra in Gujarat. Bagasra is situated (23° 3'N, 70° 37' E) in Maliya Taluka of Rajkot District, Gujarat very close to the south–eastern shore of the Gulf of Kutch. The site is currently being excavated by the Department of Archaeology, M.S. University of Baroda, Vadodara. The excavation conducted so far has revealed various interesting aspects of a fortified settlement belonging to the Mature/Urban phase of the Harappan culture.

From the habitation deposit of 4.30 m, a large number of artefacts such as an inscribed Harappan terracotta sealing, semi–precious stone beads, cubical chert weights, terracotta toys, figurines etc. have been unearthed. The ceramic assemblage comprises all the typical Mature Harappan pottery types along with other ceramics associated with Harappan sites in Saurashtra. The faunal material is represented in large numbers which besides mammals also includes marine/aquatic fauna like fish, molluscs and arthropods by (Sonawane Personal communication).

This report concerns the study of a part of the first season's shell material i.e. 1995-96 here; however, no shell objects have been examined. The shell material was examined at the Department of Archaeology, M.S. University of Baroda and were identified and classified up to the species level. Identifications have been carried out by comparison with the identified shells from the Harappan site of Kuntasi and by referring to Wye[1], Abbot and Dance[2]. These were further classified and sorted into groups comprising those reflecting human activity and those accidentally or naturally introduced.

Dimensional measurements were taken of all measurable shell. Features like breakage patterns, perforations, charring and other taphonomic features were recorded. No quantitative analysis was carried out due to the limited nature of the material taken up for analysis.

Results of this analysis have been compared with other Harappan sites of Nageswar, Kuntasi and Shikarpur. These are the only sites in Gujarat where detailed shell studies have been carried out so far.

Results

A total of 1104 marine shells comprising complete to fragmented ones were studied. From the entire collection, 19 species have been identified of which marine gastropods are 13 and marine bivalves are 6 (Table. 1). Identification was not possible in the case of 2 gastropods and a few fragmented bivalve shells hence these were identified respectively as marine gastropod sp. and marine bivalve sp. It is interesting to note that no freshwater species were present in the collection. In general the shell preservation appears to fairly good as seen by the presence of complete shells. The shells have lost their outer periostracum and therefore are creamy to grey in colour.

The NISP distribution reveals the dominance of *Turbinella pyrum* over the rest of the species. Next important species were *Paphia gallus, Thais carinifera* and *Meretrix* .

A majority of the marine species recovered from Bagasra are typical of estuarine mudflats and intertidal areas bordering the Indian west coast. These areas with their rocky outcrops, mangroves and intervening tidal flats are host to a wide variety of molluscan species. Some of the shells found form such areas are *Paphia gal-*

Table 1
List of Molluscan Species at Bagsara

No.	Name	Family	Class	Type	Number
1.	*Anadara rhombea*	Arcidae	BV	M	1
2.	*Paphia gallus*	Veneridae	BV	M	338
3.	*Meretrix meretrix*	Veneridae	BV	M	24
4.	*Placuna placenta*	Anomiidae	BV	M	1
5.	*Cantharus spiralis*	Buccinidae	G	M	11
6.	*Agaronia nebulosa*	Olividae	G	M	3
7.	*Natica sp.*	Naticidae	G	M	1
8.	*Cerithidae cingulata*	Potamididae	G	M	4
9.	*Diodara funiculata*	Fissurellidae	G	M	1
10.	*Turbinella pyrum*	Turbinellidae	G	M	447
11.	*Solen sp.*	Solenidae	BV	M	10
12.	*Chicoreus ramosus*	Muricidae	G	M	6
13.	*Tonna sp.*	Tonnidae	G	M	1
14.	*Crassostrea sp.*	Ostreidae	BV	M	2
15.	*Cypraea*	Cypraeidae	G	M	2
16.	*Pugilina buchephala*	Melongenidae	G	M7	
17.	*Thais carinifera*	Muricidae	G	M	57
18.	*Unknown sp.*	–	G	M	1
19.	*Unknown sp.*	–	G	M	1
	Unidentified fragments		BV	M	134
				Total NISP =	1104

BV = Bivalve G = Gastropod M = Marine

lus, Thais carinifera, Meretrix sp., *Crassostrea* sp. *Cerithidae* sp. *placuna placenta,* etc. They can be easily collected at low tide when their beds get exposed.

In case of the larger gastropods like T. *Pyrum* and *Chicoreus ramosus,* procurement was probably from slightly deeper waters in the nearby Gulf of Kutch. Present-day habitats of this shell are found along the Jamnagar coast adjoining coral reef areas within the Gulf of Kutch[3].

The overall shell representation reveals that shells at Bagasra have resulted primarily because of three factors,

(1) Manufacture of shell object; (2) Dietary use; and (3) Certain shells have not played any significant role and are mostly naturally occurring.

However, a majority of the shells present reflect human activity.

Shell working

At Bagasra, major shell working involved the use of the three large gastropods–*Turbinella pyrum, Chicoreus remosus, Pugilina buchephala* along with a few smaller gastropods. The entire shell material is dominated by *Turbinella pyrum* which is represented by a few complete shells, sawn columellas, obliquely sawn semi-circular spire portions and fragments from the main whorl. The nature and type of the waste present reveals the manufacture of objects like bangles, rings and inlay. Complete shells present in the average size range of 50-200·mm without any borings and encrustations suggest that fairly big sized and good quality. T, *pyrum* shells were utilised. The manufacturing shell waste resembles that of Nageswar[4] and Kuntasi[5].

Another large marine gastropod *Pugilina buchiphala* although limited in number (7) occurs as columellas, fragments from the spire and outer main whorl. This shell might have been also used for making bangles and inlay pieces as is evident at Kuntasi. In the case of *Chicoreus ramosus,* it is difficult to determine its use since it is represented only by spine fragments. However, it was probably used for making ladles or bangles as observed at species are very negligible as compared to *T. pyrum.* smaller gastropods like *Cantharus spiralis, Agaronia nebulosa* and *Cypraea* sp. are very few in number and do not display any traces of shell working. These could have been used as beads as observed at many of the archaeological sites.

Dietary use

In the past as well as in present times, shellfish has served as an important dietary component for many coastal communities. These being rich in proteins and iron had served as nutritional supplements for many of the ancient societies. At Bagasra, the bivalve shells of *Paphia gallus* and *Meretrix meretrix* represent food refuse. These are present in considerable numbers as complete to broken shells. Since a majority of the shells are complete, meat extraction probably was by either boiling or steaming the shells. These besides roasting are the commonly used methods today in coastal India adopted[7]. By these methods meat can be extracted without breaking the shell. This further suggests that food processing was done at the site itself.

Paphia gallus: This is a venerid clam having an ovate shell whose outer surface is glossy and has concentric ribs. A total of 338 shells are present. This was the most dominant edible species to be exploited at Kuntasi[8], *Paphia* sp. forms a major fishery on the Maharashtra and the Karwar coast[9].

Meretrix meretrix: Complete shells of another venerid clam consisting of a small thick ovate shell having a smooth glossy exterior are present. *Meretrix* sp. have been found at Allahadino[10] and Kuntasi[11]. Today this particular species is regularly collected on the Konkan coast for food[12].

The sizes of both *Paphia* and *Meretrix* from Bagasra compare well with their present day fishery size reflecting similar harvesting seasons.

The oyster species *Crassostrea* which was an important dietary component in the Late Harappan Period at Kuntasi is scarcely present at Bagasra. Only two shells are present and hence very little can be said about their exploitation. The *Crassostrea* sp. are commonly found attached to hard substratums like mangroves along both the west and east coast and are edible[13]. Similarly very little can be said about other edible species like *Anadara* and *Solen,* since they are also found in negligible numbers of 1 and 10 respectively.

Apart from bivalves, marine gastropod species like *Turbo, Thais, Telescopium,* etc. are also eaten in coastal India[14]. At Bagasra, complete shells along with a few broken ones of *Thais carinifera,* suggest possible exploitation. These are sturdy shells having prominent nodose whorls with fine spiral grooves and are found attached to rocks and mangroves in mudflat area. Shells in the size range of 25-45 mm were collected. *Thais* shells have also been encountered at Kuntasi and Shikarpur[15]. The modern species of the genus *Thais,* like *Thais rudolphi* and *Thais bufo* are fished on the Konkan coast[16].

Discussion

At Bagasra, presence of 19 molluscan species reflects a selective procurement strategy. Coastal location of the site was primarily responsible for the variety of species collected. Shell procurement was from estuarine mudflats and from deeper waters in the Gulf of Kutch.

Shell working was one of the major reasons for the concentration of shells at the site. It mainly revolved around *Turbinella pyrum* for the manufacture of bangles, inlay, etc. Like other Harappan sites *Chicoreus ramosus* and *Pugilina buchephala* also were being utilised for the manufacture of other objects. Comparison of the waste of all these three gastropod species with that of other Harappan sites suggests similarities in the nature of shell working technology[17]. Shell working might have been aided by the coastal nature of the site which facilitated a steady shell procurement.

Besides the manufacture of shell objects, some molluscs contributed to the food économy of the Bagasra inhabitants. The two venerid bivalves *Paphia gallus* and *Meretrix meretrix* and the gastropod *Thais carinifera* were the species consumed. In its species composition, Bagasra shares similarities with other coastal Harappan sites such as Nageswar, Kuntasi, Shikarpur, Padri, etc. as well as with present-day shell fisheries. This suggests a somewhat uniform pattern of marine molluscan exploitation on the Gujarat coast during the Harappan period[18]. Shell–fishing might have been an all-year round activity due to the easy access to different types of molluscan species.

At this juncture it is difficult to ascertain the exact role of molluscs in the over all diet. This will be possible only if other faunal and floral data is also made available.

Since this is a preliminary report, lack of quantitative analysis has not helped in determining the relative cultural layers. Therefore, a more detailed study is essential for further deduction of the degree of molluscan utilisation at Bagasra. By doing so, various aspects like dietary role, extent of shell working, local environment, etc. will be better understood.

Acknowledgements

I wish to express my sincere gratitude to Prof. V.H. Sonawane and his excavation team from the Department of Archaeology, M.S. University of Baroda, Vadodara, Gujarat for permitting me to study the shells from Bagsara. Acknowledgments are also due to the Department of Archaeology, Deccan College, Pune for enabling this shell study.

REFERENCES

1. Wye, K.R. 1991. *The Illustrated Encyclopaedia of Shells.* London: Headline Book Publishing.
2. Abbott, R.T. and S. Peter Dance 1991. *Compendium of Seashells.* London: Charles Lets and Co. Limited.
3. Nayar, K.N. and S. Mahadevan, 1974. Chank fisheries and Industrial uses of Chank in R.V. Nair and K.S. Rao Eds, *The commercial Molluscs of India* pp. 122-140, Cochin: Central Marine Fisheries Research Institute.
4. Bhan, K. and J.M. Kenoyer 1984. Nageshwar: A Mature Shell Working Site on the Gulf of Kutch (Gujarat), *Journal of the Oriental Institute of Baroda* 34: 67-75, also Bhan, K. 1992. Shell Industry in K.T.M. Hegde, K.K. Bhan, V.H. Sonawane, K. Krishnan and D.R. Shah Eds. *Excavations at Nageswar Gujarat: Harappan Shell Working Site on the Gulf of Kutch* : pp. 125-136.
5. Deshpande, A. 1995. Application of Molluscan studies in Archaeology with reference to western India. University of Poona, Unpublished Ph. D Thesis also 1996. Shell Remains, in *Kuntasi, A Harappan Emporium on West Coast* in M.K. Dhavalikar, M.R. Raval and Y.M. Chitalwala (Eds.), pp. 331-347 Pune: Deccan College Post-Graduate and Research Institute (Deemed to be a University) and Deshpande, A. 1996-97. Application of Molluscan Studies in Archaeology with Special Reference to Western India (Ph.D. synopsis). *Bulleting of the Deccan College Post-graduate and Research Institute* 56-57:pp. 355-361.
6. Deshpande 1995 op. cit.
7. Alagariswamy, K. and K.A. Narasimham 1973. Clam, Cockle and Oyster resources of the Indian coast in *Proceedings of the Symposium on living resources of the seas around India.* Cochin: Special Publication Central Marine Fisheries Research Institute. pp. 648-658
8. Deshpande-Mukherjee, A. 1998. Shell fishing and Shell craft Activities during the Harappan period in Gujarat, *Man and Environment,* Vol XXXIII (1) :pp. 63-81.
9. Alagiriswamy and Narasimham op. cit.
10. Turnbull, P. 1983. The Study of Clams and Snails from Archaeological sites in C. Grigson and Juliet Clutton Brock (Eds.), *Animals and Archaeology 2. Shell Middens, Fishes and Birds,* pp. 53-65. Oxford: BAR International Series No.
11. Deshpande 1995 op. cit.
12. Rai, H.S. 1932. The shell fisheries of the Bombay Presidency, *Journal of Bombay Natural History Society* 35 (4) : pp. 826-847.
13. Rao, K.S. 1974. Edible Bivalves, Mussels and Oysters in R. V. Nair and K.S. Rao (Eds.), *The Commercial Molluscs of India.* pp. 4-39, Cochin: Central Marine Fisheries Research Institute.
14. Sundaram, S. 1974. Edible Gastropods, in R. V. Nair and K.S. Rao (Eds.), *The Commercial Molluscs of India.* pp. 54-62, Cochin: Central Marine Fisheries Research Institute.
15. Deshpande 1995, 96–97 op. cit.
16. Sundaram, op. cit.
17. Deshpande, 1998 op. cit
18. Ibid.

Department of Archaeology, Deccan College
Post Graduate and Research Institute, Pune 411006

ARATI DESHPANDE-MUKHERJEE

A Note on the Faunal Remains from Kudatini–an Ashmound Site in Karnataka

Introduction

Kudatini is one of the major ashmound sites in Karnataka. It is located at about 22 km west of the district town of Bellary. The ashmound and artefacts from here were described town by T.J. Newbold and R.B. Foote in the 19th century[1]. The faunal material from Kudatini was collected by Dr. F.R. Allchin during his visit in 1957[2]. He has described seven fragments and their identification[3].

Archaeozoological methods have changed considerably during the last four decades. Now an archaeozoological investigations goes beyond simple names of identifiable species at a particular site and measuring bones is new addition to this field. One of the reasons for re-examining the faunal collection from Kudatini is to apply new methodology of bone analysis and to record marks left by the action of abiotic factors such as weathering and rolling of the bones. Also the faunal material from Kudatini has been compared with those from other ashmound sites such as Mallur, Utnur and Kodekal.

Table 1 List of identified bones from Kudatini

No. 1	Description 2	Weight (g) 3
KUD01	Vertical ramus of left mandible of *Bos indicus*	24.93
KUD02	Upper right side molar of *Bos indicus*	16.40
KUD03	Fragment of vertebra of *Bos/Bubalus*	2.34
KUD04	Fragment of vertebra of *Bos/Bubalus*	1.40
KUD05	Fragment of cranium of *Capra/Ovis*	0.97
KUD06	Horizontal ramus of mandible of *Bos/Bubalus*	1.56
KUD07	Fragment of scapula/pelvis of *Capra/Ovis*	1.06
KUD08	Fragment of vertebra of *Capra/Ovis*	1.04
KUD09	Mandible/Maxilla with a charred tooth	2.02
KUD10	Distal fragment of tibia of *Bubalus bubalis*	8.97
CUD11	Rib fragment of *Bos/Bubalus* (cut)	13.45
KUD12	Complete astragalus of Bos indicus that	71.34
KUD13	Shaft fragment of distal tibia of *Bos/Bubalus* (tool?)	8.63
KUD14	Symphasis fragment of mandible of *Bos/Bubalus* (cut)	14.91
KUD15	Rib of *Capra/Ovis* (cut)	2.70
KUD16	Carpal bone of *Bos/Bubalus*	9.55
KUD17	Fragment of humerus shaft of *Bos indicus*	8.42
KUD18	Fragment of rib of *Bos/Babalus* (edges rolled)	5.77
KUD19	Proximal end of second phalanx of *Bos indicus* (cut)	1.64
KUD20	Fragment of femur humerus shaft of *Bos/Bubalus*	11.13
KUD21	Fragment of femur/humerus shaft of *Bos/Bubalus*	8.80
KUD22	Bone tool with one edge charred	4.05

The Faunal Material

A total of 36 fragments were available for examination, of which 22 (221.08g) could be identified (Table 1). It was not possible to identify 14 fragments, which weighed only 11.5 g. A majority of these bones were fragmentary in nature. Surface of one fragment (KUD 21) looks heavily cracked. This indicates that perhaps this bone was exposed to bright sunlight for considerable period of time before getting buried. Margins of one fragment (KUD 18) are smooth due to rolling. Four fragments showed marks of cutting and butchering. A fragment of a jaw (KUD 09) had a charred tooth in its natural position.

One fragment of a long bone (KUD 20) has a peculiar appearance, whose surface looks reticular like a horncore surface. This bone was perhaps ingested by a carnivore and the reticular surface is due to action of digestive enzymes in the stomach.

This small collection showed presence of two bone tools, both made from shaft of long bones of cattle or buffalo. One of these (KUD 13), fashioned like a point is made from tibia. One side of the other bone tool (KUD 22) is charred.The charred edge of this tool has been used perhaps like a side–scraper.

Table 2 Mammalian species identified at ashmound sites in Karnataka

Site Reference	Mallur A	Utnur B	Kodekal C	 A	Kudatini D
Bos indicus	+	+	+	+	+
Bubalus bubalis	–	–	+	!	+
Capra/Ovis	–	+	+	+	+
Cervus duvauceli	–	–	+	–	–
Axis axis	–	–	+	–	–
Gazella bennetti	–	–	+	–	–
Sus sp.	–	–	–	+	–
Lepus sp.	–	–	–	+	–
Equus asinus	–	–	+	–	–
Canis familiaris	–	–	+	–	–
Rattus rattus	–	–	+	–	+

!: possibly present A: After Clason (1979)
B: After Alluchin (1963) C: After Shah (1973)
D: this study and Allchin (1963)

The Species

Allchin has reported presence of bovine, caprine and rodent bones in his preliminary remarks on the animal remains from Kudatini. This examination of the animal remains revealed presence of two bovine species (*Bos indicus*–cattle) and *Bubalus bubalis* - buffalo) besides *Capra/Ovis* (Goat/Sheep). Due to he fragmentary nature of the bones, it is not possible to state whether sheep and/or goats were present at Kudatini. No rodent bones were available in this collection for re–examination. Kudatini faunal material has been compared to those from other ashmound sites (Table 2). Mallur, Utnur and Kodekal like Kudatini have showed presence of cattle. Buffalo has been identified only at Kodekal[5] and Kudatini. Wild animal bones are missing from this collection. However, this collection is very small and of one field season only.

Bone Measurements (Table 3)

A few bones were preserved enough so that they can be measured. Bone measurements were taken using a Vernier caliper (least count 0.01 mm) and following the standard method developed by von den Driesch[6].

Table 3 Kudatini bone measurements (in mm)

Bone	Measurements
Bone No.	KUD 12
Bone	Astragalus
Species	*Bos indicus*
Lateral length	69.15
Medial length	63.00
Distal width	41.50
Thickness of lateral part	35.00
Thickness of medial part	32.70
Bone No.	KUD 02
Bone	Maxillary second molar
Species	*Bos indicus*
Length of M2	25.25
Width of M2	16.25
Bone No.	KUD 01
Bone	Mandibular condyle
Species	*Bos indicus*
Width of the condyle	31.35

Very few bone measurements are available for comparison with those from other ashmound sites[7]. However, none of the bones that are measurable at Kudatini have been measured so far. It has been observed that cattle size at the other ashmound sites is comparable to cattle from Budihal[8].

Cattle bones from Kudatini on qualitative basis also indicate that the cattle of all these ashmound sites were of the similar size and stature. Also it is possible to obtain a point estimate of the height at the withers of cattle based on the solitary astragalus (KUD 12) using the factor (medial length x 18.3) given by Zalkin. The estimated height is 115.29 cm. This shows that cattle at Kudatini were of at least of medium height. Such medium–tall cattle are comparable to the variety of cattle found at Deccan Chalcolithic sites like Nevasa, Daimabad, and Kaothe.

Concluding Remarks

Such a small collection of bones from Kudatini confirmed earlier observations that the ashmound builders had cattle, buffalo, sheep and goat similar to what has been observed at Budihal by Paddayya et al.[9] Mainly people at Kudatini were engaged in cattle pastoralism and also could have had also small herds of sheep and goat. More generalization is not possible due to a limited nature of the collection. However, the material has provided a fresh insight into the nature of animals at ashmound sites in Karnataka.

Acknowledgments

I am grateful to Dr. F.R. Allchin for allowing me to examine the faunal material. This work was done during my visit to Cambridge as Charles Wallace Fellow in the autumn of 1998. I also thank Dorian Fuller of the Department of Archaeology, Cambridge University for providing me necessary laboratory facilities.

REFERENCES

1. Allchin, F.R. 1960. *Kudatini Excavations. Hyderabad:* Government of Andhra Pradesh.
2. Ibid and 1963. *Neolithic Cattle Keepers of South India.* Cambridge: Cambridge University Press.
3. Ibid. p 56
4. Ibid
5. Shah, D.R. 1973. Animal Remains from the Kodekal Excavation in (K. Paddayya) *Investigations into the Neolithic Culture of the Shorapur Doab, South India* , pp. 92-95. Leiden: E.J. Brill.
6. Von den Driesch, A. 1976. *A Guide to the Measurement of Animal Bones from Archaeological Sites,* Cambridge, Massachusetts: Harvard University Press.
7. Joglekar, P.P. (in press). Re-examination of Faunal Remains from Piklihal, *Bulletin of the Deccan College Post-graduate and Research Institute.*
8. Clason, A.T. 1979. *Wild and Domestic Animals in Prehistoric and Early Historic India,* Lucknow: Ethnographic and Folk Culture Society.
9. Paddayya, K., P.K. Thomas and P.P. Joglekar 1995. A Neolithic Animal Butchering Floor from Budihal, Gulbarga District, Karnataka. *Man and Environment* XX (2): 23-32.

P.P. Joglekar
Deccan College
Pune - 411006

Agiabir – 1999: A Preliminary Report

Archaeological investigations carried out in the Sarayupar plain by the present team had resulted into the documentation of a new protohistoric culture termed 'Narhan Culture'[1]. This pre-historic culture with white painted Black–and–Red ware as the principal ceramic industry flourished in the second half of the second millennium BC. Vestiges of Narhan culture have been found, besides the type–site, at Imlidih Khurd, Dhuriapar, Bhunadih, Waina and Khairadih on the Ghaghara and its tributaries. Recently some new dimensions have been added to this culture through excavations at Raja–Nal–Ka–Tila in district Sonbhadra[2] as also at Malhar, district Chandauli[3]. However, at all these sites this culture has been noticed on small settlements (mostly village settlements not exceeding 5 hectares in size) and a transition from primitive to complex society represented by urban centres like Kausambi, Sravasti and Rajghat could not be securely documented. Therefore, in order to understand this transition an urban settlement having continuous habitation from Narhan culture to the early medieval period needed to be investigated. Agiabir perfectly foots this bill as the settlement is spread over an area of 40 acres and it has provided an uninterrupted sequence of cultures from second millennium BC (Narhan culture) to the end of the Gupta period. This site was explored by the second author in June, 1998[4]. With the above objective in mind the present team conducted excavations at this site between March and June 1999 and a preliminary account of this investigation is presented below.

Location

Agiabir (Lat. 25° 13' 52" N; Long. 82° 38' 41" E) is located on the left bank of the Ganga about 2 km south–east of Katka railway station on the Varanasi–Allahabad section of the Northern Railway, on the border of Mirzapur and Ravidasnagar (Bhadohi) districts. Katka is situated 38 km west of Varanasi on Varanasi–Allahabad G.T. Road. The ancient settlement extends in an area of more than a kilometre along the river and it has been partly eroded by it. The main mound measures about 500 m x 500 m. The excavation was carried out in the western part of the settlement (ABR–1) as also in the eastern part of the main mound (ABR2). On Mound–1 ten trenches, measuring 3m x 3m square, were excavated, while on Mound–2 only one trench measuring 5m x 5m was excavated which was subsequently restricted to only 2m x 2m area because of encountered structural activity. This trench was excavated upto a depth of 7 metres without reaching the natural soil. These excavations revealed the following culture sequence.

Period I (Narhan Culture)

Remains of Narhan culture were met with in the lowermost 60 cm cultural deposit. The main ceramic industries of this period comprised Black–and–Red ware (mostly of medium and coarse fabrics), black slipped ware (in a limited quantity but in fine fabric) and red ware. A few sherds of Black–and–Red ware and black slipped ware bear linear paintings in white as in the case of Narhan. The main types in Black–and–Red ware are bowls, storage jars, lipped basins and dish–on–stand. Some sherds of Black–and–Red ware bear cord impressions on the exterior. In black slipped ware the important shapes are deep bowls, *lota*–shaped vessels and bowls with pedestal. In red ware no kitchenware vessels were reported except for legged perforated bowls with several perforations at the base. Vases and storage jars, some bearing applique designs on the exterior, are the other types in this ware.

Inhabitants of this period lived in wattle–and–daub houses. Framents of burnt clay with reed marks and patches of floors, ovens and post–holes have been recorded. Two silos, obviously used for storage of grains, were brought to light this period. A bead manufacturing workshop is an important discovery of this period (Pl.1). Twenty-six stone beads (18 finished and 8 unfinished)together with waste chips were recovered. Other antiquities comprise eighteen net sinkers, nine bone points and sixty-three pottery discs (with ten perforated specimens). An incense burner or lamp of baked clay is a noteworthy find of this period.

A large number of bones and four charcoal samples were collected from various strata of Period I. Their study will furnish valuable information on the fauna and chronology of this period.

Period II (Pre–NBP with Iron)

The inhabitants of this period lived in wattle–and–daub houses. Traces of burnt floors, ovens, silos and post–holes have been recorded. This period is marked by the ceramic assemblage of black slipped ware and red ware but total absence of Black–and–Red ware. The main types in black slipped ware are knife–edged bowls, dishes and pedestaled bowls. In red ware dishes, knife-edged bowls, tumbler with thick core, button based goblet and vases are the principal types. Small finds comprise beads of semi–precious stone and terracotta, bone points, iron and copper objects and pottery discs.

Period III (NBP Period)

Like the preceding period, inhabitants of this period also lived in wattle–and–daub houses. Remains of post–holes, ovens, rammed floors made of pot sherds were noticed in this period. The main ceramic industries of this period were black–slipped ware, NBP ware, some of it of deluxe variety having silvery, golden, pink and golden shades, grey ware and red ware. Straight–sided and flanged bowls, dishes with incurved rim are the important types of the first three wares. In red ware bowls, lipped basins and vases are the main types. A dish of NBP ware bearing a thick slip with handle is an important discovery of this period.

The small finds from the period comprised beads of terracotta and semi–precious stones (agate, carnelian, quartz and faience), bone points, terracotta balls, copper and iron objects and terracotta discs. Mention may be made of the discovery of unusually large number of terracotta discs (236 in number) found in the limited excavatrions. Among these, three terracotta discs bear running antelope motif incised on them. Similar specimens were recorded earlier from Rajghat and Prahladpur.

A hoard of about 300 faience beads placed in a miniature vessel of black slipped ware is the other noteworthy find. The discovery of a number of beads alongwith stone chips from this period indicates that these were produced locally.

Period IV (Sunga–Kushana Period)

One room measuring 2.98 x 2.20 m with walls made of burnt bricks (size 46 x 26 x 5 cm) was found in the trench located on the eastern slope of the main mound. The northern and western parts of this structure were found to be robbed. Remains of this period comprised red ware as a principal ceramic industry with vase, ink pot lid, sprinkler, pear–shaped vase (Ahichhatra 10 A) and lugged *karahi* as the main types.

The small finds comprise two copper coins, bone points, terracotta figurines, terracotta discs, antimony rods of copper and iron objects. A votive tank of terracotta was an important find of this period.

An ivory seal with four letters engraved in Brahmi characters *(Satyanaga* or *Sandnaga)* was recovered from inside the room (Pl.2). A fragmentary terracotta nude female figurine with legs raised and spread apart is another noteworthy find (Pl.3), similar figures were reported earlier from Bhita, Kausambi and Jhunsi in the middle Ganga plain. This indicates that the cult of mother goddess was prevalent in the middle Ganga plain in the early centuries of the Christian era.

The mound continued to be occupied during the Gupta as also in the post–Gupta times. However, the remains of these periods could not be documented in the limited excavation undertaken. Fragments of stone jambs of temples with Krishna–lila scenes carved on them and broken sculptures of Ambika, Ganesa, Surya and

Ekmukha Sivalinga datable to tenth–twelvth centuries AD are lying on the present–day temple of Lutabir located south–west of present Agiabir village.

REFERENCES

1. Singh, P. 1994, *Excavations at Narhan (1984-89)*, Banaras Hindu University and B.R. Publishing Corporation, New Delhi.
2. Tewari, Rakesh, 1997. Excavations at Raja Nala–Ka–Tila (1995-96), District Sonbhadra (UP) : Preliminary Observations, *Pragdhara,* No. 7 (1996-97), pp. 77–96.
3. 1998. In Quest of Early Iron Age Sites in Karmanasa Valley, *Pragdhara,* No. 8 (1997-98), pp. 57-67.
4. Singh, Ashok Kumar, 1999. Explorations Agiabir, District–Mirzapur (UP). *Pragdhara, Journal of the UP State Archaeological Organisation,* Lucknow, No. 9 (1998-99).
5. Marshall, J.H., 1915. Excavations at Bhita, *Archaeological Survey of India–Annual Report,* 1911–12, Calcutta, pp. 24–94. Plate–XXIII, No. 40.

Banaras Hindu University
Varanasi

Purushottam Singh
Ashok Kumar Singh

Early Historic Investigations in Kalahandi District, Orissa: a Preliminary Report

Introduction

Kalahandi district is inhabited by several indigenous tribes such as the Gonds, the Khands and the Majhis. This note is based on three season's field survey (1996-97, 1997-98 and 1998-99) in the Bhawanipatna, Rampur-Madanpur and Dharmgarh sub-division of Kalahandi district. Although a few sites were reported earlier[1], no systematic research about the archaeology of Kalahandi was carried out. Our present survey has brought to light many sites belonging to the Prehistoric, Protohistoric as well as early Historic periods (Fig. 1).

The Area of Study

Kalahandi district is situated in the south-western part of Orissa (19° 3' – 21°5'N and 82° 20' – 83°47' E). Kalahandi literally means'black pot' or it could also denote 'pot of arts'. The district is bounded on the north by the districts of Balangir, Sambalpur and Raipur (of Madhya Pradesh), to the south lies the district of Koraput on the west are the districts Koraput and Raipur and on the east are the districts of Koraput and Boudh–Phulbani (Fig. 2).

The Tel, Indravati and the Jonk, which form tributaries of large rivers like the Mahanadi and Godavari are the principal rivers of Kalahandi. The Tel is the longest and most important one in the district. The most important feeders on its right bank are the Moter, Hat, Sagada, Rat, Utai and the Rahul, while on the left bank, the Tel is joined by the Udanti. Unlike the Tel and its tributaries, all flowing northward, the Indravati originating near Thuamul village of Thuamul–Rampur flows southward. Besides these rivers, the hilly tracts of the district are criss-crossed with a large number of streams, most of which are perennial. Most of the Stone Age sites are found on the banks of Tel and tributaries, whereas the confluence of two tributaries are chosen by the Early Historic settlers for habitation as they were considered sacred and good for trade and commerce.

Rich mineral wealth is the most noteworthy geological feature of the district. Precious and semi-precious stones such as diamond, cat's eye, sapphire, ruby, garnet, topaz, Alexandrite and moonstone occur in Kalahandi district. One finds mention of valuable stones in the accounts of Kautilya, Ptolemy, Yuan Chaung and Tarvenier.

Early Historic Sites and Material Culture

The chronological sub-phases of early historical urbanism in South Asia cannot be stated with precision, but following the current postulated historiographical trend, a broad distribution may be between approximately 600 BC to AD 600. This period coincides with the emergence of cities and complex polities in South Asia as well as the growth of Buddhism throughout the subcontinent[2]. The region of Orissa comprising vast deltaic plains, long coast lines with rich mineral and forest resources, which are the most essential components of urbanization, flourished well during the Mauryan and post-Mauryan periods. Both internal and overseas trade routes were opened up, linking various urban centres of South and South East Asia. Sites like Sisupalgarh, Jaugarha on the coast of Orissa and Narla Asurgarh and Manamunda Asurgarh were excavated. Since then scores of Early Historic sites have been brought to light[3]. Surprisingly no attempt has been made to investigate the genesis of urbanization in Orissa. Did the source lie outside Orissa? Was there an antecedent stage? Why no attempt has been made to investigate the Early Historic phase in Orissa using the generally accepted criteria such as the size of the settlement; an economy incorporating agriculturists and pastoralists; large urban settlements; use of stone, mud-bricks and burnt bricks; public and private hydraulic features; craft specialisation; formulation of ruling class; long-distance trade; a unified system of weights and measures and a written script[4]. The present note is a modest attempt to give an account of the early historic sites discovered and the earlier reported sites that have been re-studied by the authors.

Asurgarh

Asurgarh is an ancient fort-town 2 km from Narla village. The almost square fort (each side about 1 km) has four gates in all the cardinal directions. The river Sandul forms a natural barrier on the western side of the fort. The moat present on other three sides is fed by a huge ancient tank. The fortified city spreads over and area of 200 ha.

An Excavation of limited nature revealed paved house-floors, iron implements, weapons, beads of semi-precious stones, punch-marked silver and copper coins, Black-and-Red ware, terracota figurines, glass bangles, amulets and ornaments. The antiquities recovered from this site are more or less similar to those unearthed from contemporary Sisupalgarh. Asurgarh was occupied between the 3rd century BC and the 5th century AD.

Pottery shapes collected during this field work comprise dishes, bowls and vessels. The dishes are in burnished Black-slipped Ware and Black-and-Red Ware (both well-fired and in fine fabric). The bowls are in burnished Black-slipped Ware with slightly inverted simple rim, thin wall, well-fired and of fine fabric. The vessels are in burnished Black slipped Ware (with complex externally projected short beaked rim, well-fired and of fine fabric), and Red Polished Ware (narrow mouth, concentric corrugation on the interior, well-fired and of fine fabric with grey core) (Fig. 6).

Animal bone collection from Asurgarh (Table 1) is small (only 7 fragments), but presence of a complete second phalanx is interesting, which clearly shows that both buffalo and cattle were present at Asurgarh.

Table 1: Animal bones and their measurements (mm): Asurgarh

Bos indicus	Complete upper second molar (KAL 31)	
	Length	: 24.70
	Width	: 12.24
Bos indicus	Complete upper second premolar (KAL 32)	
	Length	: 16.34
	Width	: 12.76
Bos/Bubalus	Complete first phalanx	
Bos/Bubalus	Mandible, vertical ramus fragment	
Bubalus bubalis	Complete second phalanx (KAL 32)	
	Max length	: 45.95
	Proximal width	: 30.60
	Proximal thick	: 34.22
	Distal width	: 24.97
Bubalus bubalis	Mandible, horizontal ramus fragment (KAL 30)	
	Length	: 39.15 Premolar 4
	Width	: 17.31
Bubalus bubalis	Complete mandibular third molar (KAL 29)	
	Length	: 39.15
	Width	: 17.31

Budhigarh

The site of Budhigarh is situated 500 m to the east of school in Madanpur village. The mound (1000 x 500 m) is about 3 m in height and mostly intact in nature except in a few places. In the middle portion villagers have made a path to reach the Rahul river. The part of the mound, close to the village shrine is under cultivation. A wide range of artefacts have been recovered from this site: ceramics, coins, beads, bricks (45 x 30 x 10 cm), terracotta objects, iron implements and idols of Durga and Ganesa. A good number of animal bones and human skeletons have been noticed at Budhigarh. The artifactual evidence indicates that the site was occupied from the Early Historic to the late Medieval period.

The ceramic assemblage consists of dishes, bowls, miniature bowls, vessels, basins, dish-on-stand and lids.The dishes that are in burnished Black-slipped Ware (with inverted simple rim, thin wall) are of fine fabric; while those in Black-slipped Ware (with slightly inverted simple rim, convex body) are of medium fabric. The bowls are in dull Red Ware (with external projecting simple rim, thin wall, traces of slip on outer surface) are of fine fabric. The bowls in Red Ware (with external projecting triangular rim) are of coarse ware. A miniature bowl in Black-slipped Ware (with external projecting triangular rim) of medium fabric has been found at Budhigarh (Fig. 7). The early Mediveal pottery consists mainly or vessels in Red-slipped Ware with various complex rim forms and are of coarse to medium fabric (Fig. 8).

Faunal bone collection from Budhigarh (Table 2) comprises 27 fragments. It reveals faunal diversity attesting presence of wild animals besides sheep/goat, domestic pig, buffalo and cattle. The collection has one distal metacarpal fragment of *gaur (Bos gaurus)*, a molar of *nilgai (Boselaphus tragocamelus), chital (Axis axis)* bones and mandibular molar fragment of a wolf *(Canis lupus).*

Table 2: Animal bones and their measurements (mm): Budhigarh

Bos indicus	Fragment of calaneum
Bos indicus	Distal fragment of first phalanx
Bos indicus	Complete first phalanx (KAL 20) Max length : 64.97 Proximal width : 26.30 Proximal thick : 29.07 Distal width : 23.15
Bos indicus	Complete third phalanx (KAL 19) Max length : 67.20
Bos indicus	Distal fragment of humerus
Bos indicus	Distal fragment of metacarpal (KAL 25) Distal width : 56.78 Distal thick : 23.73
Bos indicus	Mandible, symphisis region fragment
Bos indicus	Complete deciduous lower third molar (KAL 27) Length : 18.16 Width : 9.10
Bos indicus	Complete mandibular first molar (KAL 15) Length : 31.00 Width : 21.00
Bos indicus	Complete mandibular first molar (KAL 16) Length : 26.46 Width : 12.47
Bos/Bubalus	Cranial fragment
Bos/Bubalus	Tooth fragment
Bos/Bubalus	Distal fragment of humerus
Bos/Bubalus	Mandible, horizontal ramus fragment
Bos/Bubalus	Rib fragment
Bos/Bubalus	Rib fragment
Bos/Bubalus	Rib fragment
Bos/Bubalus	Rib fragment
Bos/Bubalus	Rib fragment
Bos/Bubalus	Distal tibia fragment
Bos/Rubalus	Thoracic vertebra fragment
Bos/Bubalus	Vertebra fragment
Bos/Bubalus	Vertebra fragment
Bos/Bubalus	Vertebra fragment
Bos/Bubalus	Complete deciduous mandibular second molar
Bos/Bubalus	Complete deciduous mandibular third molar
Bos gaurus	Distal fragment of metacarpal (KAL 17) Distal width : 67.08 Distal thick : 38.63
Bubalus Bubalis	Complete astragalus (KAL 22) Lateral length : — Medial length : 60.10 Distal width : 39.19
Bubalus Bubalis	Complete first phalanx (KAL 21) Max length : 67.61 Proximal width : 29.20 Proximal thick : 31.15 Distal width : 30.00
Bubalus Bubalis	Proximal metatarsal (KAL 26) Proximal : 42.19 Proximal thick : 12.60
B. tragocamelus	Mandibular first molar fragment

Capra hircus	Proximal radius fragment	
Capra/Ovis	Mandibular molar fragment	
Capra/Ovis	Mandibular molar fragment	
Axis axis	Distal radius fragment (KAL 24)	
	Distal width	: 37.94
Axis axis	Proximal radius fragment	
Sus domesticus	Maxillary second molar (KAL 28)	
	Length	: 15.80
	Width	: 12.60
Canis lupus	Mandibular molar fragment	

Dumberbahal

The early historic mound of Dumberbahal (250 x 125m) which lies 1 km to the north of village is locally known as 'Guva'. It is situated on the right bank of Ret river. The entire mound is under cultivation and has deposit of about 10 m. Due to this cultivation, about 40 cm of the top layer has been disturbed, exposing artefacts.

Wide range of early Historic–Iron Age ceramic assemblage at Dumberbahal comprised dishes, bowls, vessels, basins, jars and dish–on–stands. The dishes are in burnished Black–slipped Ware with faceted rim showing close parallel with Rouletted Ware, bur of an inferior fabric (Fig. 9).

The faunal collection (Table 3) from Dumberbahal showed bones of cattle *(Bos indicus),* buffalo *(Bubalus bubalis)* and of *Cervus* sp. (Sambar/Barasingha).

In the previous season (1997-98) animal bones collected from Dumberbahal also showed a fauna having both domestic and wild components (Fig. 10-14).

Table 3: Animal bones and their measurements (mm): Dumberbahal

Bos indicus	Distal metapodial fragment	
Bos/Bubalus	Cranial fragment	
Bos/Bubalus	Tooth fragment	
Bos/Bubalus	Mandibular molar fragment	
Bubalus bubalis	Calcaneum fragment	
Bubalus bubalis	Complete mandibular third molar	
Capra/Ovis	Cranial fragment	
Axis axis	Complete maxillary second molar (KAL 37)	
	Length	: 17.90
	Width	: 14.05
Cervus sp.	Glenoid portion of scapula	

Concluding Remarks

The results of this investigation represent a definite stage in the continuing research process dealing with the archaeological record of a small region in Orissa. It is important to note that several early historic sites have been noticed earlier, however, information is inadequate to understand the complex social structure of Orissa during this period. Earlier more emphasis was given on large urban centres and sites with impressive art and architecture. Small and medium rural settlements which must have contributed profoundly to the growth of large urban centres had not received enough attention. So far, no attempt has been made to study the animal remains from the Early Historic sites which can throw light on the economy and chronology of this phase. This research work for the first time integrates the cultural data with those from animal remains.

The authors' preliminary survey in Kalahandi has brought to light several prehistoric, protohistoric and Early Historic sites. The discovery of extensive Mesolithic, Neolithic, Chalcolithic and Iron Age–Megalithic to Early Historic sites with fortification, surrounded by satellites in a limited geographical area shows the evolution of cultures from egalitarian hunter–gatherers to sedentary farming communities and finally to complex urbanization. The Early Historic sites have some important features like fortified settlements, structural features (both religious and secular), rich ceramic industry, terracottas, an enormous quantity of cast punch–marked coins, iron implements in considerable stones; all of which indicate that the Early Historic period witnessed a most flourishing stage comparable in many ways with that of the Ganga valley.

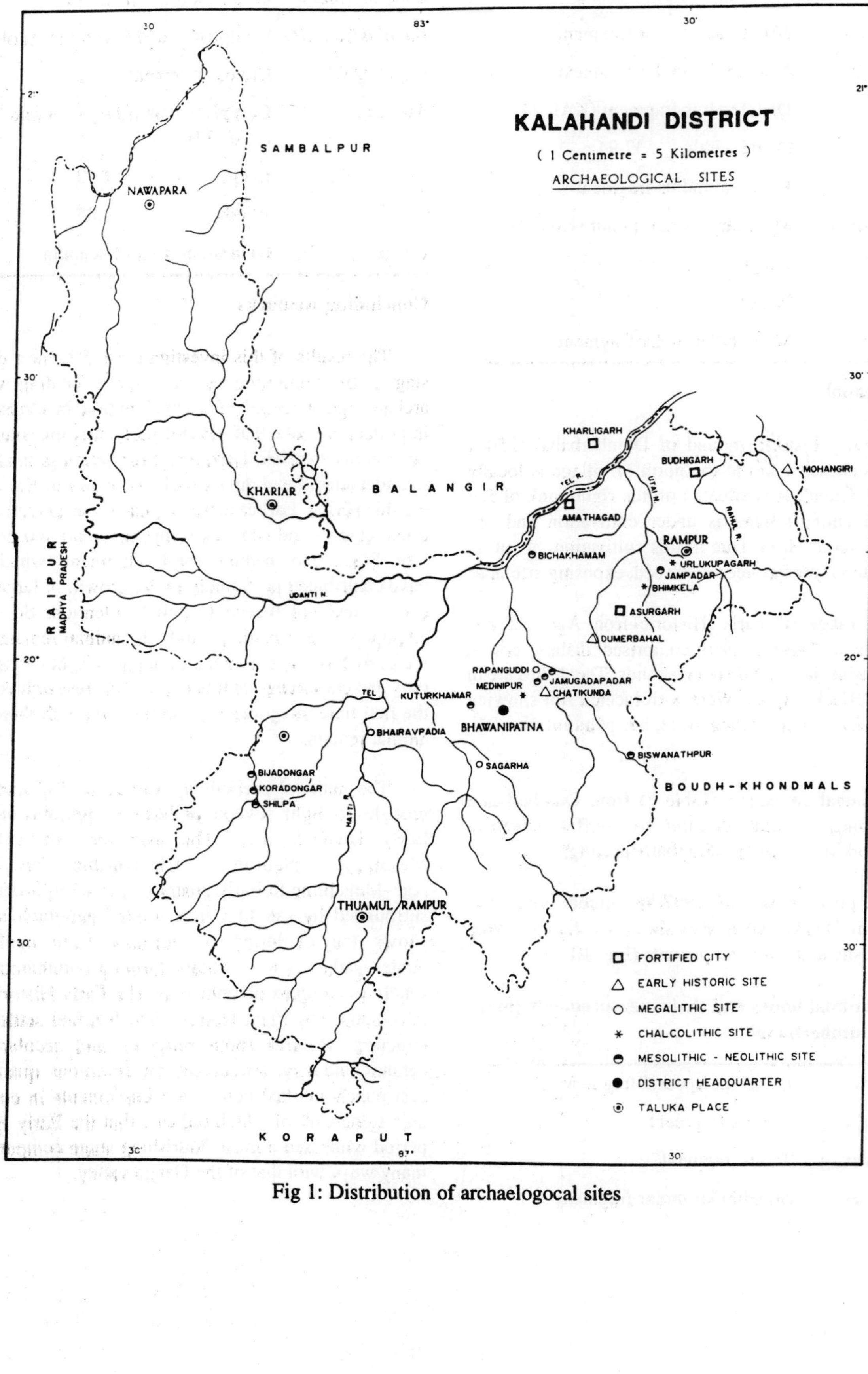

Fig 1: Distribution of archaelogocal sites

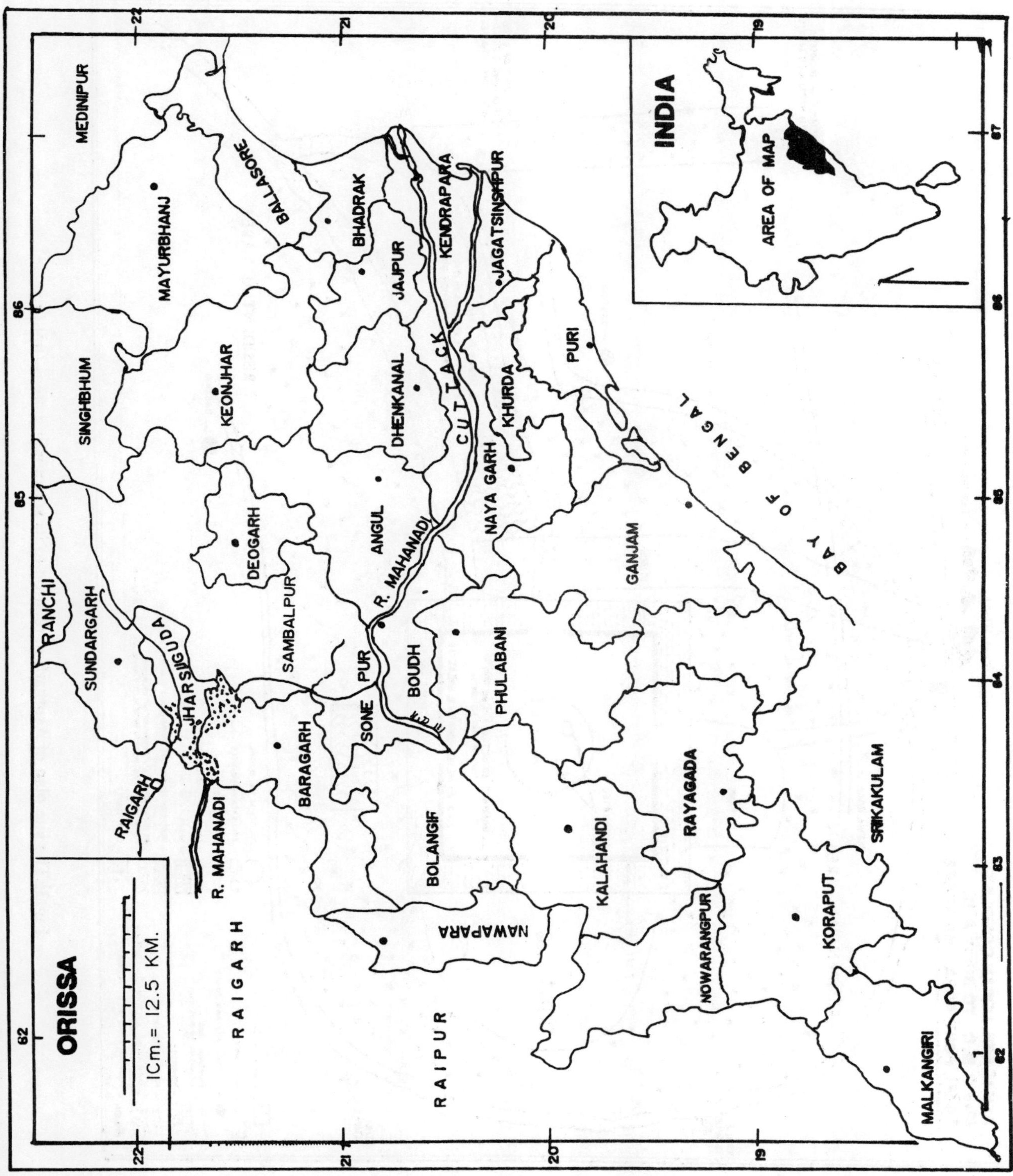

Fig 2: Location of Kalahandi

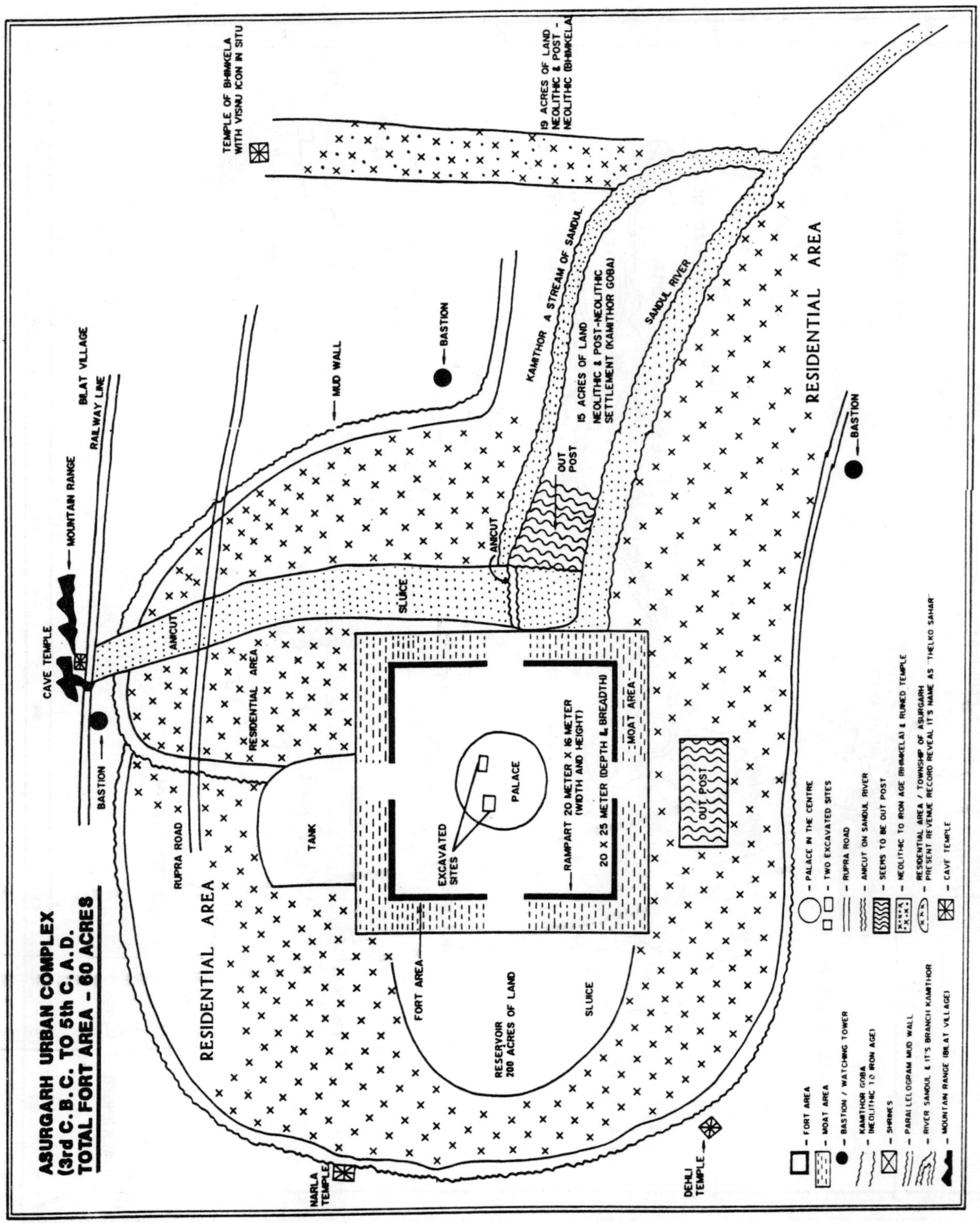

Fig 3: The site plan of Asurgarh in relation to its surrounding areas (not to scale)

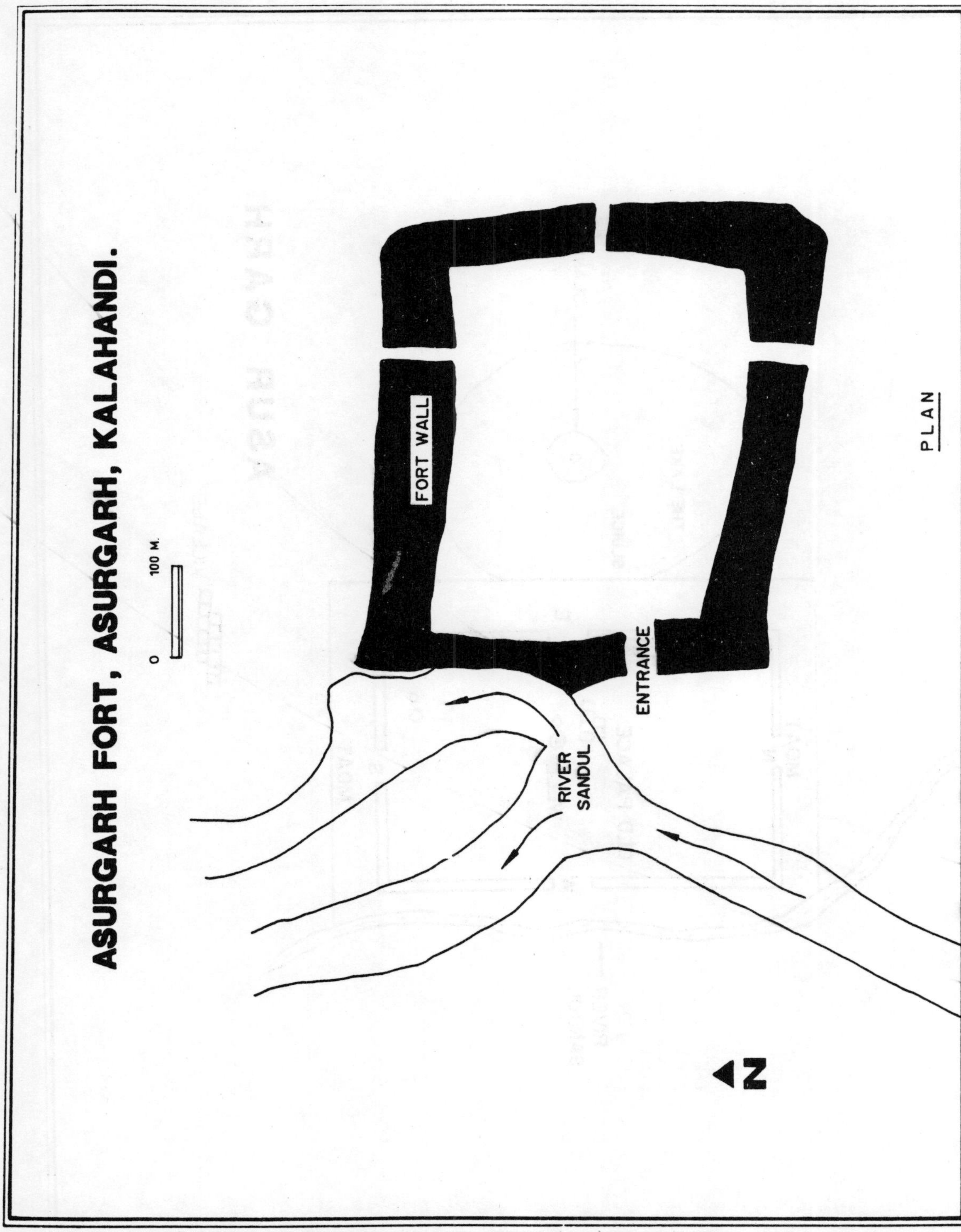

Fig: 4: The site plan of Asurgarh wth all its features

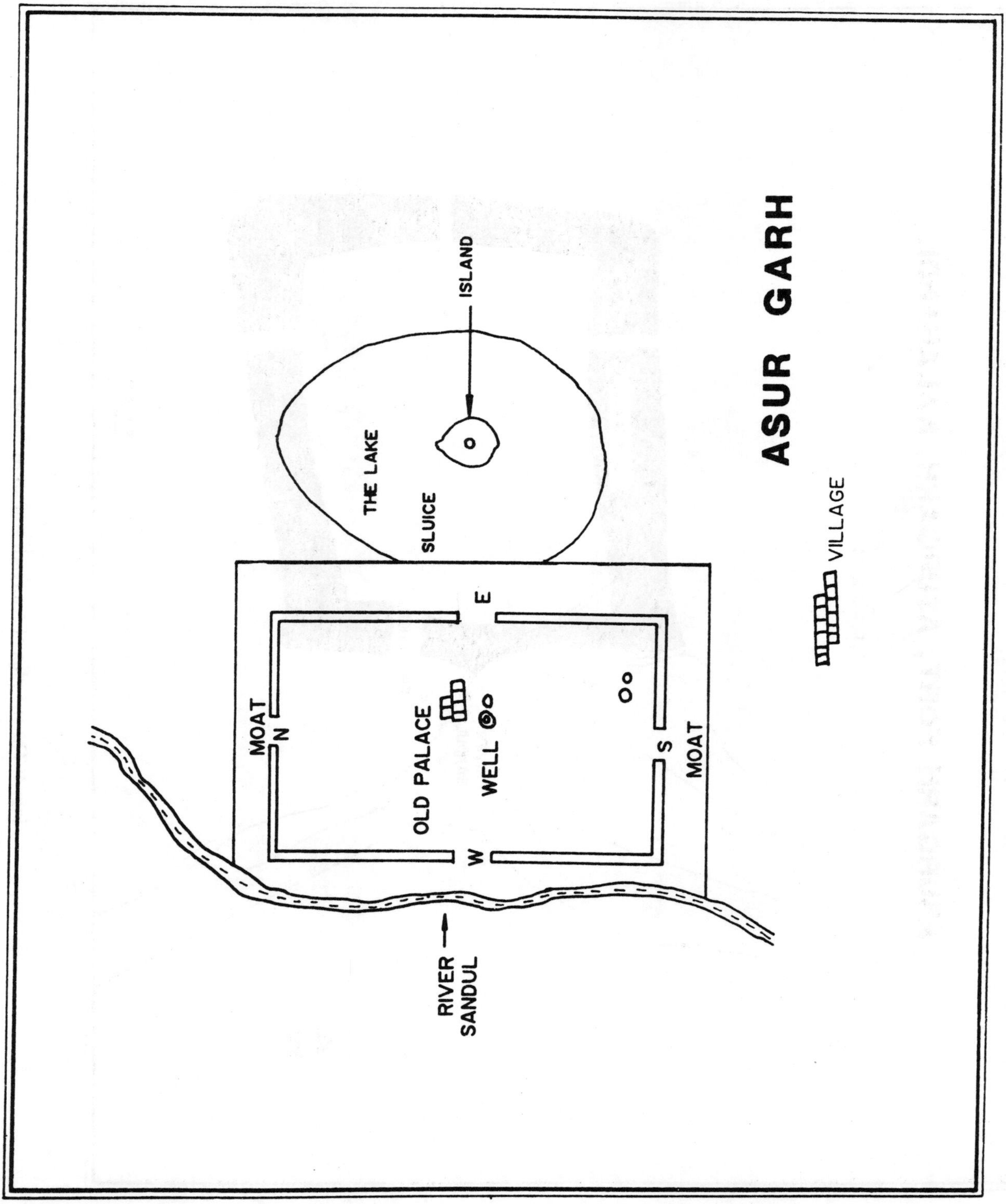

Fig: 5The site plan of Asurgarh wth all its features

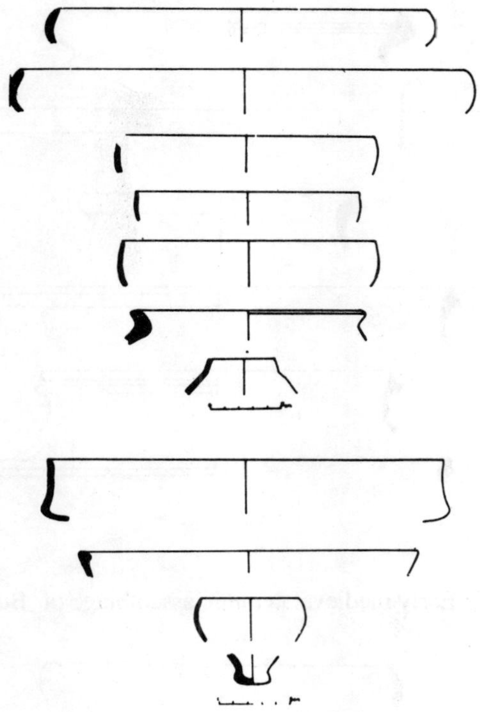

Fig 6: Early historic ceramic assemblage of Asurgarh

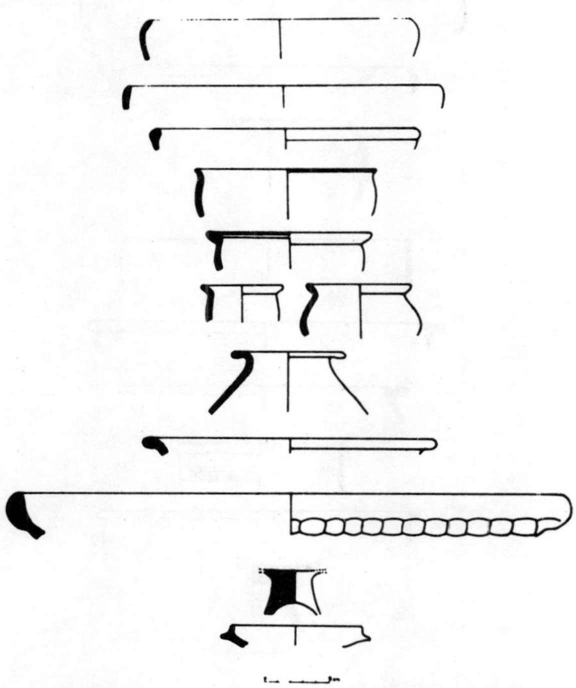

Fig 7: Early historic ceramic assemblage of Budhigarh

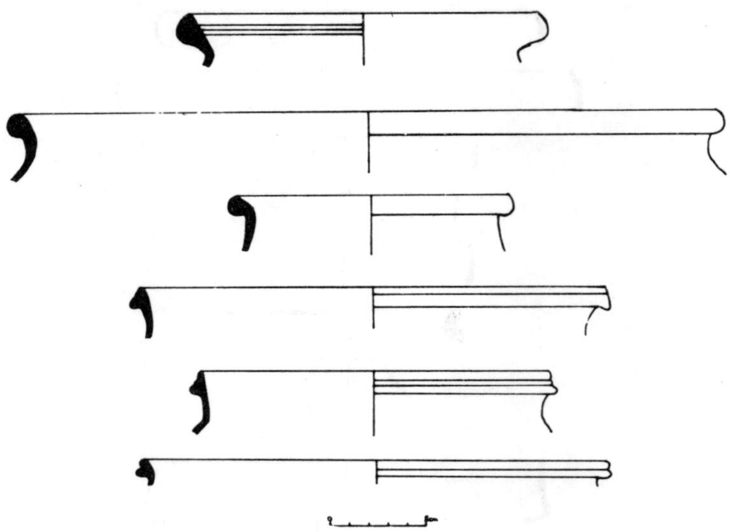

Fig 8: Early medieval ceramic assemblage of Budhigarh

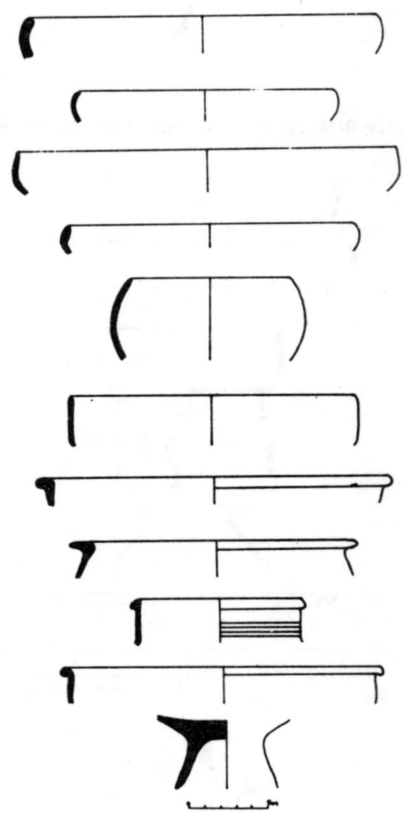

Fig 9: Iron Age - Early historic ceramic assemblage of Dumberbahal

REFERENCES

1. Sahu, N.K. 1982. Asurgarh, in *Interim Reports* (S.C. Behra (Ed.), pp. 1-8. Sambalpur; Prusty, H. 1992. Palaeolithic Vestiges from Kalahandi, *Orissa Historical Research Journal.* 37 (1-40: 55-61; and Brandtner, M. 1994. Archaeology of Western Orissa: Finds from Nehena, in *South Asian Archaeology 1993* Vol. I A. Parpola and P. Koskikallio (Eds.) pp. 101-114. Helsinki: Suomalainen Tiedeakatemia.

2. Chakrabarti, D.K. 1995. *Archaeology of Ancient Indian Cities.* Delhi : Oxford university Press; Hietzman, J. 1984. Early Buddhism, Trade and Empire in (*Studies in Archaeology and Palaeoanthropology of South Asia* K.A.R. Kennedy and G.L. Possehl (Ed.) pp. 121-138. New Delhi: Oxford; Kosambi, D.D. 1989. *The Culture and Civilization of ancient India in Historical Outline.* New Delhi: Vikas; Morrison, K.D. 1995. Trade, Urbanism and Agricultural Expansion: Buddhist Monastic Institutions and the State in the Early Western Deccan, *World Archaeology,* 27(2):pp. 203-221; Ray, H.P. 1986. *Monestery and Guild: Commerce Under the Satvahanas.* Delhi: Oxford; and Saro, K.T.S. 1990. *Urban Centres and Urbaniztion as Reflected in the Pali Vinaya and Satta Pitakas,* Delhi: Vidyanidi Oriental

3. Mohanty, P. and B. Mishra. 1998. Recent Archaeological Researches in Orissa with Special References to the Early historic Phase, *Man in India* 78(3-4) :pp. 205-221.

4. Braidwood, R. 1950. *The Near East and the Foundations for Civilization,* Oregon; Childe, V.G. 1950 (1979 ed.). The Urban Revolution, in (*Ancient Cities of the Indus*) G.L. Possehl (Ed.), pp. 12-18, Delhi: Vikas Pub. House; and Shaffer, J.G. 1993. Reurbanisation: The Eastern Punjab and Beyond in urban Form and Meaning in South Asia, (*The shaping of Cities from Prehistoric to Precolonial Times*) H. Spodak and D.M. Srinivasan (Eds.), pp. 53-67 Washington: NGA.

PRADEEP MOHANTY, P.P. JOGLEKAR* AND
BABA MISHRA*

*Department of Archaeology,
Deccan College, Pune 4110016.

**P.G. Department of History, Govt. College,
Bhawanipatna, Kalahandi 766001

Unique Carved bone piece from Chandraketugrah, West Bengal

The site of Chandraketugarh (22°41' Lat., 88°42' Long.) on the dried up bank of river Bidyadhari in district North 24-Parganas of West Bengal lies about 37 km northeast of Calcutta. This site is known for its Indo-Roman trade contact and played a major role during Early Historic period as a trading centre. in Eastern India. The excavations carried out at this site during 1955-68 by the Ashutosh Museum of Calcutta University has yielded evidence from Pre-Mauryan to Pala period[1]. Besides it was also established as the epicentre for production of Rouletted Wares and had a cultural contact with Eastern India and South East Asia[2]. The site is very extensive and covers an area of about 3 sq. km. In the last several years unauthorised diggings at various spots for antiquities hunting have destroyed the site badly. Mostly the terracotta objects particularly the plaques belonging to Kushana and Gupta periods which are very common findings of the place are smuggled out. Recently, the local police has seized antiquities which include few terracotta plaques and a unique bone piece of Sunga-Kushana period.

The present paper deals with the beautifully carved bone piece which is unique to Sunga-Kushana period. This cylindrical carved piece is prepared out of the shaft of a long bone. The length is 9.8 cm with a squarish cross section. The lower side of this object is slightly narrower than the upper side. The size at the upper and lower ends of this piece is 2.8 cm x 2.5 cm and 2.8 cm x 2.4 cm respectively. The average thickness of the bone is about 0.7 cm at the upper and 0.5 cm at the lower end of the extant portion. From the thickness of the bone and the size of the bone-marrow portion clearly suggest that it belongs to a big animal. Subsequent to the carving, the object was given fire treatment for its durability, hence the shinning surface.

The beautifully carved bone piece depicts in two upper friezes a male and a female figure under the trees whereas the lower frieze depicts wild animals in three compartments. The two upper friezes are seperated by two trunks of the luxuriant trees providing some sort of canopy above the figures. In one of the upper friezes a standing female (Pl. I) in her full bloomed youth is seen with right hand on her waist and left hand holding and bending the branch of a tree to feed a spotted deer to her left which is shown chewing the leaves. The upper part of her body is shown bare. She is shown with slightly raised belly with a delicately marked deep navel, thin waist with a soft graceful bend on right side and perfectly modelled round breasts. Her locks of hair fall on two sides. A beaded fillet on her plaited hairs is shown covering part of her forehead. She is bedecked with round flower shaped beaded *karnakundala* in her two ears and a heavy *hasuli* type beaded necklace around her neck. She is shown wearing four ornamental bangles in each hand. The soft and sensitive contour of her lower portion including the private part are covered by a diaphanous drapery tied by a *mekhala.* She is wearing three anklets in each leg. She has a radiating smile while her body vibrates in warm flesh and blood. The deer to her left is shown chewing the leaves stretching the head with a support of the forelegs on a platform.

In the other upper frieze there is a male figure (Pl. II) which is shown in a standing posture with both hands resting on his waist over the *mekhala.* He wears a scarf on his head tied by a fillet decorated in beaded patterns. The ends of the scarf are hanging on the shoulders. Like the female figure, he is also wearing a heavy necklace *kanṭhahara,* wristlets *valaya* and anklets. He is clad in a diaphanous *dhoti* with an exageration of his genital organ. Like the female figure, his waist is also narrow and the chest is 'V'shaped and masculine. He holds an ineffible smile on his face.

In the lower frieze, below the female figure is shown a standing elephant in a striding posture to right. To the left of this elephant, in another frieze, is shown a pair of jackals, seated face to face with their heads raised upwards and folded frontal legs. A panel below the male figure depicts a pair of peacocks facing each other with spread out tails. A half lotus medallion is seen at the top of the peacocks as an ornamental device. The lower panels are seperated by vertical beaded borders.

Both the male and female figures have been identified as *yaksha* and *yakshini* and find their close semblance in the contemporary terracotta art of the Sunga-Kushana period that has been found in abundance at Chandraketugarh, Tamluk and other parts of the country. What fascinates one is their closer`associations with the forest. Unlike the terracottas, the artist in this case has tried his best to create the details of a forest with the wild animals.

Acknowledgement

The authors are thankful to Shri A.K. Bandyopadhyay for going through the manuscript and making necessary corrections.

REFERENCES

1. Chakrabarti, D.K. 1989. "Chandraketugarh" in A. Ghosh (ed.). *An Encyclopaedia of Indian Archaeology,* Vol.2. Munshiram Manoharlal Publishers Pvt. Ltd., New Delhi, pp.9596.
2. Geogte, V.D. 1997. "The Chandraketugarh Tamluk Region of Bengal: Source of the Early Historic Rouletted Ware from India and Southeast Asia", *Man and Environment,* XXII (1): pp.69 85.

Archaeological Survey of India
Calcutta Circle, Calcutta

SANTANU MAITI AND S.B. OTA

Excavations at Bijamandal Mound in Khajuraho District Chhatarpur (M.P.)

The ancient mounds at Khajuraho revealed the existence of earlier brick temples. To know the further details, the Archaeological Survey of India took up further excavations.

Nourished by the meandering rivers Khudar and Kutni besides the larger river Ken, the region was blessed with much of the resources required to sustain a vibrant population. The Ken river was also instrumental in transporting men and materials from other parts of the country. This did help in the inflow of ideas and craftsman from distant lands. However, conspicuous building activity in the tract around Khajuraho from as early as 200 BC particularly at Bharhut in Satna district and in Gupta times at Bhumra, Nachna and Deogarh, shows that talent was also available within the region. With these antecedents it is no wonder that 84 temples were said to have been built at Khajuraho in a period spanning from 8th to 12th century AD.

The Archaeological Survey of India in order to ascertain the fact about the 84 temples initiated an intensive survey in 1980. The finding of 18 mounds and other associated protuberances with definite evidence of antiquarian remains gave some credence to the common belief. Perhaps many more temple remains could be found outside the ambit of 10 Km. diameter.

In the meanwhile, in 1981 the department started excavating the largest of the Satdhara mounds located east of the Western Group of Temples. The excavations which continued intermittently till 1989 brought to light the cultural sequence of the place. The remains showed clear evidence of Pratihara and Chandela periods. One of the most interesting find was the presence of a triple shrine with a common *mandapa* and *pradikshinapatha.* Significantly, the earlier structures were of bricks. The continuous occupation of the site is understood by the superimpositions of three periods on the brick structure. The presence of stone architectural fragments which were noticed in heaps at the four corners of the platform indicate that the temple might have been *panchayatana type,* though no complete structure was found.

Several sculptures including that of Mahishasuramardini, Vamana and Yamuna were found. Among the other important finds are various beads, terracotta pendants, figurines of bull, gamesman, disc and iron objects. Among the iron objects found, some remarkable ones included the tanged arrowheads, fragmentary blade of dagger and leafs-haped spear-head besides nails and other miscellaneous artifacts.

In the year 1998-99, excavation was again undertaken under my direction on the main mound of the Bijamandal group of mounds. The mound located about 3km south-south-east of the Western Group of Temples as the crow flies is approachable by a metalled road till Chaturbhuj temple. From here, at a short distance, an unmetalled road towards the old Jatkhara village would lead to the site.

This mound also known as Vaidyanath where exploration before excavation was thought to be remains of a big temple. Concealed among the conspicuous architectural remains found during the survey was a Kichak bracket and a leograff. The mound is surmounted by a small platform of coarse dressed stones which is capped by a broken marble *yonipatta.* The study also revealed intact *in situ* mouldings julting out of the rain-washed surface of the mound.

This mound with Siva linga as highest point and enclosing broken *yonipatta* has been taken up for excavation in order to expose the extant basal remains of the temple. Actual digging which started on 9-3-99 was .undertaken at the highest levels of the mound excluding the Shiva linga and *yonipatta.* During the process the topmost layer consisting of chips of stones of architectural fragments were encountered. This layer also had much cobble and broken architectural fragments and mutilated pieces of sculptures. Beneath this layer (1) huge blocks of stones were encountered. These colossal stones were laid edge to edge and perhaps formed the foundation for the pillars supporting the *mahamandapa.*

On understanding the nature of deposits in the topmost levels from the initial probings excavations were continued on the sides of the mounds so as to expose the extant mouldings. From the begining itself from the maze of partly hidden and exposed structures the entire architecture of the *garbagriha, antarala, mahamandapa, mandapa* and *ardhamandapa* was reconstrued. The extant remains observed belong to the *pitha* and *adhisthana* mouldings of the basal part of the temple. The lowest of these are resting on coarsely dressed blocks which apparently was to be below the soil. Above this roughly chiselled blocks are the mouldings of *kharasila, bhita* with frieze of floral motifs, *karnika, kumbha, kapota, karnika,* and *grasapatti.*

Broadly in almost all the trenches excluding those near the *antarala* there are only two main layers other than the lower natural soil. Layer No.(1), it appears light brownish grey to blackish in colour. It contains predominant amount of silty soil, chips of stones, possibly debitage and several architectural fragments. Other anthropogenic remains include broken sculptural parts with an occasional limb, legs, face or head etc. The total thickness of this layer is between 5 cm to 125 cm. This layer becomes increasingly thicker away from the edifice. Layer No. (2), predominantly consisting of brick-bats, interestingly thins out as it moves away from the sides of the temple and the brick-bats are not seen west of the *garbagriha.* In the *antarala* region layers of chips are found within the general layer (2) of the brickbats. The layers has several differences possibly indicating towards the nature of activities in the precincts, particularly in the *garb griha* and *mahamandapa* portions. Thus the topmost layers denoted as (1) consist of brownish silty soil, chips of the blocks from which sculptures and architectural fragments were recovered. Layer (2) is full of brick-bats with with grayish/blackish tone. Whereas lower portion of the same layer designated as layer (2a) is having reddish disposition being full of brick-bats and its powder. The underlying layer (3) is again singularly of chips which is tapering away and out from the mouldings. Layer (4) differs from the above by having brownish soil, chips of carving and brickbats. Layer (5) is again a layer of chips. However, it is much thicker and this layer is contemporary to the ornamentally carved lowest blocks. Layer (6) is again of brickbats and is contemporary with the coarse chisselled blocks. Underlying layer (6) is the layer (7) which is again of predominantly of chips of the carvings. This layer is also contemporary with the lower rough chisselled stone.

The predominance of brick-bats around the structure may have been due to either of the following reasons namely: brick-bats as remains of scaffolding built around while moulding courses were being laid. Alternatively, brick-bats may have been lain around the edifice to protect it from accidental damage during construction in which heavy stones were carrieu around. Brick-bats may be of ramp or remains of ramps which were constructed to take the structural members to the spot. Again brick-bats as remains of props which were erected to protect the dangerously poised architectural members pending completion of construction could also be possible. Alternatively some of the architectural members may have developed cracks and these may have been buttressed. Brick-bats as part of remains part of main structure like pillars of the inner core of structure or some part like of the structure particularly in the veneering like *udgama, kudas* etc.or the pyramidal tiers of roof etc. is also possible.

On searching for the staircase east of *ardhamandapa,* some brick-bats and deeper down the loose bricks were found. On further excavations eroded and weathered bricks were noticed. These, however, did not crystalize as a staircase. Possibly due to the heavier erosion in the northern half of the brick structure as also seen in the stone structure the outline in this half-side especially in the easternmost part was not discernible. However, the southern side was much better preserved. The brick structure is addorsed to the eastern mouldings which is bereft of carvings. In the line where the brick structure is coupled with the stone one the former extends almost in the same line, as the latter. However, after 1.30 m there is an offset and the structure broadens towards the south. The equivalent in the northern side is not visible; probably being eroded away, enblock. There is a niche which is 1.30 m wide and again there is another offset which makes the structure even much wider. Some continuous feeble structural remains of brick were seen upto 7.75 m from the point where it starts contiguous to the stone *ardhamandapa.* The brick size is 30x19x5 to 6 cm. Due to the incongruent nature of the structure with offsets and niche it may not have been possibly a staircase. Further on analogical grounds as seen in other temples the ratio of dimension between steps and main structure is nearly 1:6, whereas that at Bijamandal it is nearly 1:4.

A study of the moulding revealed that the highest one was about 2.25 m above the *kharasila.* At places, particularly in the northern half the mouldings were very few as these may have fallen down and rolled away. Among the main themes represented in the *antarpatta* mouldings are social scenes like music, dance, portly men being attended by male and maidservants. Other scenes include warriors on the move along with horses and elephants. A preponderance of elephants have been noticed. Most interestingly *in situ* depiction of Jain tirthankara are seen replete with several type of attributes, flanked by attendants. Curiously, whereas one of the tirthankaras has been carved in full detail including swastika etc. other one at the opposite side was left unfinished. In this panel the fact that carving was done from left to right has been lucidly shown by the fact that the attendant on the left of the viewer has been finely carved whereas the central deity and the attendant on right was in the process of being given finishing touches.

It has been observed that the sculptures of this site, belong to three distinct phases; the earliest one having simpler sculptures with lesser attributes and are more or less rotund in nature. The second phase is represented by sculptures with full elaboration of iconography executed as per the canons. The third phase sculptures are more elongate, slender with triangular ornamented head-dress, typical of the Kalchuris. Curiously many of the sculptures of divinities are either lacking in depiction of their attributes and *vahanas* or else the attributes are different from those generally attributed to them. As for instance the comparatively intact Sarasvati figure lacks its *vahana.* Incidentally, this Saraswati figure also was not given finishing touches like combing of hair, carving of particular outlines of gems on the jewellery etc. Similarly another *in situ* figure apparently of Siva was identified by headdress, and flower buds in his upper hands. There are yet many other sculptures some of which are not given finishing touches; all of which albeit have attributes which are not in concordance with those commonly in vogue.

This structure before excavation thought to be comparable with Vishvanath temple in dimension, has been found to be longer than the largest temple of Khajuraho namely Kandariya. Whereas Kandariya measures about 30 metres in length the extant Bijamandal temple remains has a length of 34.60 m. It, however, is thin in comparison to Kandariya by about 75 cm. The finding of lime coating especially over jaina figures and one chunk of lime within the brick-bats, indicate that the lime making technology was in existence when the former brick structure i.e. the ramp was in use.

In the light of the above observation and discussion following inferences can be made namely: that the temple was in the process of completion and was abandoned midway. Perhaps the *garbha griha/sikhara* was constructed to its complete height. The brick-bats were the remnants of the ramp that extended upto the *shikhara.* Part of the ramp now remains anterior to the *ardhamandapa* which looks like damaged steps extends far beyond normal staircases and, therefore, has to be remains of the ramp. The lack of sophistication in sculptures which were actually carved for the Bijamandal temple and the mix up in attributes shows these were carved in a period when the classical excellence was not there any more. Thus the temple building could be said to have continued well into 12th century AD. The presence of *tirthankaras* with halo, *srivatsa,* hairstyle and attendant, on analogical grounds may be that Hindu deities may have been placed in Jaina temples as in Parshwanath etc. is taken as dedicatory to jaina *tirthankaras.* Once the temple construction was abandoned mid way, the structural members fell down and accumulated as gravity induced deposits aided by rain water, along with chips used as filler between the moulding stones. Excavation conducted till now has revealed most of the events related to the history of this temples building. Further excavations may throw more light on construction activities of these temples.

Superintending Archaeologist
ASI, Bhopal Circle, Bhopal

P.K. Mishra

BOOK REVIEWS

L.K. Srinivasan and S. Nagaraju (Eds.). *Sri Nagabhinandanam,* (M.S. Nagarajarao Felicitation Volume, in two parts) Bangalore, 1995, pp. 889, Plates CCXXVIII, figs. 35, Price-not given.

These two bulky volumes of M.S. Nagarajarao Felicitation Volume contain 84 essays written by eminent scholars; Indian and foreign. The first has 44 articles grouped into three sections: I Prehistory, Protohistory and Anthropology, II Historical Archaeology, and III Art, Architecture, Sculpture, Iconography and Painting, while the second book incorporates 40 articles grouped under sections: IV History and Epigraphical Studies, V: Afghanistan, South-east Asia and Sri Lanka, VI Conservation of Cultural Property and VII Science and Technology in Relation to Archaeology.

The volume contains a few articles which need serious discussion and understanding others are descriptive and informative. M.K. Dhavalikar's article raises doubt about the seven "Fire Altars" at Kalibangan by calling them as simple cooking hearths of pit type even though he accepts the prevalence of Fire Worship at Harappan towns. He has, however, neither raised nor answered the question as to why seven 'hearths' were interlocked with common walls and why in each case a prominently placed brick on shorter base was higher than the top-most level of the walls of the 'altars' ?

The article by P.C. Caldwell and K.A.R. Kennedy dealing with Human Skeletal Remains from Tadakanahalli and Komaranhalli is very significant since it clearly establishes the fact that the Iron Age Megalith builders in Karnataka were not the new comers in the region, they were the same people as the Chalcolithic people of the region.

In the article "The Rigvedic People: Their Identity" by B.V. Subbarayappa has unconvincingly attempted to show that the Rigvedic People had Sumerian origin and that the Proto-Elamite system of accounting explains the nature of Harappan writing since the former has been repeatedly challenged by archaeologists and the latter does not explain the context of pictures of men, animals and vegetation on seals (of one Akkadian inscription on a Harappan type seal from Louvre Museum reads 'Goddess of Corn'). Moreover, recent discoveries at Harappa and Rehman Dheri have conclusively proved that the birth of Harappan script lies in the Early Harappan levels bracketed between 3300 BC and 2600 BC. An impression of a seal with three character has been found at Harappa in Kot Diji levels beside hundreds of pictograms on pottery.

For those interested in the historical archaeology and

history of Sri Lanka the article by Sudarshan Senevirante will be of great value. The article on Vijayanagar by P.S. Dunham will be informative for those interested in ancient town-planning. Michael W.Meister's article entitled 'Indian Seeing and Western knowing: and Art Historians Perspective' is what has been again and again said by sages of the past, Hindu of today and art historians like Coomaraswamy and Stella Kramrich that icons and temples are just *alambans* and covers, concrete forms of higher visions or abstract concepts, the 'forms' and 'lakshanas' need not always convey the hidden meaning; he rightly cites the example of Sitala icon at Amber.

There are several other informative articles on structural and rock-cut temples by several scholars. K.P. Poonacha's paper on Asokan edict at Sannati as well as early sculptures from Hasargundgi are equally informative. Sundara's paper on *Yajna Purusha* is very educative. Gorakshkar's paper on 'Metal Sculptures from Western Tibet', which contains several rare Buddhist images, conveys many new facts. L.K. Srinivasan and M.V. Visweswara have made a very detailed study of 'Pralaya varaha sculpture at Kallahalli'. Ratan Parimors' article of 'Kaliya Daman in Indian art' is a highly painstaking work. 'A Bhagavat Purana Manuscript from Mysore' by R.J. Del Bonta is a very fine study of its kind in terms of beautiful paintings. The manuscript at present is housed in the San Diego Museum. M.A. Dhaky has presented an excellent research work on the 'Umaswati in Epigraphical and Literary Tradition'. There are a few other very good papers on epigraphy as well as history of agriculture, land ownership, industries, etc. of south Indian dynasties by P. Venkatesan, M.D. Sampth, N. Pankaja, S.V. Padigar and others.

There are also very valuable papers on South-East-Asian countries, like K.V. Ramesh's paper on an inscription from Laos, Mary-Ann Lutzker paper on the narrative reliefs of Candi Jago in Indonesia, S. Nagaraju's paper based upon his own field-work of ancient Buddhist temple city in Central Sumatra; K.V. Raman's paper on India's links with Vietnam. A paper by L. Prematilleke and A. Aluwihare on the archaeological remains of an ancient hospital at Polonnaruva, Sri Lanka is very interesting and informative.

There are papers on conservation by B.M. Feilden, O.P. Agrawal, G.C. Chauley, L.K. Srinivasan and B. Narasimhaiah, each one of which gives a detailed account of works done at various sites along with problems and solutions. That of Feilden, however, focuses on the profession and its problems like teaching, International conventions, etc.

Lastly, articles on the use of Remote sensing in archaeology, Metallurgy in Karnataka, and Gemmology in ancient India, attract our attention.

The volume has indeed a compendium of articles throwing valuable light on various aspects of Indology. It has been neatly printed and beautifully produced. Everyone will benefit from it. A must for all libraries of Indian history, culture and art and archaeology.

S.P. Gupta

A.K. Seshadri , *Conservation of Monuments in India,* Book India Publishing Co., Delhi. 1997, pp 174. Plates 35, Rs. 1600/-

At a time when conservation of monuments, sites and environment has gained importance in global context, A.K. Seshadri's work on conservation of monuments in India has much significance. The defination and scope of conservation, formulation of international charters and the history of conservation of monuments during pre – and post – Independence period in India, are recounted the first chapter. Factors that cause deterioration and eventual destruction of monuments, the various branches of conservation such as preservation, consolidation, restoration, transplantation and environmental protection as well as methods of documentation of monuments are discussed in the second chapter. The conservation methods adopted for Bagh Caves, Rock Cut and Structural Temples at Ajanta, Ellora, Mammallapuram and Tanjavur as well as various forts form the subject of the third chapter. The fourth chapter deals with the nature of conservation works and cognate subjects. Chemical conservation of murals, bronze, manuscripts and stone inscriptions are dealt with in the fifth chapter. The 35 plates with a bibliography highlight the text.

Hari Shanker B.S.

Choodamani Nandagopal and Vatsala Iyenger. ***Temple Treasures*** (2 Vols.) The Crafts Council of

Karnataka. Bangalore, 1997 pp 426 Coloured Plates and Figs. 445. Rs. 2000/-.

Here is a contemplative study on the concept and significance of ritual utensils and jewellery from temples of Karnataka. This very well–documented work is in two volumes, the first discusses the rituals in temples, and examines the utensils, their significance with the prescriptions and requirements given in the *agamas* The second part is devoted to cataloguing of temple jewellery, including precious stones. The crown and crest jewels, ornaments of the face, arms, breast and waist as well as masks and ritualistic jewellery are described high lighting the symbols and motifs on them. The work throws light on metallurgy, bead making as well trade and exchange in the past.

The book is well printed with 445 illustrations. An exemplary work useful for art historians and archaeologist alike.

Hari Shanker B.S.

Helen Vallianatos, *Prelude to paleodiet: A Histological and Elementry Study of Diagenesis among Early Holocene Skeletons from North India.* Department of Ancient Indian History, Culture & Archaeology, University of Allahabad, Allahabad, 1999. pp 104. Figs 12 Rs. 300/-.

The present work deals with Palaeodietry, pertaining to the people of Mesolithic from the rock shelters at Lekhahia in the Vindhya Hills and Damdama in the Ganga Valley. A major aspect of the study in the elucidation of the problems of diagenesis which is the post-mortem physical and chemical alteration of skeletal material. Histological and trace element analysis have been adopted for the study.

In the first part, histological analysis determine bone integrity and the degree of diagenetic alteration. The qualitative description of changes in bones, the quantitative analysis of specimens as well as the statistical analysis have focussed on types of tunneling on the bones and degree of general destruction. In the second part, the diagenetic indicators on the bone samples are examined to understand variation in dietary and diagenetic values which very between sites. While suggesting new elements as diagenetic indicators and a plant diet consumed by the Mesolothic people, the author is cautious to avoid hasty conclusions. The text is supplemented with 6 tables, 12 figures, a glossary and 4 appendices.

Hari Shanker B.S.

Vandana Khanna. *Krishna Themes In The Visual Arts Of Rajasthan, 1999,* Publication Scheme, Jaipur, p.p. 158, Price Rs. 2000/-

The book entitled, 'Krishna Theme In The Visual Arts Of Rajasthan' is an attempt to tread a new path of thematic analysis of the representations in Visual Arts of Rajasthan from 200 BC to 1800 AD. It displays some rare illustrations of the Surasagar, the Rasikpriya, the Rasaraja and the Gitagovinda of Mewar School of Paintings. The plates as well as the text are beautifully brought out in the book. The book has also interesting and attractive contents as the name of Lord Krishna indicates, it *karshyatiti* Krishna (attracts readers).

The book presents the analysis and treatment of the theme in its totality in the visual arts and literature, taking the development of the theme in all its phases both chronologically and in diverse arts. An attempt has also been made to highlight some of the aspects emphasising the inter-relationship of arts and literature. In this regard those illustrations of Krishna legend in visual arts have been selected for the study whose descriptions are found in the work of Sanskrit, Braja and Rajasthani. The representative examples from both the visual arts of Rajasthan have been culled. The selection of paintings mainly centres around Mewar. In conclusion, the book observes that, it is the *saumyarupa* (pacifying aspects), awe inspiring expliots of god, and, the Vatsalya rasa that attracts the scluptors than other facets of his personality, while the painters and poets have centered their creation around the love alliances of Krishna with milkmaids and his exploits of love. The legend of Krishna has also been represented in wall paintings of palaces and in Pichhavasis at Nathadwara.

P.K. Trivedi

U.P. Arora, A.K. Sinha, and A.K. Singh (eds.) *Currents in Indian History, Art and Archaeology,* Anamika Publishers and Distributors, New Delhi pp.76, Price Rs. 300/-

The volume is a collection of 17 select research papers presented in the Annual Conference of the Indian History and Culture Society held in the Rohilkhand University, Bareilly. Each one of these is very informative and educative. Some of the subjects covered are "Use of Scientific Techniques in Indian Rock Art Studies" (D.P. Agarwal and J.Kharakwal), Geographical Horizon of Megasthenese (U.P. Arora), Models, Metaphor and Archaeology's Loss of Innocence (U.C. Chatopadhyaya), Religious Institutions as Reflected in Syncretistic Icons (P.P. Dandwate), Excavations at Fatehpuri Sikri (R.C. Gaur), The concept of Adrishta in Gandhara (Anupa Pande). Other papers are on art, architecture, archaeological discoveries and history. A very useful volume.

The printing and paper are excellent.

S.P. Gupta

U.P. Arora, *Greeks on India (Skylax to Aristoteles), ISGARS, Deptt. of Ancient History,* Rohilkhand University, Bareilly, (1996) pp.226+xiii. Figs.5 Price Rs. 450/-

Here is a book which gives a rare insight into the historiogrphy of Greek perception of India. Contrary to common belief that the Greeks hailed India in every field, they were made to believe by their writers that India was inhabited by a race of monsters who were sadow-footed, one eyed, long headed, with ears large enough to sleep in, who lived under earth. Thus, wrote Skylaxo. Ktesias talked about one footed men, dog-headed men, hairy phygmies, etc. However, they also admired Indian honesty, India's wealth, Indian animals, etc. all the information gathered here is from the original sources, translated and transliterated into English by Greek knowing scholar.

The book is divided into 10 chapters dealing with subjects like Historical Information, People and Customs, Economy, Religious Life, State Power, Medical Science, Fabulous Accounts, etc. One appendix gives translaions of original passages from the writings of Horodotos, Xenophon, Ktesias, Skylax and others.

It is a very useful book for all interested in Greek perception of India.

S.P. Gupta

K.K. Basa and Pradeep Mohanty (Eds.), *Archaeology of Orissa (two volumes)* Pratibha Prakashan, Delhi. pp. 700. Plates and Figures 200. Price Rs. 2500/- for the set.

Although a lot of work has been done on archaeology of Orissa during the last 50 years but the common knowledge about it is very little. Thus these two volumes fulfil a great need; now even the researchers of all kinds can lay their hands on the source-material for their work.

The two volumes contain 31 articles selected themtically for a comprehensive knowledge of Orissa in history and archaeology. It starts with the Geomorphology of Orissa, Historiography, New Archaeology approach to Orissa, Prehistoric cultures of different parts of Orissa, Neolithic cultures and their recent discoveries, including that of Golabai by B.K. Sinha, several Neolithic Chalcolithic discoveries on the coast and inland, discoveries of the historical period such as at Lalitgiri, Dayagiri, Radhanagar, Urban structure and change, Maritime Archaeology, Ancient Ports of Orissa, Ethnographical studies, Rock Art, Barabati Fort excavations, Ancient Potteries, Burial sites, etc.

It is a very well produced work, neatly printed on good paper. Recommended for all archaeology researchers.

S.P. Gupta

P.C. Kashyap, *Living Pre-Rigvedic and Early Rigvedic Traditions of Himalayas,* Pratibha Prakashan, Delhi pp.220 + xvi Maps3, Plates 33. Price Rs. 1200/-

This is a unique work of ethno-archaeology giving us a great insight into the Vedic and pre-Vedic Indian mythologies, feasts and festivals since in some parts of the Himalayan regions of the Seven rivers these are still being practised. amongst these are Buddhi-Diyaudi-Birtasur Mela, Jhiru, Bhunda and Bishu which affirm the survival eve today of pre-Rigvedic and early Rigvedic society. Thus, Vedic texts alone are no more the sources of knowing the Great Tradition, even the so-called Little Traditions, i.e. the folk traditions, the living rituals, contain a fair amount of lores, enactments of lores in the form of plays, beliefs and belief-systems. These lores are the exact shadows of the Vedic stories, for example with a long rope representing the serpent Vrtra.

The book is divided into five chapters : The Buddhi Diyadu : the Indra-Vrtra Legend, Jhiru : The Shisnadeva Show, The Naramadha, Khasas : the Vedic Marutas, and Himalayan Pantheon. Each one gives details of the Vedic legends, the plays in action the players, the festivals, the rituals, in words and photographs collected and taken personally after at least a decade of field-work.

S.P. Gupta

Dilip K.Chakrabarti, *Colonial Indology,* Munshiram Manoharlal Pub., New Delhi 1997. pp.258+XII, Price Rs. 250/-

It is the first book of its kind written by a senior and mature Indian scholar of history and archaeology although there are several very good books written on cognate subjects in the West and published during the last decade.. The subject of the book is rightly titled 'Socio-politics' of the Ancient Indian past since there is now overwhelming documents to prove that many of those in the West, including Max Muller, V.A. Smith and Mortimer Wheeler, who professed total objectivity in their assesment of ancient Indian history were not always that honest-racial and cultural superiority very often conditioned their perception. In addition, like the Middle Age Western explorers they too were still obsessed by their Greek knowledge of India, a place of Monsterous Races, and Christian bias of non-Christian religions in the framework of 'whiteman's burden' Anthropology and Linguistics were grossly used and misused to prove that India was civilised by the Englishmen otherwise Indian Civilization was primitive, Indian thought was a baser kind and India was a conglomeration of different races, languages, customs, belief-systems constantly at war with each other, there was nothing in its history which could make it a nation.

Chakrabarti rightly observes : "The book explores some underlying theoretical premises of the Western study of ancient India. These premises developed in response to the colonial need to manipulate the Indians' perception of their past. The need was felt more strongly from the middle of the nineteenth century onwards, and an elaborate racist framework, in which the interrelationship between race, language and culture was a key element, slowly emerged of its success is obvious from the fact that the Indian nationalist historians left this framework unchallenged, preferring to dispute it only in some comparatively minor matters of detail. This book argues that this framework is still in place, and implicitly accepted nor merely be western Indologists but also by their Indian counterparts. The image of the ancient Indian past remains the same. The persistemce of the old image is reflective of India's relationship as a part of the Third World with the West and Western historical scholarship."

One may or may not agree with all that he has to say on ancient Indian oral traditions and the supermacy of archaeology but one admit this forthright statement of facts culled from a mass of sources. Many of these may not be palatable to those still writing on India's past, some of them are serious archaeologists and anthropologists, but biased scholars, at least on two issues they all keep on arguing in favour of the non-Indian origin of the Vedic Aryan Civilization and the non-Indian origin of the Harappan Civilization. Chakrabarti has quoted them aptly to show that they argue only on very flimsy grounds.

It is a work which every scholar of Indology must read, it will be rewarding even though at several places the reviewer himself is in disagreement with the author.

S.P. Gupta

Anupama Srivastava, *The Development Of Imperial Gupta Brahmi Script,* Ramanand Vidya Bhavan, New Delhi

The *Development of Imperial Gupta Brahmi Script* is a work in the field of the palaeography of the Brahmi script by Dr. Anupama Srivastava, and is edited by Dr. T.P. Verma and published by Ramanand Vidya Bhavan, New Delhi. The book, one of its kind, is divided in eight chapters : Introduction, North Indian Styl; Kaushambi region, Eastern Indian style: region of Bengal & Bihar, Western style: Mathura region, Malwa style : Madhya Bharata, Script on Coins, Numerals and Resume. In all, fifty-seven plates illustrate the text. As many as 65 inscriptions arranged into 48 groups, have been included. These are regrouped in four, according to region and chronology, and are described in the respective chapters.

The present study describes the different stages and variations found in the Brahmi script during the period of the Gupta rulers. In the first chapter, introduction, the writer has undertaken a brief and formal presentation of the available variations and prevailing tendencies, starting from Ashokan period unto the rise of the Guptas in the North India. Eight text figures illustrate observations made in the chapter. In the second chapter, North Indian style, the style of the Brahmi script used in the Kausambi region is discussed. Twenty-three inscriptions have been studied here. Initial vowels, constants, ligatures and medical signs are described individually. They are similarly studied in third, fourth and fifth chapters. The controversy about spurious copper plate inscription, from Nalanda and Gaya, belonging to Samudragupta, discussed in this chapter. In the third chapter, eastern style of Brahmi script is elaborated. It includes the region of Bengal and Bihar. This chapter is divided in two groups, based on copperplate inscriptions, and silver and terracotta seals. Fourth chapter has a study of the western style, covering the area of Mathura region. Eight inscriptions on copper plates, iron pillar and stone are discussed here. In the fifth chapter, Malwa style: Madhya Bharat, inscriptions from central India are dealt with. The Junagadh rock inscription of Skandagupta, dated in the Gupta years 136, 137 and 138, is specially discussed under the region of Gujarat. Script on coins is studied in the sixth chapter. While presenting views of various scholars on the subject, problem of *kacha* is also touched. It is also presumed that the mints in the Gupta period were situated in the middle Ganga valley, that's why examples on the coins show uniformity in the engraving of the letters. Numerals sign unto 200 are dealt here.

Ravindra K.Vasishtha

Report of the XXXII Annual Conference of Indian Archaeological Society held at Allahabad from 14th through the 16th November, 1998

The annual session of the Societies namely Indian Archaeological Society, Indian Society for Prehistoric and Quaternary Studies and Indian History and Culture Society for the year 1998 was held in collaboration with Department of Ancient History, Culture and Archaeology, University of Allahabad, U.P. and was inaugurated by the Honable Shri Nar Singh Gaur, Minister of Education, Govt. of Uttar Pradesh on the 14th November, 1998.

After the inaugural function, Prof. V.D. Misra delivered the Presidential address of the Indian Archaeological Society; Prof. D.N. Tripathi delivered the Presidential addresses of the Indian Society for Prehistoric and Quaternary Studies and Prof. A.R. Khan of the Indian History and Culture Society. The closing function was held on the 16th November in the Allahabad Museum and the valedictory Address was given by Prof. G.C. Pandey.

The Indian Archaeological Society conferred V.S. Wakankar Award with a citation,a shawl and a cheque for Rs. 21,000/- on Dr. K.M. Srivastava, Former Director, Archaeological Survey of India, in recognition of his dedication and outstanding contribution to the growth and development of the science of field-Archaeology in India.

Programme

14, November, 1999 : Afternoon Session

Professor H.D. Sankalia Memorial Lecture by **Shri J.P. Joshi**
Harappan Civilization as seen at the Close of the 20th Century.

Conference Papers

Ravi Korisettar
Quaternary Studies in the Malaprabha Valley

Subrata Chakrabarti
The Stone Age Prehistory in Birbum

K.S. Shukla
Palaeolith from the Ganga Valley

T.P. Verma
Some Recently Discovered Prehistoric Sites in eastern U.P. & Bihar.

J.N. Pandey
The Microlithic Industries of the Vindhyan Plateau and the Gangetic Plains : their Antiquity and Possible Economic Implications

Ajita K.Patel
Prehistoric Hunters and Pastoralist in North Gujarat and Kutch, India

<u>Sunday, 15 November : Forenoon Session</u>

G.L.Badam, V.D. Mishra, J.N. Pandey and J.N. Lal
Further Research on the Palaeontology of Son Valley

A.K. Singh and Anil Kumar
The Evidence of Horse in the Indian Peninsula (Pre to Early Historic Period)

Vijay Sathe
Analysis of Enamel Ultrastructure in Archaeology

Y.S. Farswan and Vinod Nautiyal
Elemental Analysis of Anthropogenic Soil - Habitational Intensity.

K.Krishnan & R.A.E. Coningham
Petrographic Analysis of Rouletted ware and Associated ceremics of the Early Historic Period.

Ambika Patel
Metallographic Studies of Early Historic Iron Objects from Nagara.

K.S. Saraswat
Agricultural Economy at Neolithic-Chalcolithic Senuwar (*ca.* . 2200-600 BC) in District Rohtas, South Bihar

D.K. Bhattacharya
The Problem of Interpretation in Indian Archaeology

S. Bandyopadhyay·
An Exploration in District Rajnandgaon, M.P.

<u>Sunday, 15 November : Afternoon Session</u>

P. Ajithprasad, V.H. Sonawane, K.K. Bhan, S. Pratapchandaran and Abhijit Majumdar
Excavations at Bagasra - 1997-98

Abhijit Majumdar
Early Harappan Settlements in North Gujarat

Kiran Dimri
Post Urban Harappan Settlement in Central Saurashtra

V.N. Misra, V.S. Shinde, R.K. Mohanty, Lalit Pandey and Jeevan Kharakwal
Further Excavations at District Balathal, Udaipur, Rajasthan (1997-98)

R.K. Mohanty and S.B. Ota
Chalcolithic Pit-dwellers of Central Narmada Valley

Mahida Bhamini Ajitsingh
Terracotta Art of Bagasra

H.C. Mahanta
The Neolithic Pattern of Garo Hills, Meghalaya

Surgyani, Vighanesh Kumar and Chhaju Ram
Problems of Neolithic Age in Rajasthan

<u>Monday, 16 November : Forenoon Session</u>

A.S. Sundara
Rock Engravings in the Sahyadri Ghat and Coastal Region

Giriraj Kumar
Palaeolithic Petroglyphs in India : Development of Motifs and Site Use Pattern

M.L. Sharma and Vighanesh Kumar
Ostrich (?) in Rock Art and Archaeology in North-East Rajasthan

Vijay Singh
A New Interpretation of Rock Paintings

A.K. Prasad
Recent Discoveries of Rock Paintings, Palaeolithic Industries and other artefacts in Nawadah Jamui, Gridih and Kodarma districts of Bihar,

M.L. Sharma and Vighanesh Kumar
Newly Discovered Rock Art Site in Marwar Region.

Kumar Anand
Musical Elements in Indian Rock Paintings

R.K. Pancholi
Bharatiya Prag kala ka Udbhav- Bhanpura Kshera(Hindi)

<u>Monday, 16 November : Forenoon Session</u>

J.N. Pandey
A Tale of Four Cities of the Lower Gangetic Doab : Archaeological Evidence

Misra, V.D., J.N. Pal and M.C. Gupta
Excavations at Amilkoni

(Dr.) Colonel A.K. Prasad
Recent Discoveries of Rock Paintings, Palaeolithic Industries, Giridih

Bhatt, S.K.
Terracotta Art of Sai Gomati Doab

Tiwari, V.K.
Art of Nalanda

Dev Prakash Sharma
Neolithic Culture of Eastern India, Eastern Nepal & South East Asia: A Comparative Study.

<u>**Monday, 16 November : Afternoon Session**</u>

S.K. Mitra
Megalithic Excavations at Ubharia, Distt. Betul, MP.

V. Selvakuamr
Iron Age-Early Historic Cultures of the Gundar Basin, Tamil Nadu

P.S. Joshi
The Megalithic Culture of India : The Second Turning Point

D. Bhengra
Megaliths of Chotanagpur Region with Special Reference to Ranchi District

Dilip Rajgor
Evolution of Brahmi Script : A Linguistic Approach

S.K. Bhatt
Proto-Numismatic Tradition in India

Balram Tripathy
Ethnoarchaeological Perspective of Early Historic Trade in Central and Western Orissa

Surgyani, M.L. Sharma & Chhaju Ram
Fifty Years of Archaeology in Rajasthan

G. Seevalee
Irrigation and Society in Ancient Sri Lanka

NATIONAL SEMINAR

Fifty Years Of Indian Archaeology : Retrospect & Prospects

Parallel Session :

<u>**14 November 1998 : Afternoon Session**</u>

<u>**SECTION 1 PREHISTORY**</u>

V.N. Misra, Pune
The Lower Palaeolithic

K.K. Chakravarti, Bhopal
The Mesolithic in Madhya Pradesh : The Rock Art

M.L.K. Murty, Hyderabad
The Upper Palaeolithic

R.K. Varma, Allahabad
An Overview of the Mesolithic in India

Jai Narain Pandey, Allahabad
Mesolithic in the Vindhyan plateau and the Gangetic Plain

A.K. Sharma, Mumbai
The Northern Neolithic

T.C. Sharma, Guwahati
Fresh Light on Indian Neolithic Culture (Eastern Indian Neolithic Zone : A nuclear area of domestication of Rice in Asia).

J.N. Pal, Allahabad
The Neolithic of the Vindhyas

K.Paddayya
The South Indian Neolithic - with special Reference to Ash-mound

15 November, 1998 : Forenoon Session

SECTION II : PROTOHISTORY

Theme (A) : Indus Valley Civilization

V.H. Sonawane, Vadodara
Harappan Civilization in Western India with special reference to Gujarat

Amrendra Nath, New Delhi
Excavations at Rakhigarhi

Om Prakash
The question of Harappan agrarian system

K.N. Dikshit, New Delhi
The Late Harappan Culture of India and Pakistan

Theme (B) : Chalcolithic Traditions beyond the Indus

Purushottam Singh, Varanasi
The Chalcolithic of the Vindhyas and Eastern India (including Middle and Lower Ganga valley)

V.D. Misra, Allahabad
Chalcolithic cultures of the Upper Ganga Valley

Indrani Chattopadhyaya, Delhi
The Ochre Coloured Pottery and the Copper Hoards

15 November, 1998 : Afternoon Session

SECTION III : MEGALITHS, IRON AGE AND HISTORICAL PERIOD

Theme (A) : The Megalithic Traditions

A. Sundara, Bijapur
South Indian Megalithic Culture : some aspects of the studies since independence.

Theme (B) : Iron Age

M. Lal, New Delhi
Evolution of Urban Society in the Ganga Plains : Evidence from Literature and Archaeology

M. D. N. Sahi, Aligarh
Archaeology of the Historical Period I (c 600-50 BC)

V. K. Thakur, Patna
Archaeology of the Historical Period II : (c 50 BC - AD 600)

SECTION IV : PALAEOGRAPHY, NUMISMATICS AND ART

T. P. Verma, Varanasi
Studies in ancient Indian Palaeography

S. R. Dubey, Ujjain
Ancient Indian Numismatics

O. P. Srivastava, Allahabad
Fifty years of numismatic studies of Early Medieval India

R. N. Misra, Gwalior
Studies in ancient Indian Art : an overview

Pushpa Tiwari, Allahabad
Studies in ancient Indian architecture

Sandhya Mukerjee, Allahabad
Studies in Ancient Indian sclupture and iconography

H. N. Dubey, Allahabad
New dimensions in the study of ancient Indian Art with special reference to sclupture and terracotta

M.C. Gupta, Allahabad
Studies in ancient Indian minor arts and crafts

A.C. Mishra
Principal monasteries of the Madhyadesh

Rakesh Tewari, Lucknow
Prehistoric rock art

SECTION V : THEORETICAL PERSPECTIVES AND SCIENTIFIC TECHNIQUES

K. Paddayya, Pune
Theory and method in Indian archaeology : a review

Ravi Korisettar, Dharwad
Late Quaternary environmental changes in Western and Eastern India

G. L. Badam, Pune
Research in Palaeontology

P. K. Thomas, Pune
Development of Archaeozoology in India

Alok Tripathi, New Delhi
Underwater Archaeology in India : Retrospect and Prospects

R. Srivastava and V. Tripathi
Zinc metallurgy in ancient India Varanasi

B- 17, Qutab Institutional Area
New Delhi - 110016

K.N. Dikshit
General Secreatry
Indian Archaeological Society

INDIAN ARCHAEOLOGICAL SOCIETY
BALANCE SHEET AS ON 31.03.1999

LIABILITIES		AMOUNT	ASSETS	AMOUNT
<u>CAPITAL ACCOUNT</u>			<u>FIXED ASSETS</u>	
				94,15,935.52
Opening Balance	15,92,049.29			
Add:– Life Membership Fees	18,710.00			
Income Over Expenditure	37,312.70	16,48,071.99		
			<u>Current Assets & Investments</u>	
<u>Corpus Fund</u>		15,00,000.00		
			Fixed Deposits	15,75,000.00
<u>Building Fund</u>			Vardhman Construction Co.	311.00
Opening Balance	47,28,951.00		S.B.I.– 45062	15,622.73
Add:–Received during the year	33,18,312.00	80,47,263.00	S.B.I.– 45082	3,81,020.70
			Indian Bank – 460017	1,46,072.65
Dr. A.K. Narain (Award) Fund		50,000.00		
			Cash in Hand	21,872.00
Grant for Pilot Project		37,500.00		
Vardhman Construction Co. (Security)		1,00,000.00		
Indian History & Cul Soc		24,000.00		
Dr. S.P. Gupta - Loan A/C		7,000.00		
Sh. K.S. Ramachandran		50,000.00		
Sh. K.N. Dikshit		85,000.00		
Rajan Sharma & Co.		7,000.00		
TOTAL		1,15,55,834.99	TOTAL	1,15,55,834.99

Sd/
GENERAL SECRETARY

Sd/
TREASURER

Sd/
For Rajan Sharma & Co.,
Chartered Accountant

Place: New Delhi
Dated: 14.10.99

(Rajan Kumar Sharma)
Prop.

INDIAN ARCHAEOLOGICAL SOCIETY

INCOME AND EXPENDITURE ACCOUNT FOR THE YEAR ENDED 31.3.1998

EXPENDITURE	AMOUNT	INCOME	AMOUNT
To Honorarium	63,930.00	By Grant from ICHR	14,250.00
To Ground Rent	23,000.00	By Grant for Publication from ASI (Pur. 27,28)	50,000.00
To House Tax	13,500.00	By Donations	57,650.00
To Publication Expenses	64085.00	By Annual Membership Fees	100.00
To Tour & Travels	2039.00	By Sale of Publication	31,985.00
To Medical Expenses	470.00	By Bank Interest	2,84,267.20
To Telephone Expenses	12061.00		
To Conveyance	44944.00		
To Printing & Stationery	11416.50		
To Conference Expenses	20211.00		
To Office Expenses	1587.00		
To Repair & Maintenance	19874.00		
To Staff Welfare	7927.00		
To Postage & Stamps	14465.50		
To Accounting Charges	12,000.00		
To Audit Fees	7,000.00		
To Bank Charges	1831.50		
To Award	21,000.00		
To Professional Charges	17,750.00		
To Electricity Expenses	23,268.00		
To Depreciation	18,580.00		
To Excess of Income over Expenditure	37,312.70		
	4,38,252.20		4,38,252.20

Sd/	Sd/	Sd/
GENERAL SECRETARY	TREASURER	For Rajan Sharma & Co., Chartered Accountant

Place: New Delhi
Dated: 14.10.99

(Rajan Kumar Sharma)
Prop.

Plate-1. **Banawali,** Harappan Defences of Acropolis showing bastion and a flight of steps **(Bisht).**

Plate-2. **Banawali,** East Gate Complex (**Bisht).**

Plate-3. **Banawali,** Mouth of the storm water drain across East Gate **(Bisht).**

Plate-4. **Banawali,** Residential blocks of mud bricks along the street **(Bisht).**

Plate-5. **Banawali,** Apsridal Temple (**Bisht).**

Plate-6. **Dholavira,** Water reservoir to the East of Castle (**Bisht).**

Plate-7. **Dholavira,** The earliest ever Rock Cut water reservoir (**Bisht).**

Plate-8. **Dholavira,** Top of the Eastern fortification wall, provided with a stone casecade to collect the rain water. In the foreground is seen a standing stone pillar (**Bisht).**

Plate-9. **Dholavira,** The arterial storm water drain (**Bisht).**

Plate-10. **Dholavira,** Water structure in the castle-two water tanks and a well (**Bisht**).

Plate-11. **Dholavira,** The North Gate Complex of the castle (**Bisht).**

Plate-12. **Dholavira,** 9m wide Processional Pathway descending down to the stadium or Ceremonial Ground (**Bisht).**

Plate-13. **Dholavira,** East Gate of the Stadium or Ceremonial Ground (**Bisht).**

Plate-14. **Dholavira,** Arterial Street running across the middle town (**Bisht).**

Plate-15. **Dholavira,** Circular structure of stage (**Bisht).**

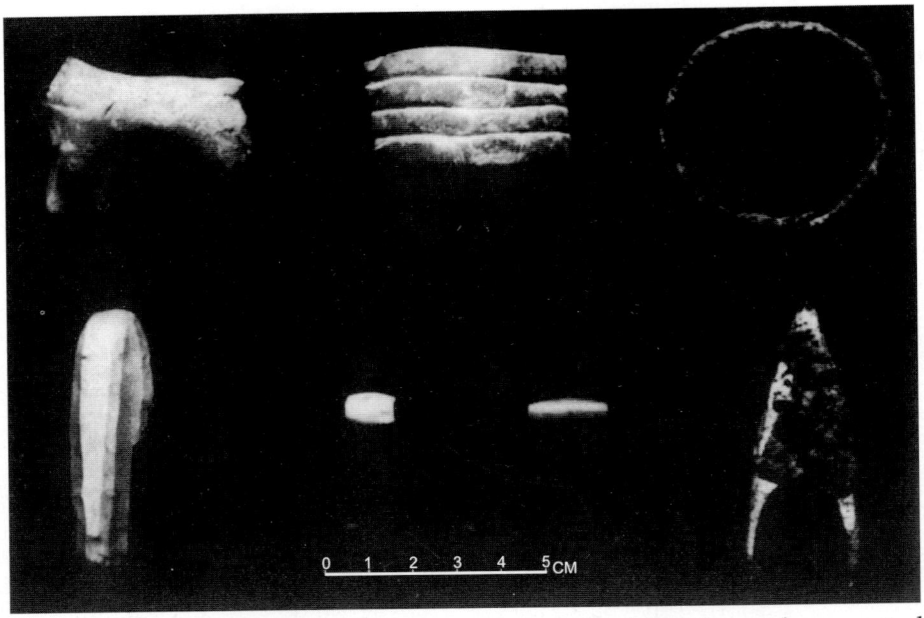

Plate-1. **Rakhigarhi,** Fluted chert core, terracotta animal figurine and segmented bangle, copper arrow head and bangle, faience beads, Early Harappan (**Nath).**

Plate-2. **Rakhigarhi,** A view of potter's klin (RGR-1), Mature Harappan (**Nath).**

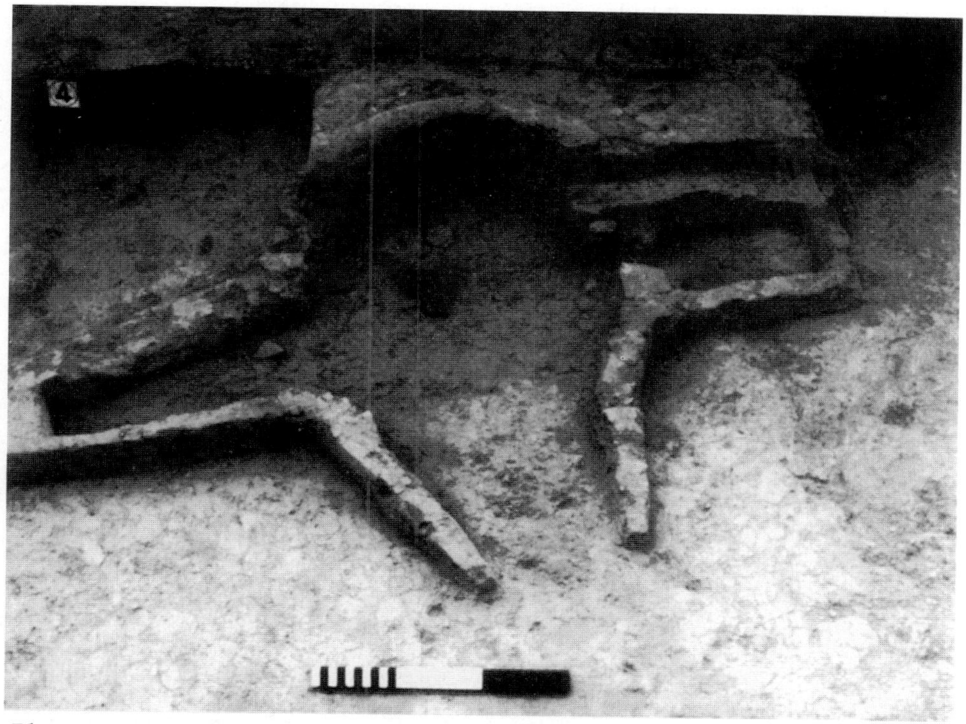

Plate-3. **Rakhigarhi,** A view of fire altar of Chiti like configuration showing stump like projection in the centre (RGR-1), Mature Harappan (**Nath).**

Plate-4. **Rakhigarhi,** A view of Yonipitha type fire altar with stump like projection in the centre (RGR-1), Mature Harappan (**Nath).**

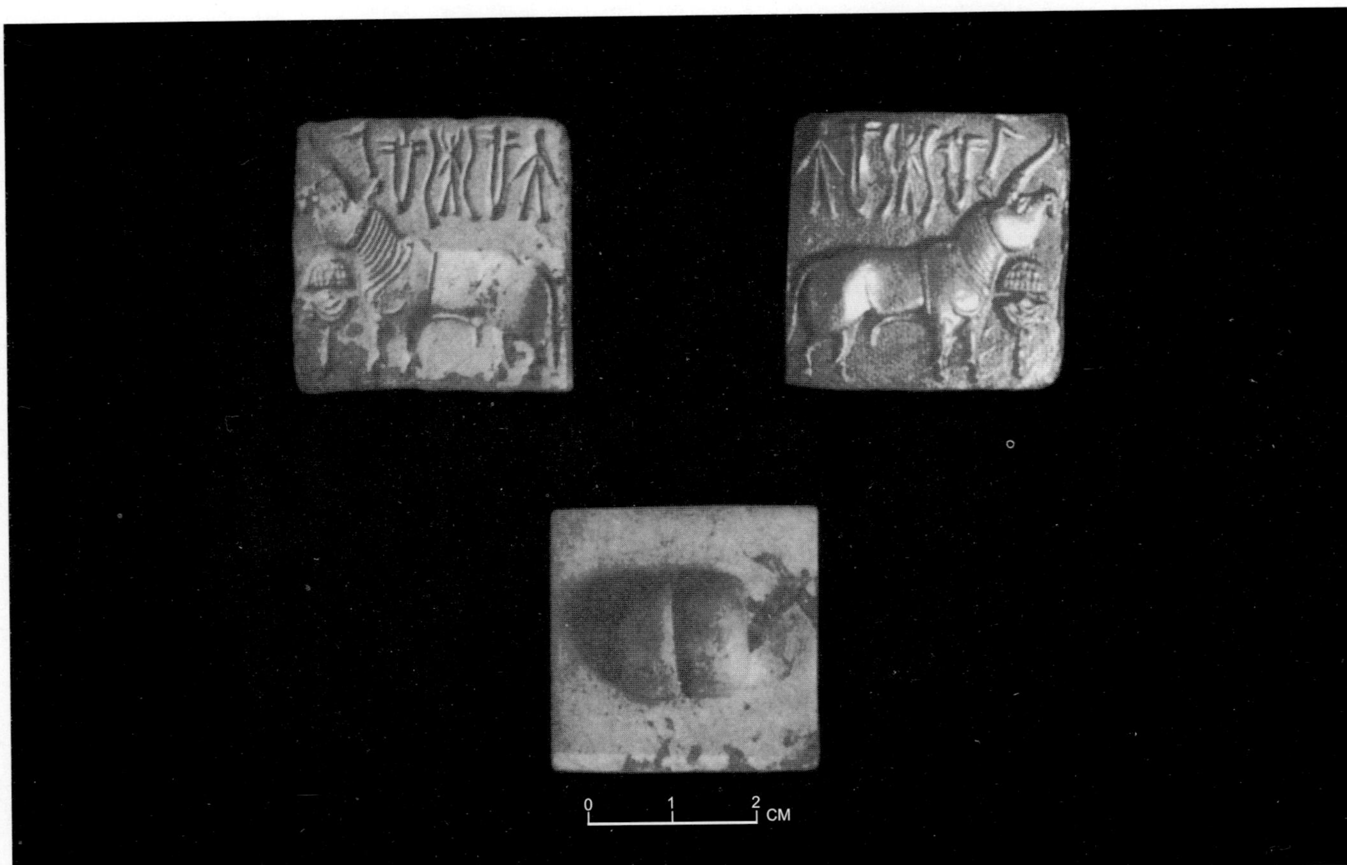

Plate-5. **Rakhigarhi,** Squarish steatite seal depicting unicorn standing in front of an altar and Harappan characters in upper segment, Mature Harappan (**Nath).**

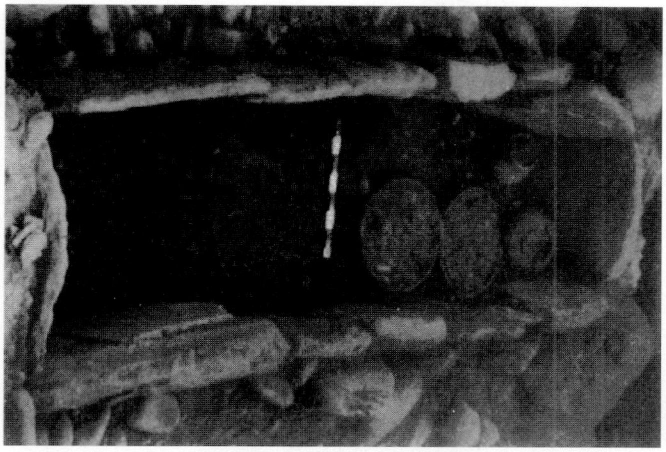

Plate-1. **Sanana,** Excavated Cist Burial (SNA-1) **(Khanduri *et al.*).**

Plate-2. **Sanana,** Megalithic Burial Complex, **(Khanduri *et al.*).**

Plate-3. **Baseri,** Cist Burial **(Khanduri *et al.*).**

Plate-4. **Baseri,** Excavated Cist Burial (BSR-3) **(Khanduri *et al.*).**

Plate-1. **Agiabir,** Bead manufacturing workshop, Period-I **(P. Singh).**

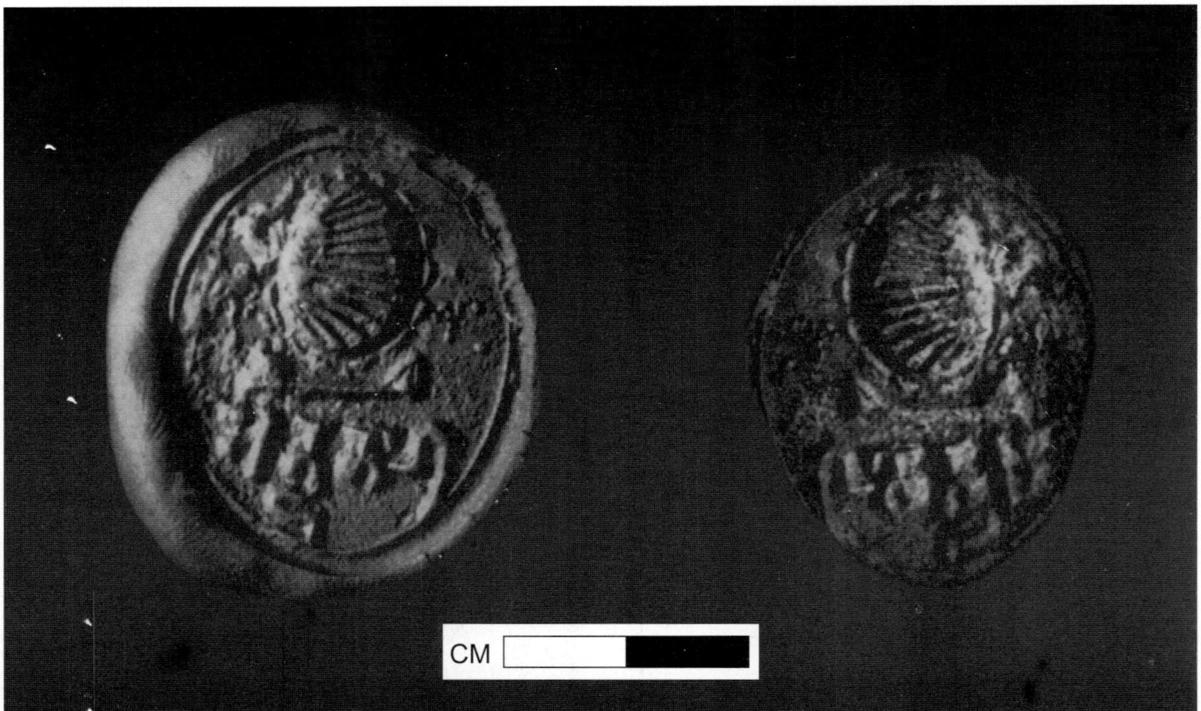

Plate-2. **Agiabir,** An ivory seal with legend *Satyanaga* or *Sandnaga* from Period-IV **(P. Singh).**

Plate-3. **Agiabir,** A nude terracotta female figurine (mother goddess) from Period-IV **(P. Singh).**

Plate-1. **Chandraketagarh,** Carved bone piece **(Maiti and Ota).**

Plate-2. **Chandraketagarh,** Carved bone piece, view of other side **(Maiti and Ota).**